$12.95

Benjamin Britten

by Michael Oliver

Phaidon Press Limited
Regent's Wharf
All Saints Street
London N1 9PA

Phaidon Press Inc.
180 Varick Street
New York, NY 10014

www.phaidon.com

First published 1996
Reprinted 2008
© 1996 Phaidon Press Limited

ISBN 978 0 7148 4771 9

A CIP catalogue record for this book is
available from the British Library

Cover illustration by Jean-Jacques Sempé
Designed by HDR Design
Printed in Singapore

Frontispiece, Benjamin Britten
and Peter Pears at
Glyndebourne, during
rehearsals for *The Rape of
Lucretia*, summer 1946

Contents

6   Preface

11   Chapter 1
      A Time There Was ... 1913–30

29   Chapter 2
      A Path of His Own 1930–34

45   Chapter 3
      Reputation Growing Steadily 1934–9

73   Chapter 4
      Europe in the Past Tense 1939–42

95   Chapter 5
      I Am Native, Rooted Here 1942–5

117   Chapter 6
      Too Much Success 1945–51

147   Chapter 7
      The Big Chariot 1952–60

173   Chapter 8
      My Subject Is War 1961–71

199   Chapter 9
      Aschenbach 1971–6

214   Classified List of Works

226   Further Reading

228   Selective Discography

234   Index

Preface

Two days after his death on 4 December 1976, an obituary in *The Times* described Benjamin Britten as 'the first British composer to capture and hold the attention of musicians and their audiences the world over, as well as at home'. One reason for this was that he was far less insular, far more aware of continental musical trends than most of his British seniors and contemporaries. To some of them the combination of his cosmopolitanism and sheer technical brilliance seemed meretricious, and although he became famous and successful at an early age the accusations of mere cleverness and of allowing technical skill to stand in for more solid musical qualities continued for many years. To many of his juniors, on the other hand, he seemed a conservative figure, at best irrelevant to a generation excitedly discovering Webern, Messiaen, Boulez, Stockhausen and Cage. As a consequence, and since he had no pupils, his influence on those juniors was slight: there has been no 'Britten school'.

We therefore perhaps expect him to seem an isolated figure, of still less relevance to today's generation of composers. But it has not proved so. In another obituary tribute Robin Holloway, a fine composer thirty years Britten's junior, admitted that when he was very young he 'learned to be supercilious' about his music, but then wrote movingly of his gradual recognition of a debt 'to a composer whose intensely personal achievement ... bears directly on the malaise of music at large – the flight to the extremes that leaves the centre empty'. Without wishing to describe Britten's style as 'central', he nevertheless thought that

in particular the combination of lucidity, emptiness and tightness in the latter works can reveal common ground between the most unexpected and unrelated sources. This music has the power to connect the avant-garde with the lost paradise of tonality; it conserves and renovates in the boldest and simplest manner; it shows how old usages can be refreshed and

remade, and how the new can be saved from mere rootlessness, etiolation,
lack of connection and communication. (*Tempo* No. 120, March 1977)

He laid down no technique or 'ism' to be imitated, but the rigour
of his solutions to his own problems can be of absorbing interest
and help to other composers confronting their own. He effectively
invented English opera and re-invented English song, and there have
been few successful operas or songs in English since *Peter Grimes* and
the *Serenade* that have not been in some way indebted to him. His
clarity, economy and simplicity (Holloway's 'emptiness'), as evident
in such masterpieces as *The Turn of the Screw* and the Third String
Quartet as they are in the joyously practical music-making of his
works for children, are too personal to be imitated, yet there is evidence in the work of numerous younger composers whose music
does not sound in the least like his that they have profited from
his example.

I was a contemporary of Britten's for thirty-nine years and although
I attended rather few of his premières – they tended to take place
in Aldeburgh – I was in the audience at many of the first London
performances which generally followed soon afterwards. The London
première of *The Turn of the Screw* in October 1954 was one of the
most memorable events of my life. The theatre was sold out, I had
to stand at the side of the stalls, and I left the auditorium during
the interval to make sure that I had a seat for the next performance.
My diary entry, written very late that evening, contains a detailed
description of every one of the opera's sixteen scenes. Of how many
operas does one retain so much after a single hearing? The discovery
of a work that so masterfully combined immediate impact with
subtle complexity, yet a complexity that was clearly both audible and
necessary, was deeply exciting to a teenager who had already experienced a good deal of music whose complexities he had had to take
on trust.

Like Robin Holloway I later 'learned to be supercilious' about
Britten's music, about some later works particularly. I was so busy
catching up on music whose complexities took some effort to compre-
hend, but of whose necessity I was by then more aware, that I took
little heed of some of the music of Britten's last period. A few of these

pieces I have studied in detail only while writing this book, and I have
found the experience almost as absorbing as the London première of
The Turn of the Screw. Some of Britten's works are minor, quite a large
number are 'occasional'. There are very few that he seems to have
written, as some musicians put it, 'with the left hand' (meaning
absently, using technique alone, while the right hand was occupied
with *real* music). And he continued to develop, refine and deepen
his language until the very end of his life.

In my teens and twenties I had very little doubt that Britten was
one of the greatest living composers. For a long time thereafter I
would have classified him with such fascinating but peripheral figures
(peripheral, that is, to the central drama of twentieth-century music)
as Martinu, Szymanowski, Weill and Varèse. Now that we are less
likely to think of this century's music as having a centre and a peri-
phery, and are beginning perhaps to see it as more like a map (Athens
is nowhere near the centre of Europe but it would be foolish to regard
it as peripheral to its history, art and thought), Britten seems more
and more like a composer of capital status.

There are two difficulties in writing about him. The first is that
he was a homosexual at a time when homosexuality was illegal in the
United Kingdom. Britten and his lover Peter Pears lived together
openly for over thirty years, but both they and their close friends were
understandably cautious about referring to their relationship. It is
hard for anyone who remembers only the relatively liberal 1980s and
1990s, with much talk of 'gay liberation' and with films and novels
discussing the preoccupations and lifestyles of homosexual men, to
imagine the prurience, censoriousness and sheer danger that surrounded homosexuals in the years before the relaxation of the law in
1967. Press reports of the arrest and imprisonment of homosexuals
were frequent. So were violent assaults ('queer-bashing'), blackmail
and police entrapment, though these were less often mentioned
by newspapers.

Britten was also attracted to teenage or pubescent boys. Some of
them have spoken of his relations with them, which seem not to have
gone further than affectionate caresses or the occasional kiss; both
would have been seen by the law, of course, then as now, as acts of
gross indecency or as sexual abuse. In such circumstances it is hardly
surprising that Britten very rarely discussed his sexuality, even with

his closest friends (Peter Pears, asked whether W. H. Auden had ever made advances to Britten, said that he was not at all sure). Inevitably such secrecy led to gossip, much of it demonstrably false, but by the very nature of the case some of the assiduously circulated rumours cannot be either proved or disproved. Where facts are available I have stated them, but in their absence I have preferred not to speculate.

Britten's silence on such matters went with a personal reticence of manner that was in part no doubt inherited from his respectable middle-class parents (the number of taboo subjects and of things that it was not 'done' to talk about was legion in the middle-class England of his period), in part due to a personal conviction, shared by many musicians, that music cannot adequately be discussed in words. Few of Britten's letters are self-revelatory; when they speak of his music they do so in purely practical or rather deprecatory terms.

He was also a man who worked exceptionally hard. Apart from a list of works longer than those of many composers who lived far longer, he was a busy performer, as both pianist and conductor, and for much of his life the director of an important arts festival. He seems to have had what is called a 'work ethic': he was unhappy and restless when not working. His holidays were almost invariably working ones, and although he travelled extensively he rarely did so for its own sake. The consequence is that the latter part of his life especially was out-wardly uneventful, an almost unbroken sequence of compositions and performances. His work, in short, *was* his life, and much of that work was done alone and in private; with many of his friends he did not discuss his music at all. He seldom wrote programme-notes on it, rarely agreed to be interviewed, and his only considered aesthetic statement is a brief pamphlet. The temptation to conclude from such meagre evidence that Britten 'must have thought' this or that is one that the biographer must resist. Nevertheless his vulnerable sensitivity, his pity for suffering and anger at cruelty, his gift for friendship and both the happiness and the suffering that his sexual nature caused him are all, I believe, reflected (not portrayed) in his music. He is a composer about whom we can learn much by listening.

Michael Oliver
Piegaro/London, 1995

I

Britten aged eight, apparently
playing four pieces of music
simultaneously

Qu'as-tu fait, ô toi que voilà
Pleurant sans cesse,
Dis, qu'as-tu fait, toi que voilà
De ta jeunesse?

Paul Verlaine: 'Sagesse'

A Time There Was ... 1913-30

Benjamin Britten's last orchestral work, written in 1974, two years before his death, was a *Suite on English Folk Tunes* with the subtitle 'A time there was ...' He had been ill for some while, a defective heart valve had been diagnosed, but he had refused to have the necessary operation until he had finished his opera *Death in Venice*, based on Thomas Mann's short novel. The obsession of the central character Aschenbach with a beautiful twelve-year-old boy had obvious relevance to Britten, a homosexual who, despite a long and happy relationship with the tenor Peter Pears, found another happiness in the company of boys.

The novelist Aschenbach's fear that his creativity was drying up had a parallel in Britten's insecure belief in his own gifts. Aschenbach's awareness of his own mortality had further resonance for an ailing composer contemplating an operation from which he might not recover. No less important than the opera's auto-biographical element was the fact that Aschenbach would probably be the last major role that Peter Pears would undertake: he was sixty as work on the opera began.

Increasing exhaustion meant that *Death in Venice* took longer to complete than expected, and Britten underwent surgery only in May 1973. The operation was of limited effectiveness; he suffered a stroke during it, which semi-paralysed his right arm.

His first new work after the operation (more than a year after it) was the fifth and last of his Canticles, written for tenor and harp since he knew that he would never again be able to accompany Pears at the piano. This was followed by the *Suite on English Folk Tunes*. Three of the ten melodies are folk tunes collected by Percy Grainger. The remainder are from John Playford's *The English Dancing Master* (1650), and much of the music indeed dances vigorously, but there is sombreness as well, and disquiet, and the suite ends in poignant melancholy. Its subtitle, 'A time there was ...', comes from a poem by

Thomas Hardy that Britten had set twenty years earlier as the darkly
eloquent conclusion to his song-cycle *Winter Words*:

A time there was – as one may guess
And as, indeed, earth's testimonies tell –
Before the birth of consciousness,
When all went well.

None suffered sickness, love, or loss,
None knew regret, starved hope, or heart-burnings;
None cared whatever crash or cross
Brought wrack to things.

If something ceased, no tongue bewailed,
If something winced and waned, no heart was wrung;
If brightness dimmed, and dark prevailed,
No sense was stung.

But the disease of feeling germed,
And primal rightness took the tinct of wrong;
Ere nescience shall be reaffirmed
How long, how long?

Nostalgia for a time of irrecoverable innocence, in short, of
'primal rightness', before 'the disease of feeling germed', when 'none
suffered … love'.

Edward Benjamin Britten (his first Christian name seems never to
have been used) was born at 21 Kirkley Cliff Road, Lowestoft on
St Cecilia's Day, 22 November 1913. The house (which still stands)
faces the North Sea, very near the easternmost point of the British
mainland. In Britten's first true opera *Peter Grimes*, based on a
poem by the Suffolk-born George Crabbe, the troubled and outcast
fisherman Grimes is asked, 'Since you're a lonely soul … why not try
the wider sea?' He replies, 'I am native, rooted here … by familiar
fields, marsh and sand, ordinary streets, prevailing wind.' Britten
was drawn strongly to the character of Grimes the outsider, no less
strongly to the landscape against which that character is silhouetted.
He was, he said, 'firmly rooted in this glorious county', and the older

Britten's family home,
21 Kirkley Cliff Road,
Lowestoft

he grew he found that 'working becomes more and more difficult away from that home.' For most of his life he lived in Suffolk, specifically in Crabbe's and Grimes's 'Borough', the small coastal town of Aldeburgh, twenty-five miles south of Lowestoft. Explicitly or implicitly Suffolk landscapes (and seascapes) are evoked in many of his works: in *Peter Grimes* itself, of course, but for *Albert Herring* a short story by Maupassant was relocated in Suffolk, for *Curlew River* a Japanese Noh play was reinterpreted in Christian terms and given a fenland setting.

He was the fourth and youngest child of Robert Victor Britten and his wife Edith. It was, said Britten, 'a very ordinary middle-class family'. Robert Britten was a dentist, well known and well liked in the town, successful enough to employ a secretary and two domestic servants and to send his children to private schools. But according to his younger daughter Beth he never intended to have children at all, and was oppressed by the expense of bringing them up. He had intended to be a farmer, but one of his brothers (the other died of drink) allowed the family dairy business to go to ruin, depriving Robert of the necessary capital. He was a rather formidable figure to his children, who were expected to stand up when he entered the room; his daughter said that they were all rather afraid of him. A

The Britten children with
their mother in 1924:
from left, Beth, Edith holding
Benjamin on her lap, Barbara
and Robert

handsome man in his youth, his face hardened with age, his mouth
wide but tight-lipped, his eyes hooded; some family friends found
his sidelong glances sinister. His letters, though, show him as an
affectionate father, proud of his gifted son, but awkwardly inarticulate
in expressing his emotions. When Robert Britten knew that he
was dying he said farewell to his children not in person but in a note
addressed to 'the 4 B's' (Barbara, Bobby, Beth and Benjamin):
'Goodbye my four! My love to you all. It's grand to have known you
and have your love. Comfort Mum.'

    His wife Edith's father was an illegitimate child, taking his surname
(Hockey) from his mother, his father being unidentified. Edith was
the eldest of his seven children, by a wife who was apparently an alco-

holic. According to Beth Britten, again, Edith dreaded that one of her children would inherit this weakness.

Robert Britten was not musical, but encouraged his wife's domestic music-making. She played the piano and had a pretty mezzo-soprano voice; Britten's earliest musical memory was of her singing him to sleep. She sang with the local choral society (the Brittens sometimes acted as hosts to the professional soloists engaged by it) and contributed songs and arias to musical evenings, mostly at a local church, some at the Britten's home. Since much of the ground floor at Kirkley Cliff Road was given over to Robert Britten's surgery and office, these were held in an upstairs sitting-room (known to the family as 'Heaven'), big enough even for very small-scale amateur theatricals. Benjamin Britten's first public performance was as an elf in a production of *Cinderella* at the age of three; at six, with 'madly curly hair and pink tights', he appeared as Tom, the little sweep (his mother played the formidable Mrs Do-As-You-Would-Be-Done-By), in an adaptation of Charles Kingsley's *The Water-Babies*. At this age he was an exceptionally pretty child, with blue eyes, pink cheeks and abundant blonde curls. His sister thought it was fortunate that he was not an only child; if he had been he could easily have been spoiled and become conceited.

Edith Britten gave her son his first piano lessons at the age of five, and he almost immediately began 'composing'. At first he merely arranged notes in patterns on the page, joining them together with

The abrupt death of the Prince of Wales was the occasion for Britten's first attempt at incidental music; his play 'The Royal Falily' [sic], written at the age of six or seven.

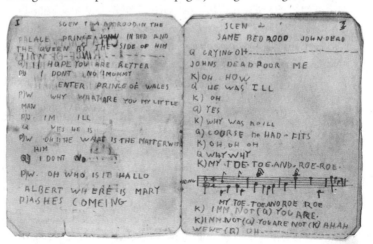

long lines, but his mother taught him the elements of notation and he was soon composing in earnest, writing 'elaborate tone-poems usually lasting about twenty seconds, inspired by terrific events in my home life such as the departure of my father for London'. There is indeed an early composition of extreme brevity entitled 'Did you no my Daddy has gone to London today?' (Britten's spelling remained fallible until the end of his life). He also wrote plays, some with music, for performance by himself, his friends and his sister Beth. Nursery plays were the idea of the children's nanny, but they were supported by their parents: Robert Britten would take his place in the 'audience' formally dressed in tails and top hat.

Britten's progress at the piano was so rapid that by the time he was seven his mother found he needed more advanced tuition than she could give. His new teacher was Miss Ethel Astle; with her sister she also ran the small 'pre-preparatory' school, Southolme, to which he was sent at the same age. He soon became skilled enough to accompany his mother in her song repertoire and to play piano duets with her ('mostly Wagner, sometimes Beethoven', according to his older sister Barbara). By the age of ten he was writing songs, many with Edith Britten's voice in mind. It was at this age also that he entered South Lodge, a preparatory school (like Southolme only a few steps from the Brittens' home) and began learning the viola.

The viola is at the centre of a string quartet or the string section of an orchestra, essential to the completeness of the texture yet unobtrusive save when the composer allows its voice to stand out. Playing the viola would be valuable for any composer, but when Britten began learning it there would have been no opportunities for him to play in an orchestra or ensemble (there was no musical activity at his preparatory school), and the viola's solo repertory is small. By this time however he was collecting miniature scores, and many of his earliest encounters with great music would have been through reading scores, deciphering them at the piano and perhaps seeing how other composers used stringed instruments by playing through the parts himself. He soon began writing music for strings and composing on a more ambitious scale: an oratorio, *Samuel*, running to sixteen pages, and a seven-page 'Sonata Fantasti' for piano. Britten remained fond of a number of these early works, of a setting of Longfellow's 'Beware!', for example, and he was sufficiently aware of the already fluent melodic gift shown in a group of 'Walztes' written between his tenth and his twelfth years to return to them twice, firstly, at twenty, drawing on them rather jokingly for his *Simple Symphony* (which he dedicated to his viola teacher, Audrey Alston), then in his mid-fifties redrafting five of the waltzes in a manner which acknowledges their precocious elegance and wit.

His remarkable gifts were obvious very early, and his mother was ambitious for him. She was fond of speaking of 'the three B's' (Bach, Beethoven and Brahms) and of predicting that he would be the fourth. By the age of thirteen he had passed the Associated Board Grade VII piano examination with honours, and was composing so prolifically and assuredly that his father sent an overture to the BBC for their comments, and his mother sought the advice of the organist of St Paul's Cathedral in London. A 'family council' was held to decide whether he should be sent to London to study music. The result of these consultations was a decision not to act hastily and to give the boy as far as possible a normal (that is to say public school) education, while making special provision for his musical studies.

Despite his evident gift and his no less striking dedication to music (throughout his preparatory school years he got up very early so as to spend an hour or so composing and practising the piano before school began), the decision was a sensible one: to send a boy of thirteen to London to pursue his musical studies would hardly have been practical. Besides, in Frank Bridge he had recently acquired a composition teacher more stimulating and less insular than most of those he could have encountered in London in the 1920s.

There were few opportunities in Britten's early childhood for him to hear orchestral music. His father, fearing that it might damage the family's domestic music-making, would not have a gramophone or a radio in the house, though the proprietor of a local record shop did not seem to object to Britten listening to his stock without buying it, and Robert Britten eventually bought a radio. His son would not have had very much time to listen to it, however, since the school hours at South Lodge (Britten was a day boy, but the timetable seems to have been designed with boarders in mind) were 7.30 a.m. to 8.30 p.m. It was Britten's viola teacher Audrey Alston who introduced him to real professional music-making by taking him, in October 1924, to the Norwich Triennial Festival, where he heard Frank Bridge

'He taught me to take infinite trouble over getting every note quite right': Britten's first composition teacher Frank Bridge

South Lodge preparatory
school, Lowestoft, with
the North Sea beyond

conducting a performance of his orchestral work *The Sea* and was, as
he later said, 'knocked sideways' by it. *The Sea* is a masterly example
of English late Romanticism, richly but delicately scored, already a
dozen years old by the time Britten heard it. At the next Norwich
Festival, in 1927, he heard a work in Bridge's later manner, the first
performance (also conducted by the composer) of his *Enter Spring*,
and he was again deeply impressed.

Frank Bridge was one of the most comprehensively gifted musicians of his generation. Initially a conservative composer, a pupil of
the Brahmsian Sir Charles Stanford, his beautifully crafted early songs
and chamber music soon became popular. But at the same time he
pursued a career as a chamber musician (his reputation as a violist was
so great that when the viola player of the celebrated Joachim Quartet
became ill, Bridge was chosen to replace him) and as a conductor,
appearing at Covent Garden and at Henry Wood's Promenade
Concerts, as well as in the USA. As a composer Bridge's style changed
radically after World War I. His later compositions, harmonically
and rhythmically more adventurous than almost anything else being
written in England at that time, received a much cooler public
response than his genial and tuneful early works. After his death his
music fell into almost total neglect and has only been rediscovered
and its high quality recognized in recent years, in part due to the
advocacy of his pupil; Britten's admiration of and gratitude to Bridge
never wavered.

Audrey Alston knew Bridge well, and introduced her thirteen-year-
old pupil to him. They spent the following morning looking through
Britten's music, and Bridge immediately agreed to give him lessons
in composition. For the next three years Britten was Bridge's only
pupil, visiting him for lessons mainly during school holidays, either in
London or at the Bridges' country cottage at Friston, near Eastbourne.
Slightly over a year later he also, on Bridge's recommendation,
began visiting London for lessons with the highly regarded pianist
Harold Samuel.

Bridge's tuition was rigorous, and his often very long lessons frequently ended with Britten in tears of exhaustion, but he later wrote
that he badly needed Bridge's strictness and his loathing of anything
sloppy or amateurish. Again and again Bridge would play at the piano

'A great little man who
was always so grand to
me': Britten's piano teacher
Harold Samuel

something that the boy had written and would demand whether the sounds that emerged were really what he meant. It was a way of insisting on good technique, on using those notes and only those notes which represented most clearly the musical ideas that his pupil wanted to express.

Bridge was also responsible for broadening Britten's musical horizons. They went to concerts together, listened to records and studied scores. Bridge was almost the only English composer of his generation who both knew and was impressed by the music of Schoenberg and his pupils, the so-called Second Viennese School. Much later Britten was with him at the first London performance in 1931 of Stravinsky's *Symphony of Psalms*, and it is hard to think of any other teacher of composition in Britain at that time who would have declared it, as Bridge did, a masterpiece.

The first fruit of Bridge's teaching was a remarkable one; indeed Britten's *Quatre Chansons françaises* are an astonishing achievement for an English schoolboy of fourteen, writing in 1928. They are filled with recollections of Ravel and Debussy and with undertones of Wagner, but all these influences are handled with assurance and with touches of harmonic adventurousness which reflect his teacher's influence (Bridge had already written his audaciously radical Third String Quartet) but may also suggest that Britten was accompanying Bridge in his explorations, not just dutifully following him.

The orchestration is of great refinement; although Bridge must have discussed scoring with Britten he cannot have given him anything resembling a detailed course in instrumentation. Britten must have picked up for himself much of his sensitive understanding of what orchestral instruments can do and how they may be combined, aided by an ear of remarkable acuteness. His selection of texts is already individual, both in the fact that the *quatre* were originally *cinq* (a setting of Gérard de Nerval's 'Dans les bois' was eventually omitted; later in life Britten's cycles or sets of songs were often selected from a larger group, some being rejected before performance) and in the poems' subject matter: a conventional evocation of nature ('Nuits de juin') by Victor Hugo, but also his sombre 'L'Enfance': a child sings over the body of his mother, unaware that she is dead (the death of his mother was one of Britten's recurring childhood nightmares; the *Quatre Chansons* were dedicated to his parents on their twenty-seventh wedding anniversary). Verlaine's 'Chanson d'automne', with its languishing melancholy:

Les sanglots longs
Des violons
De l'automne
Blessent mon cœur
D'une langueur
Monotone

('The long sobs of autumnal violins wound my heart with a monotonous languor'), but also his 'Sagesse', uncannily predicting Britten's later laments for lost youthful innocence:

Qu'as-tu fait, ô toi que voilà,
Pleurant sans cesse,
Dis, qu'as-tu fait, toi que voilà,
De ta jeunesse?

('What have you done, you there, weeping endlessly? Tell me, you there, what have you done with your youth?').

One of Britten's librettists, Myfanwy Piper, reported that towards the end of his life Britten told her that his father had been homosexual and that he sent him out 'to find boys'. As far as the recollections of all those who knew Robert Britten are concerned, this allegation is unquestionably false. To another librettist and to an American friend, Britten said that he had been raped or sexually abused by a master at school, without in either case specifying which school. It is harder to disprove this statement, but friends who were at school with him regard it as highly improbable. Were these 'recollections' mere fant- asies? Or was he dramatizing the shock of puberty and of his real- ization that he was homosexual? Nostalgia for pre-sexual innocence, for a time before sexuality is recognized, is a common theme in homosexual writing. James Baldwin's expression of it in *Giovanni's Room* is characteristic: 'I have not thought of that boy – Joey – for many years; but I see him quite clearly tonight ... For a while he was my best friend. Later, the idea that such a person could have been my best friend was proof of some horrifying taint in me. So I forgot him.'

Britten did not forget the period of his sexual innocence, that time when intense friendships were possible without realization of any sexual component they might contain, before 'primal rightness took the tinct of wrong', and in both life and art he sought to evoke or recapture that time and those friendships.

Throughout his life he was drawn to writing for unbroken male voices, and to operatic subjects in which children are portrayed. Even those operas and other vocal works in which children do not appear often dwell on the theme of innocence destroyed, threatened or unregainable. Britten was often described by those who knew him well as being more at ease in the company of children than that of adults. His nostalgia for childhood also took the form of a lifelong preference for 'nursery' food and for the public school habit of bathing in cold water. Well into adulthood he read school stories, and in his twenties planned to write music based on Erich Kästner's *Emil and the Detectives* and Jules Renard's *Poil de Carotte*, both of them encountered in filmed versions that evidently stirred him greatly. At the time he thought Gerhard Lamprecht's film of *Emil* the most perfect he had ever seen.

Britten in cap and blazer as a member of the South Lodge cricket team

After a happy period at South Lodge, where he 'loved cricket ... adored mathematics' and ended his final term as head boy, captain of cricket and Victor Ludorum, Britten began his relatively brief life as a public school boy in September 1928, two months before his fifteenth birthday, one month after finishing the *Quatre Chansons françaises*. He was intensely homesick and was saved from the worst of a schoolboy 'initiation ceremony' (being tossed in a blanket and thrown into water) by a fainting fit which alarmed the other boys. He was quite often confined to the school sanatorium, and in view of his frequent adult illnesses, often coinciding with periods of intense pressure or frustration at his work, it is hard not to conclude that some of this ill-health at school was a psychosomatic escape from school itself. After the fainting incident he was not bullied again, but at one stage during his time at Gresham's he seems to have considered some sort of protest or campaign against bullying. In his last few weeks at South Lodge he had appalled his teachers, in response to a request for an essay on the subject of 'Animals', by writing an impassioned attack on cruelty to animals, including hunting, and extending his condemnation to the cruelty of war. Britten's revulsion at the cruelty of hunting is understandable; his readiness to condemn it, as a shy child in many ways young for his years, is an early indication of the determination that was at the root of some of the most admirable as well as some of the most perplexing traits in his character.

Gresham's School was known as a 'liberal' establishment. The Officers' Training Corps, for example, was not compulsory, as it was in most public schools at that time. Gresham's took music seriously: Britten was immediately recruited to the school choir, which sang the chapel services in plainchant, and he also appeared at school concerts, as pianist and violist. There was a gramophone at the school, and Britten's housemaster, who had a radio, invited him to listen to broadcast concerts (during one of which he heard and was impressed by Schoenberg's *Pierrot Lunaire*). But his letters of this period are those of a boy rather young for his age, desperately missing his mother: he addressed her as 'my dearest darling', 'my pet' and 'angel of my heart'. The letters are also full of complaints about the school's music master Walter Greatorex, who on Britten's arrival at Gresham's had remarked 'So this is the little boy who likes Stravinsky!' Greatorex was critical of Britten's piano playing and scornful at his hero-worship of Beethoven. Britten in his turn found Greatorex's piano playing ugly and his compositions for the school chapel unpleasant.

Fairfield House, Gresham's School, Holt, where Britten was a boarder from 1928 to 1930

If Greatorex did have a somewhat disdainful attitude to Britten it would have been understandable: he might well have been offended that the most outstanding musical talent that Gresham's had recruited for many years, accepted because he had won a music scholarship to one of the few public schools to offer such things, was being taught music, outside school, by others. Two other 'old boys' of Gresham's, the poets W. H. Auden and Stephen Spender, remembered Greatorex with affection and respect, and his attitude to Britten must have softened with time, since he was the pianist in the first performance, at a school concert in Britten's second year at Gresham's, of a Bagatelle for piano trio.

Auden, who left Gresham's three years before Britten arrived and unlike him enjoyed his time there, nevertheless wrote a famous essay ('Honour', later republished as 'The Liberal Fascist') in which he concluded that 'the best reason I have for opposing Fascism is that at school I lived in a Fascist state.' His reason was the 'Honour System', still practised at Gresham's during Britten's years there, whereby each new boy was required to promise not to swear, to smoke or to say or do anything indecent. With this went an obligation to report oneself to a housemaster in case of any breach of the promise, and to report any other boy who did these things and failed to report himself. In Auden's view the system worked, but produced boys whose morality was based on fear, repressed and furtive neurotics. Britten found the 'Honour System' a 'positive failure', useless with 'boys who have no honour'. He found 'atrocious bullying on all sides, vulgarity and swearing'. He was repelled by it, and thought that it turned small and weak boys 'into sour and bitter boys, and ruined for life'. His anger was directed against the corruption of the innocent.

This anger combined with homesickness and revulsion at 'vulgarity and swearing' (Britten was at this time, under his mother's influence, a pious child, reading regularly from *The Daily Light*, an anthology of Biblical texts in diary form) to make the prospect of returning to Gresham's after each holiday away from it an appalling one. His parents had promised him that he could apply for entrance to the Royal College of Music as soon as he had passed the School Certificate. In the spring of 1930 Robert Britten told his son that he could leave school at the end of the summer term, regardless of the result of his examinations.

In May Britten submitted a number of his compositions to the Royal College, as the first stage of an application for their annual composition scholarship. In June he was invited to London to sit a written paper and to submit to an oral examination by a panel of three examiners, Ralph Vaughan Williams, John Ireland and one of the College's teachers of harmony and counterpoint, S. P. Waddington. According to Ireland, one of them remarked as they looked through Britten's manuscripts, 'What is an English public schoolboy doing writing music of this kind?' He nevertheless won the scholarship, was informed of the fact on the spot, and left Gresham's in July 1930. To his surprise (he had been dreading failure) he passed the School Certificate with credits in five subjects. Among the books he was awarded as school prizes he chose a score of Schoenberg's *Pierrot Lunaire*. In his diary he wrote that 'I am terribly sorry to leave such boys as these,' and on the day after leaving school he composed an Elegy for solo viola which combines a plangent, eloquent melancholy with an indication of how well he had absorbed Frank Bridge's training. Seemingly freely rhapsodic, the piece is in fact based on slightly modified repetitions of a very long theme.

2

Britten at nineteen returns
to his preparatory school,
South Lodge, for a game of
cricket: 'Great fun ...
eventually retiring with
bust bat!'

*Oh! Ben my boy what does it feel like to hear
your own creation? Didn't you want to get up
and shout – It's mine! It's mine!*

Letter to Britten from
his father, July 1933

A Path of His Own 1930–34

'I've got a lad under me at the moment who has such an astonishing facility he makes one feel like an old duffer': Britten's composition teacher at the Royal College of Music John Ireland ...

Britten's composition teacher at the Royal College of Music was John Ireland, fifty-one years old, an established and much-admired composer. Though not nearly as enquiring about contemporary musical trends in Europe as Frank Bridge, he was described by Bridge, in a letter to Britten strongly recommending that he study with Ireland, as 'a live composer whose activities are part of the present-day outlook with a heavy leaning towards tomorrow's!' Britten took Bridge's advice, and although he later acknowledged that Ireland and his piano teacher at the College, Arthur Benjamin, were 'very kind to me and really nursed me very gently through a very, very difficult musical adolescence', his diaries suggest a more difficult relationship with his composition teacher.

Britten's lessons with Bridge had been sporadic, largely confined to holidays and weekends. With school work to do for most of the year there would have been no possibility of him being led by Bridge through a structured and rigorous course in composition. Ireland was foolish to imply, as he later did, that Bridge gave Britten no training at all, but from his point of view the boy lacked a firm grounding in counterpoint, fugue and other essential disciplines (one of the first tasks he set him was to write a Mass for four voices 'in the style of Palestrina'). Britten found him more strict even than Bridge at his severest. He would perhaps have found this easier to accept if it had not been combined with casual time-keeping (Ireland was often late for lessons, or postponed them, occasionally forgetting them altogether) and slovenly personal habits. Ireland lived, in squalid disorder, in a house in Chelsea where from time to time he received pupils. On one occasion, a lesson having been postponed from morning until evening, Britten found him drunk and urinating on the floor.

'Studying at the Royal College of Music' might seem to imply regular attendance for lectures and tutorials. In fact Britten received only two lessons a week, one each from Ireland and Benjamin. A third, the 'music class' (ear training and musical dictation) he found so easy that he was first moved up into a more advanced class and then exempted altogether. The rest of his time he worked at home (he had moved into a boarding-house not far from the College), writing his exercises for Ireland, practising the piano (to the irritation of some of his fellow-lodgers) and composing.

... and his piano teacher Arthur Benjamin: 'Benjamin ... says that I am not built for a solo pianist – how I am going to make my pennies Heaven only knows.'

He made rather few friends at the College, the Welsh composer Grace Williams being the closest of them, and spent much of his leisure time with his sisters, both of whom were working in London, and with Frank Bridge and his wife. He was always glad to return to Lowestoft for the holidays, when diary references to 'bed at 10.00', 'walk after supper' and 'practice viola a bit after dinner' give way to records of picnics, swimming and tennis parties.

In London, though he later professed a loathing of all cities save Venice and Copenhagen, he became a frequent concert-goer for the first time in his life, and encountered a great deal of unfamiliar music. He was bewildered but impressed by a Stravinsky concert during his first winter in London, and by the autumn was describing a staged production of *Petrushka* as 'most glorious'. The following summer he bought a recording of the 'great ... marvellous' *Symphony of Psalms*. Soon thereafter he acquired Stravinsky's own recording of *The Rite of Spring*, played it almost daily and described it in his diary as 'the World's Wonder' (he used the same words to describe Wagner's *Tristan und Isolde*). Schoenberg intrigued him, but he was baffled by *Erwartung* ('Heaven knows! ... I could not make head or tail of it'). By the end of his period as a student he found Schoenberg's orchestral Variations Op. 31 'rather dull', but within a few months he was 'revelling in the romanticism' of *Pierrot Lunaire*: 'what a work – the imagination and technique!' He was angry when his suggestion that the College library should acquire a copy of the score was rejected; he had of course his own copy already.

Works like *Pierrot Lunaire* and *Erwartung*, in which Schoenberg sought to write 'atonal' music, free of any but a passing sense of key, were received in Britain at that time with distaste and his attempt in his later 'serial' works to provide a structural replacement for the sense of key was seen as aridly abstract. Since many features of the system of key and the harmony derived from it are rooted in the laws of acoustics, both atonality and serialism were condemned as unnatural. Britten later recalled that there was 'an almost moral prejudice' against

Following page, the Royal College of Music, seen from the steps leading down from the Royal Albert Hall

serial music at that time. After leaving the College at the end of
1933 he was awarded a small grant for travel abroad. Having by then
become an admirer of Schoenberg's pupil Alban Berg he was keen to
use the money to study with him. A 'coolness' was felt at the College,
and when Britten asked his mother whether he would be allowed to
visit Berg, she said that he would not, adding that Berg was 'not a
good influence'. Britten believed that the College's disapproval had
convinced his parents that he would be in moral danger in Berg's
company. Berg's sudden death not long afterwards struck Britten as
'a real and terrible tragedy'.

Mahler, at that time little valued in Great Britain ('a very tolerable
imitation of a composer' was Vaughan Williams's view) was another
enthusiasm of Britten's as a student, one which remained with him
for the rest of his life. Performances were rare, but he sought them out
and bought scores and recordings, becoming by his mid twenties
better acquainted with Mahler's music than most of his compatriots
would be for many years. Shostakovich (another admirer of Mahler)
was also a composer for whom Britten felt an early affinity. At the
time of Berg's death, regretting the small number of 'real musicians'
among contemporary composers, he listed only Berg, Schoenberg,
Stravinsky and Frank Bridge, wondering whether Igor Markevich or
Shostakovich might eventually join their number. He was more sure
of the latter when, fifteen months after leaving the College, he
heard the first British performance of *The Lady Macbeth of Mtsensk*.
The most sensationally successful Russian opera since the Revolution,
it was produced in Moscow and in Leningrad on successive days,
both productions playing to packed houses. In the two years since its
première it had been staged in three American cities and three
European ones, but in Russia it had been suppressed, apparently on
Stalin's orders, only a few weeks before the performance Britten
attended. He thought it 'idle to pretend' that it was great music
throughout, but was especially struck by the violent, even lurid
orchestral entr'actes, and was angered by the reaction of the 'English
renaissance composers' whom he saw 'sniggering in the stalls'. He
did not name them, but most of the critical response, too, was
uncomprehending, Ernest Newman in *The Sunday Times* finding the
opera scarcely worth performing, the work of a perhaps promising
'boy' (Shostakovich was twenty-eight), while the *Manchester*

Gustav Mahler (drawing by
Burkardt): 'It has the beauty
of loneliness and of pain;
of strength and freedom'
(Britten aged twenty-three
describing Mahler's *Das
Lied von der Erde*).

Dmitry Shostakovich, an influence on Britten, later a friend, later still influenced by Britten in his turn

Guardian's Neville Cardus ridiculed the idea of presenting the work in concert performance and in English translation by tortuously comparing the enterprise to an attempt to use opera to teach the Russians cricket.

Britten's contempt for such opinions (most of the London critics, only a few days before their denigration of Shostakovich, had reacted with similar scorn to Stravinsky's 'great … marvellous' *Symphony of Psalms*), and for the 'execrable' notices of Frank Bridge's *Phantasm* (whose performing parts he had helped to copy) as well as the poor reception of his teacher's other late pieces contributed to his lifelong detestation of music critics. Less fairly, his anger at Bridge's neglect as a conductor must be the reason for his almost obsessive denigration of Adrian (later Sir Adrian) Boult, the BBC's Musical Director and Chief Conductor since 1930, the year of Britten's arrival in London. 'Terrible execrable conductor' and 'that worst of all conductors (?)' are typical of Britten's descriptions of him during his years at the College.

Later that summer he described his first end-of-year composition examination as 'an absolute farce' since the examiners took only half an hour to look through the 'hundreds of things' he submitted. He was however almost immediately awarded a prize for his work. A short while before this he had been invited by a well-known authority on folk dance, Violet Alford, to a performance by Ida Rubinstein's dance company. He was not much impressed by her or by the music, but Miss Alford's object was to persuade him to write a ballet score for her, to a scenario based on a folk song, *Plymouth Town*. Britten sketched the work in a fortnight, during his summer holiday in Lowestoft, and scored it during the autumn. He promptly submitted it to the newly formed Camargo Society, the forerunner of the Vic-Wells Ballet and thus of the present-day Royal Ballet, and although they did not accept it they may have been encouraging, since the following summer Britten began (but did not finish) a second ballet score, also to a scenario by Violet Alford. *Plymouth Town* has never been performed, but it was Britten's longest work of this period, his first for the stage and, perhaps one reason he agreed to write it, concerns the archetypal Britten theme of innocence betrayed.

Despite all the new musical experiences he was subjected to in London, he still retained many of his boyhood enthusiasms: for Beethoven (later a composer he found it difficult to like, once referring to him as 'a silly old potato') and Brahms, whose 'marvellous craze for the viola' he loved and obviously shared. After hearing Ravel's *Boléro* he became 'so mad that I can scarcely keep still', but he was less impressed by Berlioz's *Symphonie Fantastique* ('not much good as music') or Prokofiev's First Violin Concerto ('didn't contain much music'). He immediately recognized William Walton (eleven years his senior) as a fresh voice in British music, after one broadcast concert finding his teacher John Ireland's recent Piano Concerto 'very loosely put together' and Gustav Holst's *The Planets* 'too sugary', and concluding that no music of their generation 'can be compared to works like Walton's Viola Concerto' (though he described Delius as 'miraculous … a wizard'). Walton's *Belshazzar's Feast* he found 'very moving and brilliant', but 'over long and too continuously loud'. His criticism of his teacher softened enough for him to find the symphonic rhapsody *Mai-Dun* 'magnificent' and the orchestral prelude *The Forgotten Rite* 'beautiful', but he was 'annoyed' by most of the music of Elgar.

To judge from his letters and diaries, indeed, the most vital parts of Britten's musical education seem to have been received outside the Royal College of Music. He later spoke dismissively of his period there, saying that he had not learned much, that exceptionally gifted musicians were not adequately catered for, and that some of the

lessons (he had in mind the 'music class', no doubt) were simply a
waste of time. On the other hand, his lessons with Benjamin were
very fruitful. Had it been necessary he could have made a career as a
pianist, and in his later recital partnership with Peter Pears he became,
in the view of Gerald Moore, the finest accompanist in the world.

His gifts were not completely unrecognized by the College
authorities. During his three years there he was awarded the Ernest
Farrar Prize for composition twice, as well as the Sullivan Prize and
the Cobbett Prize for chamber music. He twice failed, however, to
win the much more valuable Mendelssohn Scholarship of £150, the
committee each time offering him instead a 'maintenance grant' of
£50; when at last he was awarded the full Scholarship, Britten found
the committee's reduction of the award to £100 and their frank
incomprehension of his music insulting, and he refused. And
although facilities and funds were available for the public performance
of music by student composers, only two of his works were played
during his time at the College, one of those (the *Sinfonietta*, Op. 1)
only after it had received a concert performance and considerable
attention elsewhere.

His name was indeed already becoming known outside the
College. Vaughan Williams had been impressed by some of the manuscripts that he had seen, and in 1932 used his influence to interest the
violinist Anne Macnaghten (who had recently founded a series of
concerts of contemporary music with the conductor Iris Lemare and
the composer Elisabeth Lutyens) in Britten's work. She was immediately sympathetic and both the Phantasy Quintet for strings (which
had already won the Cobbett Prize) and a set of three part-songs on
poems by Walter de la Mare were publicly performed at one of the
Macnaghten/Lemare Concerts in December 1932.

The part-songs were not long afterwards accepted by the Oxford
University Press, and became his first published compositions.
Together with a group of solo songs to poems by de la Mare, also
written around this time but not published by Britten until many
years later under the title *Tit for Tat*, they have a melodic freshness
that ideally complements the lyricism of de la Mare's verse and their
shrewd insights into both the magic and wonder of childhood and
the darkness and cruelty that can haunt it: one of the *Tit for Tat* songs
is a cry of protest at thoughtless cruelty to animals, all the more

horrible because practised by a child. The part-songs were described as 'attractive' by *The Times*, but by the *Musical Record*, quite incomprehensibly, as 'reminiscent in a quite peculiar degree of Walton's latest songs'. The review must have hurt Britten, since he referred to it in an article written many years later. That the author was a fellow composer, Christian Darnton, a work of whose was given its première at the same concert (Britten helped the pianist by turning pages for him), must have contributed to his lifelong mistrust and dislike of critics.

The much more ambitious and assured Sinfonietta for ten instruments, to which he felt ready to attach the label 'Op. 1' and to dedicate to Frank Bridge, was heard at the same concert series early in 1933. These performances attracted the attention of the BBC, who broadcast the Phantasy Quintet in February 1933 and invited him to submit other works. In July he played them the Phantasy Quartet for oboe and strings that he had written the previous autumn, and his recently completed choral variations, *A Boy was Born*. Both were accepted, and within a year both these and the *Sinfonietta* were broadcast. By that time the Macnaghten concerts had performed two more new pieces (a pair of part-songs and three movements from a suite for string quartet) and the Phantasy Quartet had been accepted for performance at the International Society for Contemporary Music's annual festival to be held in April 1934. But by then, in December 1933, Britten had graduated from the Royal College of Music and returned to Lowestoft. The family home at Kirkley Cliff Road was to be his address for the next two years.

Britten was later to say of his symphonic cycle *Our Hunting Fathers* (published as Op. 8) 'that's my real Op. 1 all right', but his choice of the *Sinfonietta* for that designation is significant. Of the other large-scale pieces written during his student years he chose not to publish or give opus numbers to the String Quartet in D of 1931 or the Phantasy Quintet of the following year. Since both contain music of distinct quality as well as moments that in their melodic language and their economy of means are characteristic of him, his decision at first seems puzzling. The String Quartet in D is resourcefully worked for the medium and has music of real individuality in the outer movements. The Phantasy Quintet makes ingenious use not so much of a motto theme as of a pervasive 'tag'; it too is beautifully written for string

quartet plus added viola. Yet what both have in common is an element of lyricism, distinctly English, at times introspective or brooding, attributable to Bridge's influence and perhaps Ireland's. No doubt
Britten wanted his Op. 1 to be as personal as possible.

A lyrical, elegiac element is not absent from the *Sinfonietta*, but
there it is combined with and controlled by a quite remarkable thematic unity and economy (the entire three-movement structure is
derived from the sequence of pithy gestures set out in the work's
opening few bars) that are distinctly Britten's own, and highly
prophetic. The influence of Schoenberg's First Chamber Symphony,
both in the close thematic working and the rising horn call that is
one of the *Sinfonietta*'s most fruitful thematic cells, is obvious
and perhaps, given the College's attitude to Schoenberg and his
school, defiant.

Similarly the Phantasy Quintet's successor, the Phantasy Quartet
for oboe and strings, earns its position as Op. 2 not only by its already
characteristically Brittenesque march rhythms and ostinato figures
but by its brilliant formal ingenuity. While conforming to the basic
principles of classical sonata form, in which two contrasting themes
or groups of themes are first juxtaposed, then developed using all the
resources of tension between keys, Britten fuses this with elements
of symmetrical tripartite form and of variation. 'English' lyricism is
still present, in a beautiful viola melody sounding at times as close
to Vaughan Williams as to Bridge, but it too is now 'earned' by the
resourceful thematic economy to which it is subject.

Even so, if an Op. 1 should demonstrate not only an individual
voice but a strong sense of direction, then Britten's 'real Op. 1' was his
Op. 3, the set of choral variations *A Boy was Born*. Here his already
remarkable gift for thematic transformation provides a series of
sharply characterized but unified movements and a thread on which
the individual 'scenes' of the nativity story (Herod, the Magi, etc.)
are strung. In this it already suggests that Britten was feeling his way
towards dramatic forms (it prefigures the originality of his much later
'opera in variation form' *The Turn of the Screw*) while his choice of
poems (Francis Quarles, Christina Rossetti, Thomas Tusser and
anonymous carol texts) already demonstrates taste and imaginative
discernment. The hymn-like theme is reduced to a basic motif of four
notes, and the variations themselves are often of great ingenuity. In

particular the finale is cast as a sequence of carols in the form of a rondo (repetitions of the same or similar material separated by contrasting episodes), with a final pealing return of the original theme heralded by recollections of the earlier movements.

Variation forms were important to Britten throughout his life, especially during his earlier years. They must have come naturally to a composer who from his very earliest published compositions showed such a remarkable gift for developing the very simplest of motifs and for reducing a musical idea to an essential germ. It was in 1932, not long before beginning *A Boy was Born*, that he started writing a set of variations on a theme by Frank Bridge, a tribute to his teacher that he had long wanted to write. He abandoned the work, but was to return to the idea and the same Bridge theme five years later.

The Phantasy Quartet was Britten's first work to be performed outside the United Kingdom, at the International Society for Contemporary Music (ISCM) Festival in Florence in 1934. These annual festivals, performing works chosen by autonomous national committees, had since 1923 been the most important international forum for living composers. He travelled to Italy for the performance, by Leon Goossens and the Griller Quartet, and reported that it had been well received, but two days after the concert his family sent a cable reading 'Come today, Pop not so well'. Robert Britten had been suffering from lymphatic cancer for several months, and his son had been horrified by the agonizing progress of the disease. In fact he was already dead when the cable was sent, but Britten was not told this until he arrived in Lowestoft. He wrote in his diary: 'A great man, with one of the finest brains I have ever come across, and what a father!' The funeral took place two days later; the music, chosen by Britten and his brother Robert, included the closing chorus from Bach's St Matthew Passion and the third variation ('Jesu, as Thou art our Saviour') from his own *A Boy was Born*.

Britten still had a small travelling scholarship to spend, and in the autumn of 1934 he set off, with his mother, for Vienna. Mrs Britten used the trip to attempt to make useful contacts for her son. On the way to Vienna they spent ten days in Basel, partly in order to meet the conductor Felix Weingartner. He was 'very nice, but not much help', and Britten found a concert of music by Richard Strauss that Weingartner conducted during his stay 'VERY BAD', though he was

Felix Weingartner, the
famous conductor that Britten
found 'very nice, but not
much help' when he visited
him in Switzerland in 1934

delighted by the soloist in a group of Strauss songs, Elisabeth
Schumann, and by a 'simply lovely' performance of Mozart's *Die
Zauberflöte* at the city's opera house. Mother and son then travelled
via Salzburg to Vienna, where they stayed for nearly three weeks.
For Britten the revelation of this visit, apart from some outstandingly
fine operatic performances, mostly of Wagner, was a standard of
orchestral playing that he had not so far encountered, a revelation
to him after the generally under-rehearsed concerts he had heard
in London.

It was during this visit to Vienna that Britten began work on a
Suite for violin and piano, published as his Op. 6, that is the most
'modern-sounding' of all his early instrumental pieces, and the clearest
indication among them of his interest in Schoenberg and his school.
There is no evidence that he heard any of their music during his
trip to Germany and Austria, but the Suite strongly implies that he
was well aware of what they were doing. It is based throughout on a
simple four-note motif, but Britten uses the profile of this phrase
(ascent–descent–ascent) and its inversion (descent–ascent–descent)
much more often than the notes of the 'motto' itself. Its relatively
narrow ascents and descents are often widened, in a clear attempt
to expand the technique, already used with great confidence in the
Sinfonietta, of building an entire composition from the rigorous
exploration of a few simple cells. In particular the Suite explores the
question of how far a basic shape can remain recognizable when its
descents and ascents are radically altered. Schoenberg's dictum that
in serial practice any note may be transposed by an octave clearly
interested Britten, and the Suite's austere angularity is the result of
his first exploration of it.

Three movements from the Suite were given their first performance
in a broadcast recital in December 1934, with two further movements
added the following year. The incomplete first performance came at
the end of a very significant year for Britten and for the history of
British music. Three senior English composers – Elgar, Holst and
Delius – died during the year, and the most important of those who
survived, Ralph Vaughan Williams, dismayed many of his admirers
with his harshly dissonant Fourth Symphony. Britten's premières
during the year ranged from the exuberant *Simple Symphony* to the
masterly *A Boy was Born* and from the Schoenberg-inspired acerbities
of the Suite Op. 6 to the *Holiday Diary* for piano (commissioned
by the publisher Boosey and Hawkes, to whom Britten had moved
after the Oxford University Press had rejected his Phantasy Quartet),
which demonstrates an already personal keyboard style while frankly
avowing an admiration for Bartók and Stravinsky. As if this catalogue
of all that the twenty-year-old could do were not enough, he wrote
a setting of the *Te Deum* (in English) for a church choir in central
London which shows a perfect awareness of the strengths of the
English tradition of choral church music while easily surpassing most
of its living exponents.

Opposite, a concert given in July 1934 with a local organist and family friend. Britten's piano solos were the slow movement of Beethoven's 'Appassionata' sonata and Schoenberg's Six Little Piano Pieces, Op. 19.

𝕾𝕿. 𝕵𝖔𝖍𝖓'𝖘 𝕮𝖍𝖚𝖗𝖈𝖍,
Lowestoft.

A

PIANO and ORGAN
RECITAL

by

Mr. Benjamin Britten (Piano)
and
Mr. C. J. R. Coleman (Organ)

Monday, July 9th at 8 p.m.

PROGRAMME.

1. **Fantasia in A minor** . . . *Schumann*
2. **Piano Solos**
3. **"Moonlight" from Suite "The Sea"**
   Frank Bridge arr. B.B.
   ### HYMN.
4. **Concerto in B flat minor**
   (1st movement) . . *Tchaikovski*
5. **Prelude and Fugue in E minor**
   for Organ Solo   *Bach*
6. **Symphony in E flat (Finale)**
   Mozart arr. B.B.

Arranged by permission of the Composer

GREEN AND CO., PRINTERS, LOWESTOFT.

It should have been apparent to anyone with ears to hear that a
new and important talent had arrived. But it was equally evident that
Britten was a composer of English sensibility (the response of *A Boy
was Born* to the sound of English words and its deep awareness of
English polyphony demonstrated that) but also of an openness to the
recent music of the rest of Europe that he shared with few English
musicians of the period save Frank Bridge. Most of his early works
received favourable if perplexed reviews, but a hint of exasperation,
even of resentment, appeared in several of them. Alongside *The
Times*'s review of the *Sinfonietta* ('Mr Benjamin Britten, after taking
something from Hindemith, seems to be striking out on a path of
his own … He has already enough to say for himself to excuse his
independence of tradition') must be set the *Daily Telegraph*'s judgement: 'as provocative as any of the foreign exponents of the catch-
as-catch-can school of composition'. Although the *Observer* had no
reservations about *A Boy was Born* ('He rivets attention from the first
note onwards … one feels instinctively that this is music it behoves
one to listen to'), *Musical Opinion* had a few: 'now and then he avails
himself of his technical efficiency a trifle ostentatiously.' And *The
Times*'s judgement of the Suite Op. 6 ('the difficulty with Mr Britten
is to know whether he is being serious or not … the music did not
produce results commensurate with its cleverness') was expressed in
terms that were to recur – the use of the word 'clever' as a term of
abuse – in criticism of Britten's music for many years.

In part this was due to distrust of a composer to whom difficult
things seemed easy. Britten also ascribed it, in an article written in the
USA in 1941, to a strand in British musical life that he termed 'the
English Gentleman (who generally thinks it rather vulgar to take too
much trouble)'. Against this school, which he associated rather unfair-
ly with the name of Sir Hubert Parry, he set that of Elgar, whom he
praised as 'a most eclectic composer, his most obvious influences being
Wagner, Tchaikovsky and Franck', adding that 'Now the Elgarian
approach, with its direct admission of continental contemporary
influence, has asserted itself.' Indeed it had, in Britten's case, but in
England in the 1930s to be both 'clever' and 'unEnglish' was no recipe
for critical approval.

3

'I always feel very young
and stupid when with such
brains as these': Britten on
Christopher Isherwood and
W. H. Auden

Underneath the abject willow,
Lover, sigh no more;
Act from thought should swiftly follow:
What is thinking for?
Your unique and moping station
Proves you cold;
Stand up and fold
Your map of desolation.

W. H. Auden

Reputation Growing Steadily 1934-9

Robert Britten's will left the bulk of his estate to his wife, with bequests of £100 to each of his four children. Edith Britten would have found herself in comfortable circumstances (at her own death she left an estate not much less than her husband left her) and she would have been able to support her son had he needed it. He, however, was determined to make a living from composition: 'it was the only thing I cared about and I was sure it was possible.' He must have known, however, that very few British composers at this period were able to make a living from composing alone. Vaughan Williams had a private income and Walton had for several years been able to devote all his time to composition because of the patronage of the Sitwell family, but Britten's teacher John Ireland, a well-known and respected composer, was obliged to teach at the Royal College to supplement his income from composing. Most other 'established' composers either taught or held administrative positions in the musical profession. In the autumn of 1934, apparently with little enthusiasm, Britten was trying to obtain full-time employment of some unspecified kind with the BBC. 'I was sure it was possible', however, implies that he already had an idea of how he might make an income from composing, and although he did not begin working for the GPO (General Post Office) Film Unit until the spring of 1935 it may well be (he was already an avid film-goer) that he had the writing of film music in mind before then.

Paul Rotha, a pioneer of the documentary film movement in Britain

One account of how Britten was drawn into the still new documentary film industry suggests that John Grierson, head of the GPO Film Unit, asked the Royal College of Music to nominate a talented recent student who might write scores for him. It is certainly true that Edward Clark of the BBC, one of the pioneers of 'modern music' in Britain, had suggested Britten's name to Grierson's assistant Alberto Cavalcanti. He was tried out on the title sequence only of a short documentary called *Cable Ship* and was soon offered a full-time job writing music for the Unit at a salary of £5 a week, later increased to

£8: a good income, well above the national average, a sum on which a young man with no dependants could live in comfort. He became a self-supporting, full-time composer at the age of twenty-one.

Working at the GPO Film Unit immediately brought him into touch with a group of highly articulate and creative artists, most of them young and left-wing: among others the film directors Paul Rotha and Basil Wright, the painter William Coldstream and the poet W. H. Auden. Britten, more reticent (and younger) than any of them, said that he had 'a bad inferiority complex' in their company: 'I always feel very young and stupid when with these brains.' Auden had been, some years before Britten, a pupil at Gresham's; the two first met, to discuss a film project, at the school where Auden was then teaching (he joined the GPO Film Unit a little later than Britten). There was in fact something schoolboyish to their relationship: Auden the sophisticated senior prefect, Britten the overawed new boy, and for the next few years they were very close.

Although their temperaments and characters were very different, and the period of their collaboration short (no more than seven years) Auden's influence on Britten was deep. For a young composer to come

From left, W. H. Auden, William Coldstream and Britten, as the Three Graces or the Three Arts, at the Downs School near Malvern where Auden was teaching

into close contact with the most gifted English poet of his generation was a stroke of good fortune. Auden's didacticism and apparent omniscience might make Britten 'feel very young and stupid', but he was not, and his settings of Auden demonstrate shrewd understanding of the musical qualities of his lyric verse. Contact with Auden also introduced him to the world of avant-garde theatre: during 1935, the year of their first meeting, the Group Theatre produced *The Dance of Death* and *The Dog Beneath the Skin*, plays that Auden had written in collaboration with Christopher Isherwood, and Britten was soon asked to write music for their successors and for a production of Shakespeare's *Timon of Athens*.

The meeting with Auden also helped to mature Britten's political and social views. He was by now to some degree reacting against his middle-class background, and found Auden's 'anti-bourgeois' stance appealing. Auden and Isherwood were openly homosexual, and seem to have taken it upon themselves to draw Britten out into an

Isherwood and Auden in 1938, departing for China to report on the Sino-Japanese War; a group of Britten's cabaret songs had been sung at a farewell party for them the night before.

acknowledgment of his own sexuality. There is no evidence, however, that any relationship developed between either of them and the composer. Two of Auden's poems of this period are overtly addressed to Britten; one ('Underneath the abject willow') is an exhortation to commitment, not an avowal of love:

... Your unique and moping station
Proves you cold;
Stand up and fold
Your map of desolation ...

Coldest love will warm to action,
Walk then, come,
No longer numb,
Into your satisfaction.

while the other ('Night covers up the rigid land') seems to acknowledge that although Auden might have desired a relationship with Britten he now realized that it would be impossible:

For each love to its aim is true,
And all kinds seek their own;
You love your life and I love you,
So I must lie alone.

O hurry to the fêted spot
Of your deliberate fall;
For now my dreams of you cannot
Refer to you at all.

In the *Letters from Iceland* that Auden wrote with Louis MacNeice two years after meeting Britten, his 'testament' included the clause:

For my friend Benjamin Britten, composer, I beg
That fortune send him soon a passionate affair.

Either Britten's sexual awareness was slow to develop or he was slow in acknowledging it. A diary reference in September 1932 (he was nearly nineteen) to seeing at the Tate Gallery 'a marvellous picture of a "Dead Boy" by Alfred Stevens' seems naïvely innocent. Entries like 'Have some tea on the journey and some buns, but rather because of the very nice little restaurant boy who brings it along and talks a bit, Quel horreur!! But I swear there is no harm in it!' date from nearly three years later.

At around this time, now twenty-one, he struck up a friendship with thirteen-year-old Piers Dunkerley, a pupil at his own former preparatory school, South Lodge. They met and corresponded often. Britten described himself in his diary as 'very fond of him – thank heaven, not sexually' and added 'but I am getting to such a condition that I am lost without some children (of either sex) near me.' Britten seems to have acted the role of senior boy to Dunkerley's junior. It was no doubt an attempt to recapture something of the intensity of a schoolboy friendship, by an adult only too aware of a sexual component to that friendship; his 'thank heaven, not sexually' is surely a self warning not to let that component assert itself. Britten referred to Dunkerley as 'my foster-child'.

Britten's first compositions after leaving the Royal College were the *Holiday Diary* for piano, incorporating such boyish pursuits as 'Early Morning Bathe' and 'Funfair' and the *Simple Symphony*, based exclusively on the compositions of his boyhood. It was at this time that he saw *Emil and the Detectives* and *Poil de Carotte*, and at once planned to write works (neither of which materialized) based on both of them. A project that proceeded further was a suite for string quartet based on memories of his childhood, each movement to be dedicated to a friend from that period. It was to be subtitled (after a line in Shakespeare's *The Winter's Tale*) 'Go play, boy, play'. Only three movements were completed, originally called 'PT' (physical training), 'At the Party' and 'Ragging'; the work was subsequently withdrawn, revised and reissued as Three Divertimenti. Britten's lifelong preoccupation with the sound of unbroken boys' voices also began at this period. *A Boy was Born* is scored for mixed adult voices and a boys' choir; *Friday Afternoons* (written for the preparatory school of which Britten's brother Robert was headmaster) is a delightful sequence of songs for treble voices and piano.

It would be foolish to portray this very early preoccupation with the world of childhood as mere nostalgia. Like Walter de la Mare (the poet he chose for his earliest published vocal music) Britten was as aware of its fears and its cruelties as of its innocence and delight. And his preoccupation with this world gave him access to areas of the imagination, even to types of music, that he would perhaps not otherwise have approached. In *A Boy was Born* and many later works children's voices speak of a radiant innocence that is often Britten's image of the divine. In the Three Divertimenti, the movement originally called 'Ragging', now *Alla burlesca*, with its syncopations, glissandos and pizzicatos, is an image of rather undisciplined childhood fun. The former 'PT', now *Alla marcia*, is one of the earliest of the marches that were to recur in Britten's work. Many of the later ones are sinister, but the rhythm can also portray a drilled but not necessarily malign exuberance. There is a curious example of the ambiguity of the march in Britten's work of this period in a movement originally intended for the 'Go play, boy, play' quartet. It was replaced at an early stage by the present *Alla marcia*, but the rejected movement, a march that approaches and recedes, was later used in Britten's orchestral song-cycle *Les Illuminations*, where it evokes the 'wild parade' of which the poet (and the composer) 'alone have the key'.

Another aspect of childhood that Britten never forgot (it is very much part of *Friday Afternoons*) is its fondness for a tune that insists on being sung and, once sung, lodges in the memory. It is one of the roots of Britten's mature and highly personal melodic language, which emerges at this period, memorably and quite unmistakably in the midst of accomplished adaptations of what he had learned from his seniors, in the poised and beautiful evocation of 'Sailing', the second movement of the *Holiday Diary*.

Despite his dislike of cities Britten had clearly realized that his immediate future lay in London. He returned briefly to the boarding house near the Royal College of Music that he had shared with his sister Beth, then moved with her to a small, 'pleasant, tho' cold' flat over a garage in West Hampstead. A European war had seemed increasingly probable ever since Adolf Hitler's appointment as German Chancellor in 1933 and his suppression of opposition parties and the establishment of concentration camps shortly thereafter. Despite this, and despite political instability at home (the National Government Prime Minister Ramsay Macdonald was forced to resign

early in 1935; not long afterwards it was revealed that Britain was a
signatory to the infamous 'Hoare/Laval pact' by which France and
Britain agreed to allow Italy to annex Abyssinia), London in the
mid 1930s was a good place for a young artist to be. T. S. Eliot was
producing his first plays in verse and Graham Greene his first novels.
A new generation of socially and politically committed poets was
emerging, headed by Auden. The works of Anthony Tudor, Ninette
de Valois and Frederick Ashton were beginning to establish a national
school of ballet. Modern art and modern design were no longer
imported exotica, with the work of Paul Nash, Ben Nicholson, Henry
Moore and Barbara Hepworth arousing heated discussion.

Britten was evidently enthralled by the artistic life of London,
going to the ballet, theatre and cinema as well as many concerts and
opera performances, and he was much less homesick than during
his student years. His mother had now moved to a smaller house in
Frinton, a seaside resort much frequented by retired and prosperous
middle-class people. He visited her for occasional weekends, but
found the wealthy and rather snobbish atmosphere of the town not
to his liking. Although still deeply attached to her he allowed an
occasionally critical note to creep into his diary entries. When in the
summer of 1936 he played his sketches for *Our Hunting Fathers* to her
and she expressed strong disapproval of the opening song 'Rats Away!',
he described her reaction as 'almost an incentive', but of her attitudes
to his mostly left-wing friends he said as little as he did of her by
now devout adherence to Christian Science.

Britten joined the GPO Film Unit in May 1935, and by the end
of the year had written eleven short film scores for them. News of his
talent for this sort of work spread fast, and he was soon in demand
by other documentary makers and the BBC, as well as the theatre
companies to which he had been introduced by Auden. Thus in 1935,
apart from his work for the GPO, he wrote three film scores for the
Gas Association and the incidental music for two plays: the Group
Theatre's *Timon of Athens* and, for the Left Theatre, *Easter 1916*, a play
by Montagu Slater about the Easter Rebellion in Ireland.

For the next four years, until 1938, Britten devoted most of his time
to writing music for cinema, theatre and radio, nearly fifty scores in
all. They were invaluable experience for a composer who would later
turn to opera, but in them he demonstrated not only a gift for dra-

matic imagery and timing but a remarkable understanding of the new media of film and radio. His film scores, often written to a tight schedule and on a very low budget (most of them used only a handful of musicians) make brilliantly original use not only of music but also of sound effects used musically. *Night Mail*, for example, uses an instrumental ensemble of ten players, a poem by Auden spoken in strict rhythm as well as a 'rhythm section' designed to evoke the sounds of steam trains and to unite them into an integrated whole with the music, the words and the screen images. It consisted of a

Night Mail: a page of Britten's manuscript, incorporating parts for sand paper block and wind machine

compressed air cylinder (to suggest escaping steam), a sandpaper block rubbed on slate, a small trolley rolling on a steel rail, metal bars struck together, a drill piercing aluminium sheet, the sound of a hand-cranked cine-camera, a length of metal conduit struck by a hammer, a siren, and the sound of coal sliding down a shaft. There were also special effects, such as a recorded cymbal stroke played backwards at high speed to accompany the image of a train suddenly entering or emerging from a tunnel. The entire score was written in four days and recorded in four hours. Far more time was needed for the laborious process of editing, ensuring the precise synchronization of music, words and images. Britten's talent for this extremely exacting work was greatly respected by his colleagues.

The function of documentary film was to inform and to educate, and for many of those involved these functions were broadly but essentially political. That there was an implicit conflict of interest between documentary film-makers and established authority was demonstrated in April 1936 when Paul Rotha directed a short film, *Peace of Britain*, which had been commissioned by the League of Nations Union with the support of several prominent Labour Members of Parliament and trades union leaders; Britten wrote the music for it. The film did little more than assert the dangers of rearmament and urge the establishment of an international peace-making body, but the British Board of Film Censors refused it a licence, ostensibly because the filming of a tank was a breach of War Office copyright (in fact the tank was American). There was a brief but determined flurry of protest in the press and the ban was withdrawn; 'Never has a film had such good publicity!' was Britten's comment.

He had been a convinced pacifist since his school days, perhaps partly due to the influence of Frank Bridge, who was haunted by memories of World War I and of the friends who had died in it. Bridge's political views were left of centre, though Britten seems only to have discovered this when showing the older man some poems by Auden that he was planning to set. Britten's diary entries of this period are filled with worried and angry reactions to the political situation both abroad and at home. They are dismissive or scornful of British Conservative politicians, especially Stanley Baldwin, the Prime Minister, and the newly appointed Foreign Secretary, Anthony

Eden. During the 1930s Britten wrote a number of overtly political works: the incongruously martial *Pacifist March*, composed for the Peace Pledge Union (of which Britten remained a member for the rest of his life), settings of texts by such socialist writers as Randall Swingler and Montagu Slater (later the librettist of Britten's first opera, *Peter Grimes*) and, for a concert given in 1936 by the London Labour Choral Union, a work for wind band called *War and Death*, subsequently renamed *Russian Funeral*. This impressive symphonic funeral march is based on a Russian revolutionary song, a lament for those who had died in the struggle (it was much later used by Shostakovich in his Eleventh Symphony, subtitled *The Year 1905*). The piece is thus as overt a statement of Britten's political sympathies as the *Ballad of Heroes*, written three years later to a text by Auden and Swingler in memory of the British volunteers who had died fighting for the Republican cause in the Spanish Civil War.

The *Ballad of Heroes*, despite a nobly funereal opening theme, some eloquent lyricism and a haunted conclusion, suggests that for all the sincerity of Britten's views, he was not really at home writing what would become known as 'agitprop' music. *Advance Democracy*, written rather later at the time of the Munich crisis, begins strikingly, with a smooth wordless melody over a rapped-out staccato: an effective parallel to the poem's opening image of searchlights hunting for bomber planes. But 'the big bosses plotting their biggest coup of all' understandably awakens nothing in Britten, and 'Time to arise, democracy!' no more than conventional banality.

His strongest political statement of these years is his 'real Op. 1', the symphonic cycle *Our Hunting Fathers*. It was commissioned by the Norfolk and Norwich Triennial Festival, and Britten asked Auden to devise the text. The three central poems (two anonymous, the third by Thomas Ravenscroft) describe three aspects of man's attitude to animals: as abhorred vermin ('Rats Away!'), as pets ('Messalina', a lament over a dead monkey) and as victims in the name of sport ('Dance of Death', Britten's and Auden's retitling of Ravenscroft's 'Hawking for the Partridge'). Auden himself provided an Epilogue (an already published poem that gives the work its title) and a specially written Prologue.

It is an astonishing work, audibly the result of what Britten had learned from the close motivic working of its predecessors and from

the apprenticeship in dramatic writing of his work in film, radio and
theatre. Its subtitle 'symphonic cycle' is significant: it is his first song-
cycle, a form that he was to make peculiarly his own, as well as his
first attempt at a multi-movement symphonic structure for orchestra.
It was also his first collaboration with Auden on a concert work,
his first publicly performed orchestral composition and his first
major commission.

Britten himself conducted, with the Swiss soprano Sophie Wyss
as soloist; until Britten met Peter Pears she was to be a regular performer of his music. He was distressed when members of the London
Philharmonic Orchestra laughed at the work during rehearsals.
Boorish though this treatment of a young composer was (Vaughan
Williams, whose own *Five Tudor Portraits* received their première
on the same programme, reproved them for it), it is possible to understand their perplexity. The orchestral writing, with many difficult
solo passages and much use of chamber textures, is unprecedented in
British music and must have seemed at first sight almost unplayable.
Even so, Britten reported that after the troubled first rehearsal the
orchestra 'improved a lot' and at the first performance itself played
'better than I had dared to hope'. The vocal writing is equally
extreme, both in its tongue-twistingly rapid mutterings and florid
coloratura and its ferocious expressiveness. The gravity of the
Prologue and Epilogue increases the vivid impact of the three central
movements, but the entire work is unified by a 'motto' as brief as but
far more cunningly used than those Britten devised for *A Boy was
Born* and the Suite, Op. 6. Indeed, the resourceful use of this motif
is one justification for the adjective 'symphonic' in the work's subtitle.
It appears in many guises, like an obsession, in the headlong 'Rats
Away!', a depiction both of a house swarming with rats and a hyster-
ical attempt to exorcise them. More lyrically extended it underlies
both the melodramatic over-statement of 'Messalina' and its genuine
pathos. It is however almost absent from the 'Dance of Death', a
scherzo that expresses both the violence and the sheer physical excitement of hunting. The excitement is fuelled by obsessive rhythmic
repetition of the hawks' names and by the incessant rolling of the 'r'
in the huntsman's call ('Whurret!') to them.

The unifying motif is heard at last at the movement's climax –
the kill – and then repeatedly throughout the savage orchestral

interlude that links it with the ensuing funeral march. The hawks' names include 'German' and 'Jew'; their juxtaposition in the coda, and Britten's and Auden's reason for thus linking them in 1936, were not remarked upon by any of the numerous reviewers of the first performance. The work had a single broadcast in the following year, 1937, and was then not heard again for a quarter of a century. Britten described himself as 'pleased' by the adverse review in *The Times* (by H. C. Colles) 'because what could be the use of a work of this kind if the narrow-minded, prejudiced, snobbish Colles approved?' Colles's review was uncomprehending ('we are unable to say … we wish we knew …') and attributed the warmth of the audience's reception to their sharing with Britten 'some sense of music or of humour, or both, to which we are strangers'. The *Observer* found the music 'dire nonsense … hardly worth doing', only the *Daily Telegraph* finding much that was positive – though scarcely perceptive – to say about it: 'Puck-like music, fantastically nimble and coruscating … a kind of orchestral prank.'

That a work of such stature and of such bitter, towering eloquence should have achieved at best a minor *succès d'estime* or *de scandale* and should then have been all but forgotten is evidence of how provincial the standards of musical life in Britain were at that time, and it makes one understand some of Britten's withering contempt for critics. But having, as he must have known ('my Op. 1 all right'), written his finest work so far, how must he have reacted privately to the almost total lack of understanding which greeted it?

Our Hunting Fathers was written in two months, mid May to mid July 1936, and some have heard in it the influence of a work that Britten heard a short while earlier, on a visit to Barcelona for the first complete performance of his Suite Op. 6 at the ISCM Festival. The major event of the Festival was the posthumous première of Alban Berg's poignantly expressive Violin Concerto, a work inspired by the sudden death at the age of eighteen of Manon Gropius, the daughter of Mahler's widow by her second husband Walter Gropius; the concerto is dedicated 'to the memory of an Angel'. Britten described it as 'shattering' and made a point of hearing both its British première, less than a fortnight later, and another London performance not long afterwards. There may be an echo in *Our Hunting Fathers* of one of the concerto's moods, that of bitter protest, but a more direct influence is the suite of orchestral fragments from Berg's opera *Wozzeck*, which Britten already knew and was on the same programme with the concerto at its première. Britten's motto phrase could be inserted without much difficulty into the most eloquent of the *Wozzeck* interludes. Like 'Messalina', that interlude is in the key of D minor; Berg's opera, like Britten's cycle, is an expression of pity for helpless suffering.

The *Temporal Variations* for oboe and piano were written very fast towards the end of the same year; they are among the most strikingly individual of his works of this period. All the variations have titles, but the theme itself is of such an agitated character that the listener wonders in advance whether it can possibly assume the grace of a Waltz or the sprightliness of a Polka. It can, but the real strength of the work lies in the bigger emotions that it reveals in such variations as the first ('Oration': boldly declamatory, later almost beseeching), the fourth ('Commination': severely plain phrases from the oboe supported by rhetorical piano gestures) and the extremely quiet, almost visionary 'Chorale' that follows.

The *Temporal Variations* were withdrawn after a single performance and were not published or heard again during Britten's lifetime; as with a number of other withdrawn works it is impossible to tell whether he was dissatisfied with the piece or merely planned to revise it but never found the time. Many of Britten's scores of this period for film and theatre are unknown and difficult of access. Although a few of the documentaries have become famous and have enjoyed revivals in specialist cinemas and on television, most have not, and a great deal of music to which Britten devoted great pains remains inaccessible. In the case of the plays and radio features on which he collaborated with writers of the distinction of Auden and Louis MacNeice, revival of text and music has sometimes been feasible; in recent years concert suites have been extracted from his more extended early dramatic scores. From the little that has so far been made available it is obvious not only that Britten's 'incidental' music is of high and imaginative quality but that it was the workshop in which he formed his operatic language. It was at this time, too, that he wrote his only feature-length film score. *Love from a Stranger* demonstrates that Britten could easily have made a distinguished career in the specialist field of dramatic film music; its opening storm sequence is a

Lennox Berkeley: 'He is a
dear, and is helping me a lot.'

clear anticipation of the storm music he would write nine years later
for *Peter Grimes*.

At the beginning of 1936 Britten summed up his creative, material
and emotional situation as he entered his twenty-fourth year: '1936
finds me infinitely better off in all ways than did the beginning of
1935 ... having a lot of success but not a staggering amount of
performances, tho' reputation (even for bad) growing steadily ...
being comfortably settled in a pleasant, tho' cold, flat in West
Hampstead with Beth, with whom I get on very well.'

It was in Barcelona in April 1936 that Britten began two very
significant friendships. The first was with the composer Lennox
Berkeley, ten years his senior, who was also at the ISCM Festival for
a performance of one of his works. He too had been at Gresham's
School, but unlike Britten had gone from there to university and
then not to a college of music but to study privately in Paris with the

most famous trainer of composers of the period, Nadia Boulanger.
He returned a composer more Gallic than English in his elegant
craftsmanship. He and Britten soon became close; they shared a
working holiday that summer and collaborated on a suite based on
Catalan dance tunes. They called it *Mont Juic*, after the hill on the
outskirts of Barcelona where they had heard the original melodies.
Neither composer would reveal which of them was responsible for
which movement, pointing out in their preface to the score that the
form and orchestration of each piece were discussed in detail, and it
would have been difficult even for them to be sure which feature was
first suggested by whom. Apart from a grieving 'Lament' (subtitled
Barcelona 1936, a reaction to the Civil War that broke out in Spain
shortly after their visit) it is an agreeable and highly accomplished
piece of light music.

Berkeley, who subsequently married and had children, was
sexually attracted to Britten and told him so but, as Britten's diary
firmly records, 'we have come to an agreement on that subject.' They
remained friends until Britten's death. His friendship with Peter Burra
was of much shorter duration. Burra was a talented writer and critic
who was in Barcelona covering the ISCM Festival for *The Times*.
He had been at school with Peter Pears (who at this time Britten had
not met) and for some time during 1936 the two shared a house.
Britten became fond of Burra, seemingly confided in him about his
homosexuality, and was deeply shocked when he died in a light
aeroplane accident a year after their meeting. Britten first met Pears
when both had volunteered to help sort out Burra's papers.

Three months before that, in January 1937, Britten had been still
more deeply shaken by another unexpected death, that of his mother.
Her daughter Beth had fallen seriously ill with influenza, she
travelled to London to nurse her, contracted the disease herself and
died of bronchial pneumonia after an illness lasting several days.
Britten was grief-stricken and overwrought, not least because his
sister was still so ill that she could not immediately be told about her
mother's death. Nearly a year later a friend remarked in a letter to a
mutual acquaintance that Britten's depression as Christmas
approached was due to the fact that 'he really hated growing up'
and that his ideally happy childhood only truly ended when Edith
Britten died.

Her death ended his childhood, and also released him from it.
It seems probable that Britten only began to consider the possibility
of some physical sexual relationship, as distinct from an idealized,
platonic one, in the months after his mother died; he was by then
twenty-three. Barely a month after her death his diary reflects on the
necessity 'to decide something about my sexual life'. Two months
later his acquaintance with Peter Pears began.

Pears was three years older than Britten, but as yet making only a
modest career as a singer. Coming from a rather conventional middle-
class family, many of them clergymen or army officers, he had drifted
into teaching after being sent down from Oxford University for

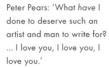

Peter Pears: 'What *have* I
done to deserve such an
artist and man to write for?
... I love you, I love you, I
love you.'

failing his first important examinations. He had then been rejected by a school of singing on the grounds that his voice was too slight for a professional career. Subsequently, however, he won a scholarship to the Royal College of Music, but left after a year because he was dissatisfied with the tuition and was in any case finding enough work to live on. But his voice, although musically and intelligently used, was still small and of restricted range: useful for professional choral work or in a madrigal group, quite unsuited to major roles in opera or oratorio (Britten first heard him, though seems not to have noticed him, singing a very minor part in Shostakovich's *The Lady Macbeth of Mtsensk*). Britten later claimed that he recognized Pears's latent abilities much more clearly than he did himself, and Pears would probably have agreed. Britten's love for Pears inspired a remarkable succession of works written for his voice, but from the very beginning challenged that voice to realize its potential.

In his later years at least, Pears was more open about his sexuality than Britten, and said that he thoroughly enjoyed his life at public school partly because the attitude to schoolboy 'crushes' at Lancing College was relatively relaxed. Another reason would have been the remoteness of his parents: Arthur Pears was a civil engineer who spent much of his time abroad, his wife often accompanying him. Pears was sent to a boarding school at the age of six, and his schoolfriends were closer family than his parents, whom he seldom met between his nursery years and his teens. Many of his friends have commented on how much less shy Pears was than Britten, how much more obviously at home in a group, but they have also often added that Pears was the more difficult to get to know.

As yet Pears and Britten were no more than affectionate friends. Although Britten soon described Pears as 'a dear' (also his term for Burra) it was a year before the two set up house together, and more than two years before their relationship was fully consummated. Immediately before they met to arrange Burra's papers Britten had spent three weeks on another 'composing holiday' with Berkeley, and not long afterwards it was Britten and Berkeley, not Britten and Pears, who made plans to live together (though with a continuance of their 'agreement') in the Old Mill at Snape, near Aldeburgh, that Britten had bought with the money his mother had left him. After conversion work had been done (including arrangements for two pianos, to be

The Old Mill at Snape

placed as far apart as possible), he moved almost simultaneously to the Mill and into a London flat that he was to share with Pears (in April and March 1938 respectively). A reference in his diary to 'Sleeping with Peter P.' is however without its modern connotation, and almost certainly means that he was sharing Pears's borrowed flat for a night; similarly, in 'He's a dear – and I'm glad I'm going to live with him', 'live with' is surely meant literally, not as a circumlocution.

It was at the Old Mill that Britten pursued a brief and unsuccessful attempt to adopt a twelve-year-old Basque refugee boy. It was from the London flat that he wrote to an eighteen-year-old whom he had met briefly four years earlier during the ISCM Festival in Florence. The meeting took place during an excursion from there to Siena; in a sudden storm they shared Britten's raincoat (the trip took place on the day of Robert Britten's death). Learning that the young man was now living in Cambridge, Britten suggested that they might meet. There was an immediate response, and they were soon seeing each other often. Encouraging letters from Berkeley and from Auden imply that this was almost certainly Britten's first sexual experience.

Since *Our Hunting Fathers* he had continued to collaborate with Auden, on radio features and a group of cabaret songs for the actress and revue artist Hedli Anderson. She also took part in Auden's and Isherwood's play *The Ascent of F6*, for which Britten wrote extensive incidental music. It makes colourful use of very restricted forces (piano duet and percussion) and parallels the irony of the text with adroit reference to popular idioms. In his setting of Auden's choral blues ('Stop all the clocks') in particular Britten managed the precise fusion of wry cabaret number and troubled funeral dirge that the words imply. For a 'highbrow' play, largely in verse, *F6* was very successful, with a run of two months at the small Mercury Theatre, followed only a fortnight later by a five-week revival at a slightly larger theatre.

Britten found his friend's poems harder to set than the songs in his plays. After setting a couple of poems from Auden's recent collection *Look, Stranger!*, he promised Sophie Wyss, his publisher and the BBC to add several more, but it was only after repeated attempts ('about six versions ... all of them NBG') that he finally produced a setting of

The Ascent of F6: the original production of Auden's and Isherwood's play, designed by Robert Medley

'Let the florid music praise'. Eventually he set eight Auden poems but published only five of them as *On This Island*, Op. 11. The original edition of the score referred to it as 'Vol. I', as though a second were in preparation, but although Britten made several attempts to set further Auden poems none was ever finished and Britten was never again to use Auden's verses as song texts.

The opening song of *On This Island*, 'Let the florid music praise' (that 'fanfare poem' as Britten called it) is as perfect a matching of Auden's artifice as could be imagined: indeed a neo-Baroque coloratura vocal fanfare. Purcell's influence is often traced in it; that of Stravinsky is at least as strong. 'Now the leaves are falling fast' uses four descending chords and a lyrical vocal phrase to encompass a range from simplicity to grandeur. 'Seascape' easily parallels Auden's richness of marine imagery but subjects it to subtle structural discipline and thematic economy, while in 'Nocturne' Britten's majestically unhurried melody supports the text but is not directed by it. In the final 'As it is, plenty' the music echoes the spirit of the words so accurately that the result verges on the trivial.

One of Britten's 'incidental' scores of this period that has been rediscovered recently is *The Company of Heaven*. The BBC had already produced, for various seasons of the Christian year, anthologies of prose and verse with interpolated music. For a programme scheduled for Michaelmas 1937 they sought greater unity by inviting Britten to write all the music. They were rather disconcerted when he produced a full-scale cantata for two soloists, chorus and orchestra with interpolated readings. It seems that Britten had it in mind to convert it into an independent concert piece, but the score was long thought to have been lost, and it was not heard again in its entirety until 1989. Apart from its interest as an example of a whole area of Britten's music that has remained largely unknown, it contains the first music that he ever composed specifically with the voice of Peter Pears in mind, a lilting setting over a light, trilling string accompaniment of Emily Brontë's 'A thousand, thousand gleaming fires'. The striking unison string theme with quiet drums that opens the piece, the poised serenity of the soprano solo with chorus 'Heaven is here' and the boldly declamatory male voice chorus 'War in heaven' are all intriguing glimpses of Britten's 'hidden' music of this period; the serenely gracious 'Funeral March for a Boy' is one of the clearest indications we have of his obsession (not too strong a word) at this time with Mahler.

Britten's finest work of 1937 shrewdly used the circumstances of a commission to write what he wanted and needed to write. Boyd Neel, who had conducted Britten's score for *Love from a Stranger*, had founded what was then the only virtuoso chamber string orchestra in Britain. The Boyd Neel Orchestra's reputation had spread as far as the Salzburg Festival, and the orchestra was invited to appear there on condition that they bring with them a new work by a British composer. The invitation arrived in May, with the date of the concert fixed for 27 August. Neel, who had been impressed by Britten's 'extraordinary speed of composition', was nevertheless astonished at his response: he turned up at Neel's house ten days later with a complete composition sketch. The *Variations on a Theme of Frank Bridge* were fully scored a month later. Britten could not be present for the première, but Pears was on a European holiday at the time and reported that the *Variations* had been a great success. The Salzburg papers confirm Pears's impression, one describing the work as 'quite splendid', another, though evidently disconcerted by the 'Wiener Walzer' variation, as 'a great success ... a very dexterous piece'.

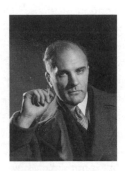

Boyd Neel, whose shrewd recognition of Britten's ability to work extremely fast resulted in one of his masterpieces, the *Frank Bridge Variations*

Like the *Temporal Variations*, the Frank Bridge set have titles; they originally also had subtitles, which were never made public. The Introduction and Bridge's own theme (from his Idyll No. 2 for string quartet) were inscribed 'To F B – himself', the first variation was entitled 'his integrity', the second 'his energy', and so on. Britten seems to have changed his mind several times about these private superscriptions, and was only with difficulty persuaded by Bridge himself to suppress them. The older man was undoubtedly right: variation 6, 'Wiener Walzer', tells us more about Britten's ability to sum up every cliché of the Viennese waltz in a few pages than about Bridge's 'gaiety'. 'His tradition' seems a curious title for variation 5, 'Bourrée Classique', unless Bridge and Britten had laughed together at some of the Stravinsky-derived neo-classicism that was then fashionable in Paris. And the annotation 'his sympathy' is a feeble understatement of the bitterly grieving Funeral March, variation 8.

Far more even than the *Temporal Variations*, the Frank Bridge set represent the first climax of Britten's mastery of motivic development. Even before the variations 'proper' begin, the basic elements of

Bridge's theme are subjected to close analysis and its crucial intervals and melodic curves refined to a series of brief germinal motifs. Concentrating on the latter half of the theme Britten first demonstrates, in a darkly scored Adagio, that the wistfulness of the melody his teacher had written at an age not much greater than his own has an impassioned eloquence beneath its surface. It is followed by a March which some have seen as a satire on Germanic militarism, but its subtitle referred to Bridge's 'energy', and it is brisk rather than sinister. The Romance is a not quite serious sidelong glance at French elegance, the Aria Italiana a burlesque on all things Italian – strumming guitars, coloratura display – that would have delighted Rossini, while the 'Wiener Walzer', as one of the Salzburg reviewers noticed, approaches the Viennese waltz via Ravel's parody of it, *La Valse*.

No credit for the composer: *Love from a Stranger*, for which Britten provided the music

The Moto Perpetuo does precisely what it was intended to do with great efficiency – to show off the athletic virtuosity of Neel's players – but it also serves to increase the shock value of the Mahlerian Funeral March which follows. This abruptly changes the character of the work: its harmonic instability is never satisfyingly resolved, its brooding melancholy rises to impassioned eloquence. This sombre mood affects the Chant that follows it: broken phrases for Britten's and Bridge's own instrument the viola (in three parts, all muted) supported by glassy harmonics and high pizzicatos. It is one example among many of the extraordinary range of string sonorities that Britten discovered in this single work. The Finale begins with a virtuoso fugue whose angular, syncopated subject is discussed in no fewer than eleven parts. The fugue subject, still flickering in the corners of the orchestra, is then made the background for a return of Bridge's theme, before a homage more heartfelt than all Britten's awkward subtitles: quotations from five of Bridge's other works are woven into the elaborate texture. None of the works quoted was at all well known; until a Bridge scholar recently pointed them out, they had remained a secret between pupil and teacher.

Many years earlier, after he had conducted a work by Ravel and a friend had asked whether England would ever produce a composer of that stature, Bridge had replied, 'You will hear of one: Benji Britten.' Perhaps his questioner meant 'an English composer of *European* stature'. One of the reasons for the *Variations'* impact in the 1930s is their very European-ness. A composer at home with Bartók and

Stravinsky, Mahler and Schoenberg, in a way that very few of his compatriots were, found an evident response in Europe, but was mistrusted by many English critics. After the London première, though several of the individual variations were applauded, *The Times* demurred that 'it would perhaps have been more creditable to develop the theme seriously', the *Observer*'s anonymous critic announced that he had not the slightest wish to hear the *Variations* again 'because they exemplify Mr. Britten's particular weakness, that neither his seriousness nor his levity is intense enough.'

Critical response to his next major work was to be still less favourable. It has been said of the Piano Concerto (his only work in this form, despite his skill as a pianist and the fact that it was originally published as 'Piano Concerto No. 1') that it is a relative failure because it does not sufficiently depart from the model of the Frank Bridge Variations. It is in four movements, but each has a title: Toccata, Waltz, Recitative and Aria (replaced six years later by an Impromptu) and – we are beginning to expect it – March. These titles have been held to imply that Britten was avoiding the formal problems of composing a true concerto by writing instead a set of genre pieces, a 'mere' suite or even (since in the original version all four movements were linked by brief melodic motifs) yet another set of variations. The work has been derided, on the one hand by critics seeking to demonstrate that Britten's central talent was for vocal music and that his instrumental works are of secondary importance, and on the other by those trying to prove that he found such large-scale Classical forms as symphony, concerto and sonata less sympathetic to his talent than the brilliant but essentially short-breathed strategy of variation.

This argument ignores the fact that the Concerto's opening Toccata is a sonata-form movement of considerable length and skill. Britten was soon to make much more personal use of the form, but the opposition of the soloist's brilliant clatter and the orchestra's lyricism is assured, at times witty. The piano persists not only in its own material but in attempts to convert the orchestra's theme into something more toccata-like. The movement succeeds both in doing what is expected (soloist and orchestra, and their two respective 'subjects', are eventually heard in perfect concord) and what is not: after a brilliant cadenza the piano takes up the lyrical idea and at last plays it

rhapsodically and romantically, for all the world as though the
concerto were by Rachmaninov.

The Waltz ambiguously treads a line between pastiche and disturbed parody: the transformation of the quiet waltz into something
harshly wild after the sinister, whirling central trio section is particularly striking. Even finer, the replacement slow movement is let down
only by its title. It is in no sense an 'Impromptu', but was written in
a form of which Britten, by 1945, the date of the revision, was a
master: a passacaglia or chaconne. It is a set of variations in which the
un-varied theme is repeated throughout, often in the bass, with
embellishments above or around it. Britten's variations are separated
by florid piano solos that freely 'modulate' between the variations'
often strongly contrasted moods. It is a fine piece, but it emphasizes
by contrast the uneasy glitter of the showy march-finale. Curiously
enough, the finale seems more satisfactory when heard after the
original third movement which, despite its suppression by the composer, has been heard again in recent years. In its sequence of recitatives for wind instruments, each hinting at a theme but greeted
derisively by the soloist, it makes a convincing rejoinder to the
preceding scherzo, while the edgy grotesquerie of the finale seems a
more apt sequel to the original Aria's ambiguous 'big tune' (Prokofiev-
like in its opulence) than to the earnestness of the Impromptu which
replaced it.

The two major works that followed the Piano Concerto, both
begun in the year of its completion and first performance, were not
completed until Britten's move to the USA in the following year,
1939. But 1938 also saw a number of important dramatic scores whose
rediscovery and reassessment in recent years has cast new light on
Britten's development immediately before his American period.

Johnson over Jordan was Britten's only important score for the com-
mercial West End theatre. J. B. Priestley's Johnson is a bowler-hatted
Everyman, subjected after his death to a dream-like examination of
his conscience and a reliving of crucial events from his past. Britten's
music is extensive, including a ballet sequence, an expressionist
night club scene (incorporating a dance-band blues, 'The Spider and
the Fly') and haunting use of a wordless solo soprano.

For the BBC, Britten followed the Michaelmas sequence *The
Company of Heaven* with a very similar project, *The World of the Spirit,*

for Whitsuntide. He described it in a letter at the time as 'an Oratorio in the grand style'. Also for the BBC, for a six-part dramatization of T. H. White's Arthurian novel *The Sword in the Stone*, he wrote a score of comparable scale for full orchestra and a chorus of male voices. Concert versions or suites from *Johnson over Jordan* and all three major BBC scores have been published and performed in recent years, and they show Britten developing his talent for dramatic music that is more than merely illustrative and for the subtle use of linking motifs to give a sense of unity.

J. B. Priestley, author of the 'modern morality' *Johnson over Jordan*, which was one of Britten's most important theatrical collaborations of the 1930s

Enjoyable and well-paid though this work was, there was little satisfaction to be found in the reviews of the Piano Concerto, first heard at the Proms in August 1938 with Britten himself as soloist. The finale was accused by *The Times* of 'angry blatancy'. The *Musical*

Times adopted a tone that the composer must have found intolerably lofty: 'Mr. Britten's cleverness, of which he has often been told, has got the better of him and led him into all sorts of errors, the worst of which are errors of taste.'

More wounding still, perhaps even a factor in his decision to leave England, was the adverse reaction of Frank Bridge's circle. One friend of Bridge's wrote to another of how 'we all utterly agree with the drastic criticisms of *The Times* ... dear Benjy doesn't know how deeply disappointed we all are.' But he must have sensed something of this when he took an off-air recording of the Concerto to play to Bridge and a group of friends a short while later. The writer of that letter, Marjorie Fass, was in other respects a warm and loving friend to Britten, and she was presumably too tactful to let him know her opinion that 'in one way, because he has so many young friends who adore and flatter him for his brilliant talent and who only live on the superficial side of life, it won't hurt him at all, but pull him up, if the criticisms in the papers are harsh.' But her reference to him in this same letter as 'poor little boy' (he was approaching twenty-five) suggests an attitude that she may have found harder to hide than her opinions.

Britten's reasons for undertaking what was at first envisaged as a visit to the USA, not a prolonged stay, were numerous. Frank Bridge had enjoyed a greater success there than in his own country. Pears had visited the USA twice, on tours with a madrigal group, the New English Singers. Britten was feeling restless. During the previous winter his doctor had ordered him to spend Christmas in bed after a number of fainting spells. Some of his friends thought that overwork and lack of sleep were the cause, and that he was risking a nervous breakdown. Auden and Isherwood, as the political situation in Europe grew graver, had moved to New York. Britten said later that 'many of us young people at that time felt that Europe was more or less finished.'

Thus by the time that he had made the decision to go, the possibility of staying in the USA was already strong; his sister recalled that he spoke of seeking American citizenship. In a letter written on the ship to Aaron Copland he said that 'I got heavily tied up in a certain direction, which is partly why I'm crossing the ocean!' This presumably refers to the eighteen-year-old of whom he had been seeing so

'We had many of the same sympathies ... and we knew we faced similar problems.': Aaron Copland at the time of his first meeting with Britten

much. Copland was a recent addition to Britten's circle of friends in America; they had met at the 1938 ISCM Festival in London, and Britten had tried (successfully) to interest his own publisher in Copland's music. There was also some talk, in the event fruitless, of him being asked to write the music for a Hollywood film on the subject of King Arthur.

Before the decision to travel was final, Montagu Slater and his wife gave him a copy of Carl Sandburg's anthology *The American Songbag*. In his letter of thanks Britten said that he was humming the tunes and muttering the words of the songs all day, describing himself as 'definitely into my "American" period'.

4

'I do think about you a lot';
for some while after his return
to England, Britten had a
photograph of Bobby
Rothman on his desk.

*L'amor me prende, e la beltà mi lega;
La pietà, la mercè con dolci sguardi
Ferma speranz'al cor par che ne doni.**

Michelangelo: Sonetto XXIV

*Love captures me, beauty binds me,
compassion and mercy with their sweet
glances give my heart secure hope.

Europe in the Past Tense 1939–42

Britten and Pears set sail on the Cunard Line's SS *Ausonia* on 29 April 1939. Frank Bridge saw them off, and as a parting gift gave Britten his own fine Italian viola, with a message wishing him not only 'bon voyage' but also 'bon retour'. Bridge died, aged only sixty-two, less than two years later, and never saw his pupil again.

On 9 May the two arrived in Quebec, where the interest of the newspapers and of the national radio station (CBC, who soon commissioned a work from Britten) must have been flattering, and encouraging if Britten was already considering a permanent move to America. The fact that, unlike Pears, he had made no definite plans to return to England implies that he was prepared to remain in the USA alone, at least for a while. It was after a month's stay in Canada, on a brief holiday trip to Grand Rapids, Michigan, on their way to New York, that the relationship changed. In a letter many years later Pears referred to Britten 'giving himself' to him on that trip. It is impossible to say precisely what happened between them at Grand Rapids, since neither of them ever discussed it with others. But it was as a couple that they travelled to New York, and after a brief stay there rented a studio together at Woodstock on the Hudson River in order to be near Aaron Copland and his lover Victor Kraft. A letter from Britten to Copland after leaving Woodstock concludes, 'love to you both from us both.'

Britten was completing a violin concerto begun in London, and was also working on a song cycle on texts by Rimbaud, *Les Illuminations*, intended for Sophie Wyss. One song from the cycle, 'Antique', was dedicated to and surely intended as a portrait of the young man of whom Britten had seen so much during the preceding year. Another, 'Being Beauteous', was dedicated to Pears. The work commissioned by CBC, however, *Young Apollo*, was also inspired by the nineteen-year-old left behind in London ('you know whom that's written about,' Britten wrote to him) and it was composed after the visit to Grand Rapids.

Young Apollo is a glittering fanfare of a piece, a toccata for piano, string quartet and string orchestra, in which some of the brilliant writing of the Frank Bridge Variations is recalled, with the addition of hurtling glissandos for all the instruments including the piano. It is 'rather inspired by such sunshine as I've never seen before,' said Britten, but it is also based on Keats's 'Hyperion': 'the new dazzling Sun-God, quivering with radiant vitality ... his limbs celestial.' It has a feeling of incompleteness, as though it were a first movement of or preliminary fanfare to a longer work, and Britten, perhaps sensing this, withdrew it after a single performance. It was not heard again until after his death.

Whether Britten deliberately chose the poetry of Rimbaud in order to expand his music's expressive range or simply came across it while investigating suitable texts for the French-speaking Swiss Sophie Wyss, *Les Illuminations* is a remarkable step forward even from the Frank Bridge Variations. Part of the reason for this is the at times flamboyantly flexible vocal line, a clear response to the sound of the French language and the extravagant imagery of Rimbaud's verse. After the fanfare-like opening, there is pride to the soloist's cry, repeated like a motto throughout the work, of 'J'ai seul la clef de cette parade sauvage' ('I alone possess the key to this wild parade'). Since two of the ensuing songs had private meanings for Britten, it is tempting to hunt for 'keys' to the others. The headlong images of crowded cities in 'Villes' are self-explanatory, but the slow ascent to a high B flat at 'et je danse' in 'Phrase' could be either an artist's or a lover's image of ecstasy (Britten himself described the poems as 'the visions of heaven that were allowed the poet, and I hope the composer'). 'Antique' is an archetypal example of Britten's gift for a simplicity so beautiful that analysis can give little impression of it. 'Royauté' is a neo-Baroque march evoking glittering but empty pomp. 'Marine', an exuberant seascape, leads to an instrumental interlude and a repetition of the motto, now hushed, to introduce the passionate 'Being Beauteous'. 'Parade', once an attempt to describe the bracing discipline of PT, works far better as a rather spectral procession. The motto returns again, finally, to introduce 'Départ', another song of extreme simplicity: a very plain, almost monotone vocal line over a sequence of ordinary chords, yet the timing of each move from chord to chord,

each vocal inflection, is masterly. Sophie Wyss gave the cycle its first
performance in London early in 1940; Peter Pears gave its American
première in May 1942.

Apart from meeting Copland again, and renewing acquaintance
with Auden and Isherwood, Pears and Britten soon made new friends
in the USA. On an earlier visit Pears had met Elizabeth Mayer,
whose psychiatrist husband was Medical Director of the Long Island
Home at Amityville, Long Island; the Mayers had left Germany after
the rise of the Nazis. Pears and Britten visited them for a weekend
in August 1939, and when war broke out a fortnight later Mrs Mayer
invited them to stay for as long as they chose. Both soon became very
attached to the Mayer family, to the very musical and sympathetic
Elizabeth especially, and Britten was soon addressing her in terms
more restrained but no less affectionate than those he had used to his
own mother; she in turn addressed him as 'my darling'. She became
indeed a second mother to him, a warm and deeply understanding
one, and the Mayers a second family. Britten's period with the Mayers
at Amityville may well have been the happiest of his adult life.

Among the Mayer circle was a local shopkeeper, David Rothman,
who was also chairman of a semi-amateur orchestra and an
acquaintance of both the physicist Albert Einstein and his cousin the
musicologist Alfred Einstein (Britten and Pears took part in
impromptu music-making with both of them). The Rothmans, as
musical as the Mayers (Mrs Rothman sang and played the violin, their
daughter was a fine pianist) became a 'third family' for Britten, the ties
to them intensified by David Rothman's sympathetic understanding of
his occasional bouts of depression and creative uncertainty – during
one of these he told Rothman that he wanted to give up music and go
to work in his store – and by Britten's strong attachment to Rothman's
young son Bobby. It was to Bobby Rothman that Britten dedicated
one of the first of his arrangements of folk songs, 'The Trees They
Grow So High' ('O father, dearest father, you've done to me great
wrong, you've tied me to a boy when you know he is too young').

The conditions for a new career in America, now that war had
broken out and the British authorities were recommending expatriates
in the USA to stay there, seemed favourable. Apart from the CBC
commission, Britten maintained good relations with the BBC
(a number of his 'American' works were given European premières by

'She is one of those grand people who have been essential through the ages for the production of art ... one of the few really good people in the world': Pears and Britten with Elizabeth Mayer

them) and his publisher, Boosey and Hawkes, had a new and lively New York office. The Frank Bridge Variations were very well received on their first performance in New York, as was the Piano Concerto when Britten gave it its US première in Chicago. Once the Violin Concerto was finished arrangements were made to give its première in New York, with the Spanish violinist Antonio Brosa (an old friend of Britten's: they had played the Suite Op. 6 together at its first complete performance and subsequently), conducted by another British expatriate, John Barbirolli. Commissions were soon received from the exiled Austrian pianist Paul Wittgenstein and from the Japanese government. Wittgenstein had lost his right arm in World War I and had made a new career by commissioning music for the left hand only: Richard Strauss, Ravel and Prokofiev had already written works for him. The Japanese, whose expansionist war with China would in 1940 lead them into an alliance with the Axis powers (Nazi Germany and Fascist Italy), were anxious to preserve and spread belief in the antiquity of their Emperor's lineage. Magnificent celebrations were planned for the 2600th anniversary of his dynasty on 11 February 1940 (in fact both the name of his founding ancestor and the date of his accession to power were purely legendary) and these included commissions to a number of Western composers for works to be performed at commemorative concerts.

Britten's Violin Concerto is a great advance on that for piano. At the time he described it as 'without question my best piece. It is rather serious, I'm afraid.' Like Beethoven he begins his concerto with a drum rhythm. Brosa identified it as a 'Spanish rhythm', and although the elegiac opening melody is soon joined by a harsher one, it is the drum rhythm that is the movement's true 'second subject'. The central scherzo is a hectic *moto perpetuo*, becoming wilder as it proceeds. A cadenza links this to the finale, but also brings back the seeds of the first movement's conflict, in particular the drum rhythm, before a grave trombone melody begins Britten's first use of a form that he was to return to often, especially for utterances of great seriousness, the passacaglia or chaconne. He treats the sombre melody quite freely, altering it slightly on each repetition and, tellingly, lowering its pitch each time. The conclusion is a lament, leaving in its wake an inevitable question about the significance of the 'Spanish rhythm', in a concerto begun during the Spanish Civil War, for an expatriate Spaniard, and concluded in a World War for which the Spanish conflict seemed to many like a sinister rehearsal.

The Concerto was neglected for many years, partly no doubt because of the adverse reviews it received from British critics after its London première (in New York, Britten reported in a letter to his brother-in-law, the press response was 'pretty violent – either pro. or con.', but the *New York Times* found 'many and positive virtues' in the work). It may also have suffered from being an almost exact contemporary of William Walton's Violin Concerto, which has a more suave melodic grace and makes more flattering use of virtuosity. Both works, and both composers, are 'conservative', but Britten's Violin

Concerto is more aware than Walton's of how a conservative idiom
can be refashioned into a music that reflects its time. Walton's concerto reminds one of Elgar's, written in 1910; Britten's 'reminds' one
of Shostakovich's first, ten years in the future. Another work that
reminds one of music not yet written, in this case of the clean textures
and 'open-air' scoring that Britten's friend Aaron Copland was soon
to develop in his popular ballet scores, is the *Canadian Carnival* or
Kermesse canadienne. Brightly scored, a sequence of brief and exuberant settings of Canadian folk songs, it was written immediately after
the Violin Concerto, and sounds like a relaxation from it.

Britten's mind was divided at this time between a feeling that he
should burn his boats and settle in the USA for good (he tried to
persuade his sister Beth and her family to join him) and a deep nostalgia not so much for England as for his part of it. On the way to the
Mayers' home at Amityville he had passed a sign informing motorists
that they were entering Suffolk County. By a further coincidence a
nearby town was called Southold, which must have reminded Britten
not only of Southwold, not far from Aldeburgh and Snape, but
of his schooldays at Southolme and South Lodge. In 1941 he was
appointed conductor of the semi-professional Suffolk Friends of
Music Orchestra, while Pears trained and conducted the Southold
Town Choral Society; Britten received $10 per rehearsal, Pears $15.
Undertaking this work indicates not only an eagerness to take part
in practical music-making but a need to supplement incomes that,
despite prestigious commissions and warm public and critical
reaction, were far from stable. During 1940 the British government
blocked the transfer of sterling overseas.

In February 1940, not long after travelling to Chicago for the
American première of his Piano Concerto, Britten had an attack of
influenza followed by a severe streptococcal infection which kept him
in bed for nearly six weeks; he was convinced that it was only the
nursing of Mrs Mayer's daughter Beata which saved his life. The
effects of the illness were to be felt for nearly a year but, as was usually
the case with Britten, it seems not to have slowed down his output of
work, almost as though he had been composing feverishly in his head
during the period of enforced rest, and could thus write down the
resulting music with great speed once he was back at his desk. He
wrote the symphony commissioned by the Japanese government in a

little over two months immediately after his illness, and finished the
work for Wittgenstein during a brief summer holiday in Maine.
By the autumn he had finished his first major composition for Pears's
voice, the *Seven Sonnets of Michelangelo*, and begun a string quartet.
Soon thereafter he embarked on his first full-length stage work.

The Japanese authorities were clearly hoping for a festive piece,
but the key to the power of Britten's *Sinfonia da Requiem* is that it
was his intention from the outset to 'combine my ideas on war and a
memorial for Mum and Pop', as he wrote to his sister. Six months
earlier, when the commission arrived, he used the very phrase *Sinfonia
da Requiem* to indicate what he proposed writing, and his assumption
that such a work 'sounds rather what they (i.e., the Japanese) would
like' was surprisingly not contradicted by his publisher; nor, apparently, did the Japanese demur at this stage. They subsequently
expressed surprise that a work with Christian subtitles to each movement and of a mournful nature should have been thought suitable
for a tribute to the Emperor, and although Britten was paid his full
commission fee it was diplomatically announced in Japan that the
score had arrived too late to permit adequate rehearsal.

The commission was received at a time when Britten's country was
at war with Japan's principal ally, when the European war that he had
dreaded seemed inexorably to be expanding into a world conflict,
and when he was deeply worried about the safety of his family. These
feelings were undoubtedly in his mind when the commission gave
him the opportunity to write his first major work for orchestra alone.
That he should wish to dedicate it to his parents' memory is equally
natural, and the titles that he chose for his three movements, all from
the Latin Mass for the Dead – 'Lacrymosa', 'Dies irae' and 'Requiem
aeternam' – are as appropriate to a symphony of mourning as they are
to one about the horror of war.

The title and the subtitles imply a programmatic, that is to say a
dramatic work, one with a literary subtext or even a plot. As in the
case of the Piano Concerto, some have seen this as a contradiction –
how can a symphony, an abstract musical form proceeding by purely
musical logic, be programmatic without renouncing its claim to be
symphonic? Britten's answer to the question 'symphonic or dramatic?'
is a resolute 'Both!' It is of the first movement's dramatic essence – a
procession of grieving mourners – that it should be repetitive, and

what analysis would call the 'first and second subjects' are alike, both pervaded by similar wailing figures. It is both inspired symphonic thinking and vivid dramatic strategy that the climax of the movement should demonstrate the implacable irreconcilability of what had seemed kindred ideas.

The undischarged electricity of this conflict is released in the central scherzo, the 'Dies irae'. Here the impression is of a headlong rush to the abyss: the music is almost without thematic substance, a series of frenzied twitchings. A second idea in the trumpets is overtly militaristic, but in the trio section, more dismayingly still, the saxophone leeringly mocks the grief-stricken phrases of the first movement; muted trumpets, with a phrase that we have not heard before, add to the derision. The twitchings return, now rooted to the spot with terror, before the music flies to pieces like a machine out of control. The fragments fall to earth, one of them rocks desolately to and fro, and it is from this motion that the lulling rhythm of the 'Requiem aeternam' is generated. But only two bars after we have realized how the possibility of salvaging something from destruction has been suggested, we hear a serenely consolatory theme (for three flutes) that we only gradually recognize as a transformation of the trumpets' odious sneering that had brought about the dissolution of the 'Dies irae'. One final transformation remains, that of the mourning procession of the opening movement into an expression of radiant hope.

Perhaps surprisingly, after such a masterly demonstration that 'dramatic symphony' is not a contradiction in terms, the work for Paul Wittgenstein is in no sense a concerto. The *Diversions*, as he called them, are another of his sets of resourceful variations: Romance, Chant, Badinerie, Burlesque and so on. The nature of the theme itself, though, is new, and seems to promise a work in more 'symphonic' style, closer in stature to the Violin Concerto and the *Sinfonia da Requiem*. First heard in the orchestra, the theme at once contradicts any expectation that in writing for a one-armed pianist Britten will confine himself to ideas of narrow range: his angular sequence of fifths and fourths stalks boldly across a compass of five octaves. It is, to be frank, too big a theme for mere 'diversion', and Britten's ingenuity is instead devoted to choosing elements from it for development.

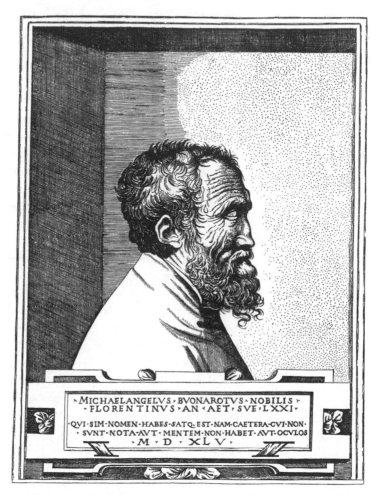

·MICHAELANGELVS·BVONAROTVS·NOBILIS·
·FLOREN TINVS·AN‹AET·SVE·LXXI·
·QVI·SIM·NOMEN·HABES·SATQ·EST·NAM·CAETERA·GVI·NON·
·SVNT·NOTA·AVT·MENTEM·NON·HABET·AVT·OCVLOS
·M·D·XLV·

Michelangelo Buonarroti at the age of seventy-one, an engraved portrait attributed to Giulio Bonasone

That Britten's gift for mimicry – at times in the *Diversions* and the earlier sets of variations close to burlesque – could be put to far more deeply creative ends is demonstrated by the work that immediately followed. In the *Seven Sonnets of Michelangelo* he used the Italian language to refer, without ever quoting or betraying any obvious influence, to the long tradition of Italian vocal music. There are unmistakably Italian rhythms in his setting of Sonnet XXXI and an Italian grace to Sonnet XXXVIII. Italianate, too, are the cycle's wonderfully ardent, curving lines; but the huge vocal gestures of the opening Sonnet XVI and the noble keyboard rhetoric of the concluding

Sonnet XXIV are pure Britten, a side of him revealed by the Italian
language, by Michelangelo the visual artist as well as the poet and
by the artistry and the personality of Peter Pears.

The *Michelangelo Sonnets* are love songs of great intensity, but
also a remarkably shrewd analysis of Pears's voice and musicianship.
Although they were completed by October 1940 their first public
performance did not take place for another two years. Caution at the
Sonnets' overt homosexuality may have been one reason for this delay
(Michelangelo wrote religious sonnets, and chaste ones addressed to
the poetess Vittoria Colonna; Britten chose none of them), but Pears
did not feel ready for a public performance of such taxing music. In
the USA he worked hard with vocal coaches to increase the range and
power of his voice, and when the first public performance did arrive
Edward Sackville-West in the *New Statesman and Nation,* apart from
praising the songs very highly indeed, said of Pears, 'it is long since
we heard an English tenor with a voice at once so strong, so pure and
so sweet.'

Despite the major works of 1940, and his long illness early in the
year, Britten managed not only to take on several pieces of work
intended primarily to make money (a reduced orchestration of *Les
Sylphides* for the New York Ballet Theatre; a volume of violin passages
from standard orchestral works for the use of students – edited in
collaboration with Antonio Brosa) but also to collaborate with Auden
on a couple of radio features and to write (though he suppressed it
before it reached performance) a full-scale piano sonata. In fact, along
with the manifest maturing of Britten's language during his American
period, a number of abandoned or suppressed works suggests that
the maturing process had many frustrations and uncertainties as well.
Apart from the Piano Sonata ('Sonata Romantica') and *Young Apollo,*
these included a set of part-songs to texts by Gerard Manley Hopkins,
an abortive clarinet concerto for Benny Goodman, an orchestral
piece for Georg Szell that got no further than sketches and a projected
harp concerto that may not have proceeded even that far.

Also in the astonishingly productive year of 1940 he began a
series of short works for the British piano duo Ethel Bartlett and Rae
Robertson, who had settled in California. None are of major
importance, though the *Introduction and Rondo Alla Burlesca* Op. 23
No. 1 is efficiently and virtuosically written for the medium, filled

with angular interplay between the players. The *Mazurka Elegiaca* Op. 23, No. 2 was conceived as a memorial to the great Polish pianist Ignacy Paderewski, and pays tribute to him and to his country with references to Chopin's Mazurkas.

In November 1940 Britten and Pears, perhaps thinking that they had trespassed long enough on the Mayers' hospitality, and in any case feeling the need to be closer to Auden (Britten and he were about to begin a major collaboration) moved to the remarkable household at 7 Middagh Street, Brooklyn Heights, where Auden was then living with his American lover Chester Kallman. The house belonged to a journalist friend of his, George Davis (who later, after the death of Kurt Weill, married his widow Lotte Lenya). It was run as a kind of artistic 'commune', with Auden as its informal but sometimes punctilious leader. Its residents at and around the time that Britten and Pears were there included the novelist Carson McCullers, the stage designer Oliver Smith, the novelist and composer Paul Bowles and his wife, Thomas Mann's son Golo, Louis MacNeice, Salvador Dalí and the revue artist and dancer Gypsy Rose Lee.

Britten installed a grand piano in the common living-room but found it almost impossible to concentrate amid the noise and disorder. He retreated frequently to Amityville to work in peace. Middagh Street was 'a trifle too Bohemian for my liking – I like the ordinary dull routine more and more, the older I get,' wrote the 27-year-old, primly, to his sister.

The initial impetus for Britten's first major stage work seems to have been a need to make money. An American associate of his publishers suggested that he write simple music for string orchestra or wind band which could be marketed through the extensive network of American high school bands, or that he might write a high school operetta. By the end of 1939, much more ambitiously, he reported that he was working with Auden on *Paul Bunyan*, an 'operetta for Broadway'. He worked hard on it, with enthusiasm for Auden's text ('a breath of fresh air'), but although the operetta was eventually performed every night for a week at Columbia University, the reviews were unenthusiastic. The *New York Times* found the music shallow and derivative. Virgil Thomson in the *New York Herald Tribune* wrote that 'its particular blend of melodic "appeal" with irresponsible counterpoint and semi-acidulous instrumentation is easily recognizable as that considered by the British Broadcasting Corporation to be at once modernistic and safe ...

Opposite, Paul Bunyan:
playbill for the first (and until
thirty-three years later the
last) production

Mr. Britten's work in *Paul Bunyan* is sort of witty at best. Otherwise it
is undistinguished.' That this critical coolness was not shared by
audiences is suggested by the laughter and applause on a private
recording of one of the original performances.

Auden and Britten called *Paul Bunyan* a 'choral operetta'; it is in
fact a musical. At the very end of his life Britten was persuaded to
look over the score and with a few modifications and cuts he allowed
firstly a broadcast, then a staged production at the Aldeburgh Festival.
He was moved by hearing it again, and said that he 'hadn't remembered that it was such a strong piece.' Despite many flaws, he was
right. It was perhaps a false step on Auden's and Britten's part to
choose such an archetypally American myth for their subject. Paul
Bunyan, the legendary giant who led the pioneering lumberjacks into
America's virgin forests, is as American a figure as Paul Revere or
Billy the Kid, and although the reviews of the first production do not
condemn the two young and recent exiles for their cheek, some such
resentment must have been felt. Auden's text is ingenious, fast-moving
and characteristically rather didactic, with some passages which almost
defy setting to music. A burlesque love song, for instance – one of the
numbers that Britten omitted from the 1974 revision – includes an
endless sequence of lines whose only function is to provide pretexts for
elaborately improbable rhymes:

Appendicectomy
's a pain in the neck to me
Anthropomorphosis
Owns several offices
Psychokinesia
Never gets easier
Papal Encyclicals
Are full of pricklicles
Plenipotentiaries
Endure for centuries…
and so on, for about four pages.

It was risky to choose as the central figure of an operetta a character
who literally cannot appear on stage (Paul Bunyan was legendarily at
least a mile high) and is thus represented by an off-stage voice, his

exploits recounted in narrative ballads placed between the scenes;
the real central character, a projection of Auden himself, is Johnny
Inkslinger, Bunyan's 'book-keeper' or mythographer. The absence
from the stage of Bunyan himself prompted the inclusion of many
small roles (over thirty of them, plus a chorus representing trees,
lumberjacks, farmers and frontier women); this and Auden's sheer
exuberance gave the composer opportunities that range from blues
and simple ballads with folk-style guitar accompaniment via ensembles for cats and wild geese, quasi-operatic aria and grotesque operatic
parody, to a scene in which, to strange music, the moon turns blue.

This passage, in which a melodic motif is heard at several different
speeds simultaneously, is based on Britten's recent experience of
gamelan music. Among the other artists who had been guests of
Elizabeth Mayer's at Amityville Britten had become friendly with the
composer Colin McPhee, who had spent much time in the Far East,
and with him had played and recorded a number of McPhee's
transcriptions for two pianos of music that he had collected in Bali.
Britten's fascination with the complexities of this music surfaced
intermittently in his music until, fifteen years later, he visited Bali
himself and was strongly influenced by what he heard.

Britten also enjoyed the opportunities *Paul Bunyan* provided to
write music of a distinctly American cast; it was for this reason that
Pears, deeply involved in copying parts and coaching singers for the
production, did not himself, with his distinctively English diction,
take part in it. Some of the early reviewers attributed this 'American-
ness' to the influence of Marc Blitzstein, whose 'play in music' *The
Cradle Will Rock* had been produced on Broadway four years earlier.
There is no evidence that Britten knew it, and it is unlikely that he
would have relied on a single source for the idiomatic Americanisms
of his score. It was much more likely a sharp ear for the American
tone of voice, in folk music, in Copland and in what he had heard
of the Broadway musical (Pears was fond of singing show songs at
parties). But the use he made of this 'mimicry' is startling: the best
pages of *Paul Bunyan* are indeed as good as a musical, and better
than most that were available for imitation in 1941.

By May, after the brief run of *Paul Bunyan*, Britten and Pears
moved from Middagh Street to California, having received an
invitation from Bartlett and Robertson to spend the summer with

them in a house they had rented at Escondido. The summer was productive – Britten completed his series of pieces for his hosts (the exuberant but rather noisily scored and over-extended *Scottish Ballad* for two pianos and orchestra) as well as a string quartet, his first, commissioned by the wealthy patroness of the arts Elizabeth Sprague Coolidge. But it was not an especially happy time: it seems that Ethel Bartlett fell violently in love with Britten, to her husband's perfect equanimity.

Britten's First String Quartet has suffered from comparison with its two superb successors. In fact among his earlier chamber works it is as climactic as the *Sinfonia da Requiem* among the works for larger forces, but it lacks the dramatic 'programme' of the *Sinfonia* and its originality is more reticent. It has a similar preoccupation to the larger work: to investigate classical formal models and where necessary refashion them to suit Britten's growing awareness of the nature of his own gifts. Like the 'Lacrymosa' of the *Sinfonia da Requiem,* the quartet's first movement is in sonata form, but with no great conflict between its subjects. Instead a slow introduction of shining, quivering high chords with fitful pizzicatos in the cello part returns twice, at the movement's mid-point and just before its end. The two intervening faster sections discuss not contrasts between dissimilar ideas but the harmonic and tonal ambiguities present within a single one, ambiguities dramatized by presenting the basic material in two guises. The scherzo makes deft, varied use of minimal material, and the way in which the sombrely nocturnal slow movement derives its calm opening from a radical simplification of the recurring slow music from the first movement is both ingenious and formally satisfying. After it has built considerable tension from a refusal until the last moment to confirm what key it is in, Britten allows himself a brief, jesting, Haydn-like finale.

Soon after returning from California to Amityville, Britten received a commission for a short orchestral work from Artur Rodzinski and the Cleveland Orchestra. It was for some reason never performed and Britten left the manuscript of what was then called *An Occasional Overture* in the USA (it was later renamed *An American Overture,* to avoid confusion with another *Occasional Overture,* written in 1946). The work was presumed lost until the manuscript was found towards the end of Britten's life. He did not remember having written it and even denied having done so until he recognized the handwriting as his own. A rather ceremonious, march-like slow introduction gives way to a central allegro with a distinct, rather Copland-like flavour of folk fiddle-playing to it. The introduction returns, rather grandly. As a piece of genially likeable light music it lives up to both its titles, but its hasty composition was followed by one of the worst of Britten's occasional 'blocks': he found himself unable to write music at all, and seems to have made his first folk-song arrangements as an attempt to cure this.

It was in California in July 1941, during the composition of the quartet and the *Scottish Ballad,* that he came across an edition of the BBC's weekly magazine *The Listener* in which he read an article by E. M. Forster about the East Anglian poet George Crabbe. Crabbe had been born in Aldeburgh, very close to Britten's mill at Snape. The article began, 'To talk about Crabbe is to talk about England', and concluded, 'Crabbe … is entirely of England. Aldeburgh stamped him for ever.' It aroused in Britten both intense homesickness and a desire to read Crabbe. Pears found an edition of his poems in an antiquarian bookshop, and almost immediately Britten wrote to Mrs Mayer that he was 'very excited – maybe an opera one day …!!' Many years later he recalled that on reading Crabbe's poem *The Borough* and especially the section about the fisherman Peter Grimes, 'I suddenly realized where I belonged and what I lacked … I had become without roots.' Talk of staying in the USA now ceased, but at that stage of the war crossing the Atlantic was out of the question.

There is no reference in Britten's and Pears's published letters to the controversy that had surrounded their absence from Britain. Auden and Isherwood had been the subject of angry articles and correspondence in the national press, even an indignant question in the House of Commons suggesting that their British citizenship should be withdrawn. Britten's exile was the subject of a letter to the *Sunday Times* from the Treasurer of the Royal Philharmonic Society who resented the fact that the paper's music critic Ernest Newman was continuing to write articles praising Britten despite his taking no part in the war effort. There was also a long correspondence in the *Musical Times,* opened by an Air Force officer who alleged that concert pro-moters, especially the BBC, were giving Britten 'particular favour' which his avoidance of military service should have denied him; he

'Cradled among the rough sons of ocean ... was born and reared the Poet of the Poor' (*Life of George Crabbe* by his son).

was 'thriving on a culture which [he has] not the courage to defend.' Other correspondents were more sympathetic, but the editor, Harvey Grace, showed his sympathy with the attackers in his reference to 'having saved one's art and one's skin at the cost of failure to do one's duty'.

Such an attack, in a specialist journal of small circulation, might not seem much of a threat, but Britten's publishers regarded it as one. They feared that there might be a boycott of his works, and with some reason: the Royal Philharmonic Society had refused to give the British première of his Violin Concerto, giving the composer's exile as the reason for his 'unpopularity'. Even the BBC, until now so sympathetic to Britten, declared a ban on the employment of men who had registered as conscientious objectors to military service; Britten and Pears both did so immediately on their arrival in England, but by then the prohibition had been withdrawn. Angry feeling against conscientious objectors and those who were seen as having deserted their country in its hour of need did not vanish with the closure of the *Musical Times* correspondence on the subject. Indeed it contributed to the ill-feeling that marred the otherwise triumphant success of *Peter Grimes* in 1945.

The delay in finding a transatlantic passage was in fact fortunate. It enabled Britten, in January 1942, to go to Boston for the local première of the *Sinfonia da Requiem*, conducted by Serge Koussevitzky. The work had been little noticed by the press after its first hearing in New York and roundly abused in Chicago, but Britten was thrilled with Koussevitzky's performance. The conductor, impressed by the work's dramatic force, asked why he had never written an opera. Britten explained that he had a subject in mind for one, but it would need a period of time free from the need to take on other work, a luxury that few young composers could afford. Not long afterwards the conductor, who had recently set up a Koussevitzky Music Foundation in memory of his wife Natalie, offered Britten $1000 as a commission fee for an opera. It was understood that Koussevitzky himself would present the work at the Boston Symphony Orchestra's summer home, the Berkshire Festival at Tanglewood.

By March it was considered safe enough to cross the Atlantic, and on the 16th Britten wrote in Elizabeth Mayer's visitors' book 'The end of the weekend' – he and Pears had arrived at the Mayers' house, ostensibly for a weekend, two and a half years earlier. Although the sea crossing took only twelve days, he and Pears were on the Swedish merchant ship *Axel Johnson* for five weeks, as it sailed, in convoy with other vessels, slowly up the coasts of the USA and Canada.

Britten took with him in his luggage an unfinished setting of some poems by Auden and a farewell message from him. Expressing his great admiration ('I think you are the white hope of music') Auden went on to give Britten several pieces of advice because 'I think I know something about the dangers that beset you as a man and as an artist because they are my own':

> *Goodness and Beauty are the results of a perfect balance between Order and Chaos, Bohemianism and Bourgeois Convention.*
> *Bohemian Chaos alone ends in a mad jumble of beautiful scraps; Bourgeois Convention alone ends in large unfeeling corpses.*
> *Every artist except the supreme masters has a bias one way or the other. The best pair of opposites I can think of in music are Wagner and Strauss. (Technical skill always comes from the bourgeois side of one's nature.)*

*For middle-class Englishmen like you and me, the danger is of course
the second. Your attraction to thin-as-a-board juveniles, i.e. to the sexless
and innocent, is a symptom of this. And I am certain that it is your
denial and evasion of the demands of disorder that is responsible for your
attacks of ill-health, i.e. sickness is your substitute for the Bohemian.*

*Wherever you go you are and probably always will be surrounded by
people who adore you, nurse you, and praise everything you do, e.g.
Elizabeth, Peter ... Up to a certain point this is fine for you, but beware.
You see, Bengy dear, you are always tempted to make things too easy for
yourself in this way, i.e. to build yourself a warm nest of love (of course
when you get it, you find it a little stifling) by playing the lovable talented
little boy.*

*If you are to develop to your real stature, you will have, I think, to
suffer, and make others suffer, in ways which are totally strange to you at
present, and against every conscious value that you have; i.e. you will
have to be able to say what you never yet have had the right to say – God,
I'm a shit.*

Britten's reply has not survived; a short note from Auden in
response to it suggests that he objected to what he saw as an implica-
tion that his relationship with Pears was 'on a schoolboy level'. But if
he was offended by the letter's general tone, there is no evidence of it,
and indeed an approving echo of Auden's 'Order/Chaos' dichotomy
appears in a letter Britten wrote barely a month later to his brother-in-
law Kit Welford.

After their separation by Britten's return to England, composer and
poet continued to discuss plans to collaborate. Auden's poem 'For The
Time Being' (referred to by both of them as a 'Christmas Oratorio')
was written with the intention that Britten would set it to music, and
for at least two years he spoke of the project with enthusiasm while
making very little progress with it: he set only the concluding Chorale
and a brief Shepherds' Carol. Auden was hurt by this abandonment
of the project, and by Britten's failure to use another of his poems, a
Litany for St Matthew's day that had been commissioned (by St
Matthew's Church, Northampton), again with the specific intention
that Britten would set it.

Since Auden later showed himself to be a brilliant opera librettist,
above all in the imaginative dramatization of Hogarth's *The Rake's*

Progress that he wrote, with Chester Kallman, for Igor Stravinsky, the fact that he and Britten never collaborated on another dramatic work is a sad loss. The barrier may have been Britten's shyness before what he regarded as Auden's superior brain, together with the fact that at this period Auden, as Stephen Spender much later put it, 'extended his imagination into other people's worlds' (meaning that he had strong and perhaps bossy ideas about the way his artistic colleagues should develop). It is curiously significant that it was on the ship taking him back to England that Britten wrote his last major Auden setting, one that he had found it difficult to come to grips with while he and its poet were on the same continent.

5

'I am native, rooted here': Britten on the beach at Aldeburgh

Various and vast, sublime in all its forms,
When lull'd by Zephyrs, or when rous'd
by Storms,
Its colours changing, when from Clouds
and Sun
Shades after shades upon the surface run;
Embrown'd and horrid now, and now serene,
In limpid blue, and evanescent green.

George Crabbe: *The Borough*

I Am Native, Rooted Here 1942-5

After the controversy surrounding Britten's and Pears's absence from their native country for the first two and a half years of the war, they were pleased to encounter little overt antagonism on their return. Pears found no difficulty in obtaining concert and operatic work, the latter often separating him from Britten for weeks at a time. Both applied for registration as conscientious objectors. Pears easily gained absolute exemption, his work being regarded as a contribution to public morale in wartime. Britten was at first registered only conditionally, which would have obliged him to work in agriculture, fire-fighting or some other non-combatant duty. He appealed, however, and the appellate tribunal granted him unconditional exemption. He and Pears undertook to give recitals for the recently formed CEMA (Council for the Encouragement of Music and the Arts, the forerunner of the Arts Council), and they toured extensively, giving recitals in churches and village halls.

Somewhere to live was initially a problem. Britten's and Pears's London flat had been at first let to a friend, then relinquished. Britten had lent the Old Mill at Snape to his sister Beth, as somewhere safe from air raids to bring up her young family. They stayed briefly with Pears's parents in London, then with friends, and did not find a flat of their own until ten months after their return. By then, however, both were travelling extensively, and as soon as it was possible to do so Britten did most of his composing at Snape.

If he thought that he would be welcomed back with some reserve, he must have been heartened by his first major première after his arrival. The Wigmore Hall was full on 23 September 1942 for the first performance of the *Michelangelo Sonnets*; the audience was hugely enthusiastic and the critics almost unanimously favourable. Edward Sackville-West shrewdly recognized that Britten had matured during his time in the USA and pronounced the songs the finest that had been written in England since Purcell and anywhere in the world since the death of Hugo Wolf. The *Sinfonia da Requiem*, too, given its

European première at a Promenade Concert earlier that summer, was cordially received, and the *Hymn to Saint Cecilia*, completed on the Atlantic crossing, was given a broadcast première by the BBC, who also commissioned music for several features. The Decca record company expressed interest in the *Michelangelo Sonnets*, actually approaching the composer as he stepped off the Wigmore Hall platform. The records, made little more than a month later, were issued with remarkable promptitude and, Britten reported to Elizabeth Mayer, 'sold enormously'.

The three Auden poems that are the basis of the *Hymn to Saint Cecilia* were dedicated to Britten, and are full of lines that Auden must have realized that he would hardly have been able to resist. The heart-stopping moment in the third song at which soprano (or treble) voices separate themselves from the choral mass for an image of vulnerable innocence:

O dear white children casual as birds,
Playing among the ruined languages

is as masterfully picked up by the composer as it had been cunningly laid in his path by the poet.

It is, however – and Auden was no less acute in realizing how Britten would respond to this – a lost innocence, and the sweetness achieves aching poignancy at

O weep, child, weep, O weep away the stain,
Lost innocence who wished your lover dead.

Of Auden's evocations of musical instruments it is not the drums of the law, nor the 'flute that throbs with the thanks-giving breath of convalescents', but the trumpet,

O trumpets that unguarded children blow
About the fortress of their inner foe,

that Britten chooses for the tenors' fanfare of

O wear your tribulation like a rose

to bring about the final, heartfelt plea to the Saint to

come down and startle
Composing mortals with immortal fire.

Variants of that invocation end each of the preceding movements, the first of them a beautiful image of timelessness (upper and lower voices, in perfect accord, move at two speeds simultaneously), the second a pattering scherzo, childlike in its repetitions, coming to rest on a final beseeching cry of 'Love me'. It is a masterpiece that always seems to occupy more space than the mere eleven minutes it takes to sing.

Also on the ship bringing him back to England Britten wrote the much simpler *A Ceremony of Carols*. It is for treble voices and harp, and has a touching innocence, free of artfulness or irony. The *Ceremony* sets nine carols between a plainchant Procession and Recession, with a central interlude for solo harp based on the same chant: a magical, wintry pastoral with an indication in its delicate chiming repetitions that McPhee's gamelan music had remained in Britten's memory. The *Ceremony of Carols* combines a shrewd under-standing of what children's voices can do with a highly original perception of the bright purity that results from combining them with the sound of a harp.

Britten was in poor health during his first months back in England. No doubt the hectic activity of his life at the time, the frequent separations from Pears and the strain of living in a city threatened with bombardment were among the causes. In March 1943, while still trying to finalize the libretto of *Peter Grimes*, he contracted measles so seriously that he was confined to hospital for several weeks. Quite typically, he wrote much of the *Serenade* for tenor, horn and strings in hospital and during his convalescence, followed it with another work for Boyd Neel, written even faster than the Frank Bridge Variations, and managed to master the difficult keyboard part of Michael Tippett's song cycle *Boyhood's End*, written for and dedicated to Pears and Britten after Tippett had been greatly impressed by the *Michelangelo Sonnets*.

'I think that all of us who were close to Ben had for him something dangerously close to love. And it gave us, perhaps, an anguished sensibility for what might happen to this figure': Michael Tippett at the time that he and Britten first met

Britten described Tippett, after their first meeting in 1942, as 'an *excellent* composer, and most delightful and intelligent man'. In his autobiography and elsewhere Tippett said that Britten was 'the most musical person I have ever met'. They became close friends for a while (according to Tippett they spent one chaste night in bed together) and dedicated major works to each other: in 1963 Tippett's Concerto for Orchestra marked Britten's fiftieth birthday; two years later, for Tippett's sixtieth, Britten inscribed *Curlew River* to him 'in friendship and admiration'. By his own account Tippett later found Britten 'less accessible' among his group of friends and associates at Aldeburgh, and deliberately stayed apart from that circle.

Edward Sackville-West, author of *The Rescue*: 'A good many critics thought [Britten's music] the best part of the programme, and I shall not quarrel with their opinion.'

The remarkable cantata *Rejoice in the Lamb* was completed shortly thereafter, and although there were many concerts to give and work on the *Peter Grimes* libretto still continued, Britten found time in the remainder of the year to write the very extensive music to *The Rescue*, a radio dramatization by Edward Sackville-West of the concluding passages of Homer's *Odyssey*, and to respond with a work of real substance when a group of British prisoners of war in Germany asked him to write something for a choir they had founded.

The *Serenade* was as warmly received by critics as the *Michelangelo Sonnets*, and public response was even more enthusiastic. Sackville-West had been provoking as well as acute when he described the *Michelangelo Sonnets* as the finest 'English' songs since Purcell, but the real point of the comparison was made when, after Michelangelo's Italian and Rimbaud's French, Britten returned in the *Serenade* to English.

Not many of the texts are obvious choices for musical setting. Tennyson's 'Nocturne' ('The splendour falls on castle walls') has an awkward rhythm – spoken aloud it seems to alternate pairs of four-syllable lines with others of ten. Cotton's 'Pastoral' ('The day's grown old') seems too elaborately sustained a conceit for music, with its catalogue of things whose shadows are magnified by a sinking sun. Blake's 'Elegy' ('O Rose, thou art sick!') is surely too brief for anything more than an epigrammatic setting: it is a single sentence of thirty-four words. Does not the anonymous fifteenth-century 'Lyke-Wake Dirge', with its insistent repetitions and remorseless warnings of judgement, demand an unsustainable crescendo?

Britten solves these problems partly with the knack of a born
dramatist. Cotton's poem is not broken up by successive musical
images of 'brambles like tall cedars show, mole hills seem mountains,
and the ant appears a monstrous elephant', but unified by variants
of the long opening phrase. Blake's tiny poem is set as the almost
unpunctuated single sentence that it is, but the setting is embedded in
a slow, throbbing depiction, for horn and strings without voice, of a
painfully endured high fever. The mounting tension of the 'Dirge' is
powerfully sustained by delaying the entry of the horn until the solo
voice almost breaks under the strain of depicting the 'Brig o' Dread'
where judgement is pronounced. Many of the other beauties of this
work are due to the intimate attention Britten pays to prosody, to
individual words or even syllables. The Tennyson 'Nocturne' owes its

Three of Britten's poets:
(left) Tennyson,
(above) Blake and
(right) Christopher Smart

beautiful colour to its scoring, but its evocation of a legendary past ('castle walls and snowy summits old in story') to a precise response to the poet's potentially square rhythm. The first syllable of 'excellently bright', Ben Jonson's epithet for the goddess Diana, is extended into a virtuoso cascade of notes, the very image of excellent brightness and an affectionate exploitation of Pears's by now effortless command of coloratura.

The work for Boyd Neel, a Prelude and Fugue for eighteen-part string orchestra, is scarcely of the stature of the Frank Bridge Variations, but matches them in ingenuity. Neel and most of his players were in the armed forces, but he managed to assemble about half of them for a London concert celebrating the orchestra's tenth birthday. He mentioned this to Britten, and five days before the concert received a work tailored to the precise number of available players. A sonorous introduction gives the impression of a far larger group; elements of it then accompany a solemn melody. In the fugue each instrument, from the second double bass upwards, enters in turn and each has its own solo; after the working-out of the fugue the noble opening melody returns *fortissimo.*

The 'festival cantata' *Rejoice in the Lamb* is one of the freshest and most lovable of Britten's 'occasional' pieces: it was commissioned for the fiftieth anniversary of St Matthew's Church, Northampton, whose vicar the Revd. Walter Hussey strongly believed in a revival of the church's patronage of art; he had already commissioned a beautiful *Madonna and Child* from Henry Moore and a mural from Graham Sutherland; at Northampton and subsequently as Dean of Chichester he went on to invite Chagall, John Piper and Ceri Richards to design windows, and to commission music from Berkeley, Leonard Bernstein, Edmund Rubbra, Tippett and Walton.

The cantata combines the renewed delight in setting English words of the *Serenade* with something of the bright innocence of *A Ceremony of Carols.* That it can do so is due to Britten's choice of text: it is a selection from *Jubilate Agno,* written by the eighteenth-century poet Christopher Smart during his long incarceration in an asylum for the insane. His friend Samuel Johnson observed, when the poet's habit of stopping strangers in the street and asking them to pray with him was put forward as evidence of his madness, 'Faith! I would as lief pray with Kit Smart as any man living.' What inspired Britten was the

poet's ability to see evidence of the glory of God not only in the
stories of the Old Testament, in flowers and in the sounds of music
but in the lazy stretchings of his beloved cat:

For I will consider my Cat Jeoffry,
For he is the servant of the Living God, duly and
                    daily serving him.
For at the first glance of the glory of God in the
                    East he worships in his way,
For this is done by wreathing his body seven times
                    round with elegant quickness

in the letters of the alphabet:

For K is king and therefore he is God.
For L is love and therefore he is God.
For M is musick and therefore he is God.

even in his own confinement

For I am under the same accusation with my Saviour –
For they said, he is besides himself.

Smart called the poem, almost every line of which begins with the
words 'For' or 'Let', 'My Magnificat', and Britten treats it so, with an
almost martial syncopated toccata associating each of a sequence of
biblical heroes with an emblematic beast, David and a bear signifying
'the beginning of victory to the Lord'. This is saluted in a Hallelujah
chorus that bears a marked resemblance to a passage in Stravinsky's
Symphony of Psalms, a work that Britten had loved since his student
days. There is solemnity as well as sweetness to the treble solo evoking
the cat (accompanied by feline writhings in the organ part), a nimble
march for the mouse ('a creature of great personal valour'), a bleak
four-note ostinato represents Smart's persecutors, crying 'Silly fellow!
Silly fellow!', and an innocent jubilance his association of musical
instruments with particular rhymes:

For the cymbal rhimes are bell well toll soul and the like.
For the flute rhimes are tooth youth suit mute and the like.

This last section ends with a rapt vision of the peace that will ensue after 'GOD the father Almighty plays upon the HARP of stupendous magnitude and melody', before the gracious Hallelujah returns.

Rejoice in the Lamb is in fact not an 'occasional' work at all, but a crucial work in Britten's final maturing. Nor is the piece written for the prisoner-of-war captives of Oflag VIIb 'occasional'. *The Ballad of Little Musgrave and Lady Barnard*, based on a folk ballad of adultery and revenge, is a swift-moving miniature drama, combining the strophic repetitions of a folk-song with graphic interludes and asides, the piano accompaniment also seasoning varied repetition with vivid scene-painting.

London in the blitz: St. Paul's Cathedral seen from Cannon Street: 'The City of London is a terrible sight ... looking rather like the gaps where teeth have been pulled out.'

The Rescue also dates from this astonishingly prolific period. The BBC, who commissioned it, have revived it with commendable frequency (there have been seven productions so far), and in 1996 an arrangement for concert performance was published as *The Rescue of Penelope*. It is the most important of Britten's radio scores, and by far the longest, with eighty separate music cues lasting in total nearly an hour and a quarter. Britten's contribution is notable for its strong characterization and its combination, envisaged from the start by his collaborator, of song and speech with orchestra. It contains fine examples of his ability to vary and transform melodic ideas (Penelope's mournful theme, lamenting saxophone with strings and arresting harp chords, becomes a serenely joyful vocal quartet after Odysseus's return) and its sea music is powerfully evocative.

Britten's continuing preoccupation throughout this period was *Peter Grimes*. After unsuccessfully trying to persuade Christopher Isherwood to write the libretto, Britten selected Montagu Slater for the task. They had worked together before the war, and kept in touch during it. Slater was a slow worker, often in poor health, and he was besides employed by the film unit of the Ministry of Information. Britten was involved with the opera from very soon after his arrival back in England in April 1942, but he was not able to start the composition sketch until January 1944.

Pears had been engaged as a principal tenor by the Sadler's Wells Opera Company not long after he and Britten had returned to England. After an early career in which his voice had seemed incapable of the demands of opera, he became one of the company's most versatile and popular artists, a development that Britten had shrewdly predicted and perhaps aided in the *Michelangelo Sonnets*. Britten saw many of the company's productions, and was introduced by Pears to its artistic director, the soprano Joan Cross. Invaluable though Koussevitzky's commission fee had been, there was now no immediate prospect of his being able to perform Britten's opera, his festival at Tanglewood having been discontinued for the duration of the war. As soon as the composition sketch of Act I was finished, therefore, Britten played it to Cross and her fellow directors. They were enthusiastic, and immediately made plans to produce the opera at their London theatre as soon as the war in Europe was over.

Britten seems to have been delighted with Slater's libretto when
he received a draft in September 1942, but six months later he wrote
to Pears that he was sure it was 'not *fundamentally* hopeless'. He was
evidently already considering having it rewritten by another poet; in
fact he modified it quite extensively himself, helped by Pears (they
had together drawn up a draft scenario in the USA), and asked a new
friend, the poet and playwright Ronald Duncan, to revise one scene
very thoroughly.

These delays and modifications were due in part to Slater's lack of
experience as a librettist, but also to the fact that the libretto Britten
needed could not be a simple dramatization of Crabbe's poem. That
section of *The Borough* that deals with Peter Grimes is brief, has a
single thread of plot and no developed characters other than Grimes
himself, presented as a pathological if pitiful brute, guilty of the
deaths of three workhouse orphans bound to him as apprentices. In
the opera he is loved by the schoolmistress Ellen Orford, and is shown
to be misjudged for the accidental death of his first apprentice, harsh
to his second but not guilty of his murder. Gossip and xenophobia,
however, poison 'the Borough's' mind against him, and he accepts the
advice of Balstrode, a sympathetic retired sea-captain, to take his own
life. He was thus transformed into an outsider, a victim of prejudice,
one with whom Britten could identify.

For most of Britten's lifetime homosexual activity of any kind
was illegal in the United Kingdom. In 1957 the government rejected
the recommendation of a Home Office committee that homosexual
acts between consenting male adults in private be decriminalized.
The consequence was that Britten and Pears, like all practising
homosexuals, were breaking the law until it was finally changed in
1967. Apart from the possibility of arrest, and there were numerous
prosecutions during the post-war period, any homosexual ran the
severe risk of blackmail. That Britten and Pears were lovers was
obvious, and widely known, but the fact was referred to covertly, if at
all; in Great Britain the word 'homosexual' was not used in print to
describe Britten during his lifetime. But prejudice and gossip were
widespread and the risk of scandal very great. Britten himself spoke
of his sexuality, even in private, very rarely. Some of his friends
interpreted this as evidence that he felt guilt or shame, but Pears
warmly denied this: 'Ben never regarded his own passionate feelings

for me or his earlier friends as anything but good, natural and pro-foundly creative.' At the time of the first broadcast of *Peter Grimes*, in March 1946, Pears wrote an article about the opera for the BBC's magazine *Radio Times*. 'Grimes ... being at odds with the society in which he finds himself, tries to overcome it and, in doing so, offends against the conventional code, is classed by society as a criminal, and destroyed as such.' When Britten and Pears, at the very time that *Grimes* was being planned, decided to return to Britain as pacifists and as a homosexual couple, they were facing a not dissimilar prospect. Pears's paragraph about Grimes's character ended, 'There are plenty of Grimeses around still, I think!'

Britten spent the greater part of 1944 writing the opera, the only major interruptions being the composition of a stirring *Festival Te Deum* and his concerts with Pears and the necessary practice and rehearsal for them. Their recital repertory was expanding – they gave their first account of Schubert's *Die schöne Müllerin*, an interpretation that was to become famous, in April 1944. It was also in this year, for a recital with Pears, that Britten wrote the first of his 'realizations' of Purcell, arranging the *Evening Hymn* for voice and piano.

Rehearsals of *Peter Grimes* began under difficult conditions. The Sadler's Wells company was still on tour, giving eight performances a week, and several of the principal singers both disliked the work and disapproved of the fact that its composer, principal tenor (Pears) and producer (Eric Crozier) were all conscientious objectors. Others thought that the reopening of their London theatre should have been marked by a new production of a repertory piece. A group of singers protested to the management that staging such a 'cacophony' was a waste of time and money; the baritone chosen for the role of Balstrode withdrew from it during rehearsals because of his distaste for the idiom; a week before the première a group of the more determined objectors petitioned the governors to appoint them as an executive committee, able to override the decisions of Cross and her fellow directors.

Britten was apprehensive about the effect this open rebellion might have on his opera; he later said that after the dress rehearsal he was convinced that it would be a disaster. In fact its success was overwhelming. With one or two exceptions the critical response was enthusiastic, *The Times* and the *Observer* most unusually devoting two articles to the opera, a week or so apart, Ernest Newman in the *Sunday Times* returning to it for three successive weekly articles. He found the orchestral interludes in particular to be 'of great power and masterly musicianship'. William Glock in the *Observer* repeated the word 'masterly' several times, and concluded 'a most thrilling work. Don't miss it.' The *Birmingham Post* described the opera as 'a work of genius', the *News Chronicle* declared it 'a work that must not be ignored' and the *Evening Standard* said of Britten 'young as he is, this opera will outlive him.'

The audience's reactions must have been even more heartening. Newspaper accounts speak of jewels and furs mingling in the auditorium with Sadler's Wells 'regulars'. The theatre, far away from the fashionable West End, had always drawn a substantial part of its audience from the predominantly working-class area surrounding it. If *Peter Grimes* was successful – and the theatre was full for all nine performances of the initial run – it was so with a genuinely broad public. Pears was fond of telling the story of a bus conductor on a route passing the theatre calling out, 'Sadler's Wells! Peter Grimes! Any more for Peter Grimes the sadistic fisherman?'

Peter Grimes was welcomed as the first important English opera since Purcell. It also established opera as a possible art form for a British composer. Before the war operas by British composers had been rare in the repertory at Covent Garden, not much commoner in that of Sadler's Wells, and most had been undistinguished or unsuccessful. Sadler's Wells had demonstrated a public appetite for opera by its pre-war seasons and its wartime touring, and now by the success of *Peter Grimes* it showed that there was a public also for modern opera. The Covent Garden Opera (later renamed the Royal Opera) was not established as a full-time repertory company until 1946 (before the war it had mounted only winter and early summer 'international seasons' with long periods of closure between them). In the twenty years between the two World Wars it had given premières to only five operas by British composers. By the end of its second post-war season it had staged *Peter Grimes*, and in the following decade it mounted important premières of operas by Ralph Vaughan Williams, Arthur Bliss, William Walton and Michael Tippett as well as commissioning two more operas from Britten himself.

Although the language and the setting of *Peter Grimes* are indeed
English, another of its qualities is the amount that it learns and adapts
from European sources. Its structure is Verdian: it is essentially a
'number opera', divided into arias, ensembles and choruses, but its
divisions grow naturally from dialogue. The power of its five orchestral interludes (the *Four Sea Interludes* and *Passacaglia* that were soon
published separately and have been widely performed ever since)
owe something to the great D minor interlude in Berg's *Wozzeck*,
something to those in Shostakovich's *The Lady Macbeth of Mtsensk*,
both operas greatly admired by Britten.

Peter Grimes has occasionally also been described as Wagnerian,
because of its extensive use of recurring motifs. Britten's use of motif,
however, is his own, and often quite un-Wagnerian. It can encompass
sharp irony: Grimes's moment of bitterest despair, when he strikes
Ellen Orford and cries in anguish, 'So be it, and God have mercy
upon me!' is a parody, of the church service that is taking place off-
stage (the congregation has just reached the Amen of the Creed), but
it is itself parodied by the ensuing chorus, savagely proclaiming
to exactly Grimes's own notes, 'Grimes is at his exercise!' It is then
made the subject of the tragic and impassioned *Passacaglia*, a portrait
of Grimes and his doomed aspirations.

Even a single interval, the difference of pitch between two notes,
can be used in this way. The rising, yearning ninth of Grimes's 'What
harbour shelters peace?' is almost the same (but crucially not quite:
this time it is a minor ninth, a semitone narrower) as his grim recollection of the day that his first apprentice died ('We strained into the
wind') – there can be no harbour from that memory. Similarly but
more disturbingly still, Grimes's dream of a future life with Ellen, but
an Ellen perhaps changed to suit him ('And she will soon forget her
schoolhouse ways') is almost literally repeated, but with an ambiguous
new harmony, as the nightmare returns ('Sometimes I see that boy
here in this hut'). A deliberately sentimental, drunken waltz-tune
heard at the village dance in Act III is later transformed into an
exultant wordless chorus: the Borough, baying for vengeance.

There are many such subtleties in *Peter Grimes*, and they are one
reason for the immense power that it exercised over audiences from
the beginning. The use of such techniques was to be further refined in
Britten's later operas. What was already fully mature, and announced

Sadler's Wells Theatre
shortly after its reopening in
1945 with the première of
Britten's *Peter Grimes*

Britten in 1944: drawing by
Kenneth Green, who the
following year designed the
scenery and costumes for
Peter Grimes

Kenneth
Green
1944

Britten as a born opera composer, was his ability to sketch character
with graphic economy. Grimes's 'difference' from the townspeople of
the Borough, as represented by the Town Clerk Swallow (his fussily
self-important theme opens the opera) is exemplified in his very first
words. At the inquest into the death of Grimes's first apprentice he
repeats the words of the oath after Swallow, singing each monotone
phrase lyrically, impatiently interrupted each time by Swallow hurry-
ing him on to the next phrase. This monotone, an image of the side of
Grimes that the Borough fears because it does not understand, returns
at his most visionary moment ('Now the Great Bear and Pleiades').
One pompous phrase of Swallow's, no more than a rising scale ('Do
you wish to give evidence?'; fragments of it pepper his discourse), later
acquires a gleeful viciousness as the mob ('Him who despises us we'll
destroy') turns on Grimes.

The two principal 'characters' of the drama are Grimes and the
Borough. The others are more briefly but pungently sketched.
Swallow's self-satisfaction is obvious even when making drunken
advances to one of Auntie's 'nieces' – in legal jargon, and to much
the same sort of phrases that he used to give lofty advice to Grimes.
Balstrode is sympathetic but a little cynical: his 'We live and let live,
but look: we keep our hands to ourselves' is addressed to the
'Methody wastrel' Bob Boles, but might he not have said much the
same to Grimes? Auntie, publican and 'madam', is an outsider herself,
but for that reason lives by the rules, and her sing-song delivery
('That is the sort of weak politeness makes a publican lose her clients')
proclaims it; her 'nieces' are an inseparable, comically timorous pair,
even more given to see-sawing repetitions of very few notes. Grimes's
persecutors, Boles and the laudanum-addicted widow Mrs Sedley,
are respectively characterized by a high-pitched, fanatical chanting and
an obsessive muttering, circling on itself.

As a teacher Ellen Orford is another 'outsider', a cut above the
other townspeople, but more likely to know her place and keep to it
than (except at a crucial moment) stand up against the majority.
Of her three arias, only the third ('Embroidery in childhood was a
luxury of idleness') tells us much about her. But it seems quite natural
that such a reticent woman should already have told us far more in
dialogue scenes (especially with Grimes and, although he never speaks,
his new apprentice, John) and in ensembles.

'Child, you're not too young
to know where roots of
sorrow are': Joan Cross as
Ellen Orford with Leonard
Thompson as John, the
new apprentice, in the first
performance of *Peter
Grimes*, 7 June 1945
Below, Britten and Eric
Crozier examining set
model for Peter Grimes

If as a first opera *Peter Grimes* has a fault, it is that it is too rich: rich in all the expected ingredients of a 'number opera' (arias, choruses, set piece finales, even a 'mad scene'), rich in incident and illustrative detail. The opera would probably work perfectly well with the roles of the Rector, Hobson the carter, even perhaps Ned Keene the apothecary omitted. But that would come close to meanly objecting that no opera needs as many as five symphonic interludes or quite so many crowd choruses. All the richness is in the service of the drama, and 'generous' would be a more accurate as well as a more charitable description of it than 'ostentatious'.

6

'Let's Make an Opera!': the
final Coaching Song at the
first performance, Jubilee Hall,
Aldeburgh, 14 June 1949

*Much good has been shown me and much evil,
and the good has never been perfect. There is
always some flaw in it, some defect, some
imperfection in the divine image, some fault
in the angelic song, some stammer in the
divine speech.*

E. M. Forster: *Billy Budd* (libretto)

Too Much Success 1945–51

*I am a bit worried by my excessive local success at the moment – the
reviews that the Sonnets, St Cecilia, the Carols, and now the Quartet
have had, and also the fact that* Les Illuminations *is now a public draw!
It is all a little embarrassing, and I hope it doesn't mean there's too much
superficial charm about my pieces. I think too much success is as bad as
too little …*

That letter was written by Britten to Elizabeth Mayer in 1943,
two years before the overwhelming success of *Peter Grimes*. Within
a very few years the opera was performed in most West European
countries with an operatic tradition. By 1950 it had had three
productions in Germany, two in France and others in Belgium, Italy,
Switzerland, Finland, Hungary, Sweden, Denmark and the USA. No
more than two years after its première it received a new production
at London's 'senior' opera house, the newly reopened Covent Garden.
Britten must have been pleased at the enthusiasm which greeted his
opera. It may also have increased his anxiety at 'too much success'.

'Thou art slave to fate,
chance, kings and
desperate men, '
And dost with poison, war
and sickness dwell':
John Donne, whose *Holy
Sonnets* Britten set to
music under the influence
of a visit to Belsen

The year of *Peter Grimes* was an extraordinary one. The opera was
finished in February, and had been copied, rehearsed and given its
successful première by the beginning of June. Britten then began his
The Holy Sonnets of John Donne, but broke off work to act as Yehudi
Menuhin's accompanist on a tour of Germany, including the
Belsen concentration camp. He returned, profoundly affected by the
experience, to complete the *Sonnets* by the middle of August. His
Second String Quartet was finished two months later; it and the
Donne cycle were first performed on consecutive days in November,
by which time Britten was already at work on a new opera, *The Rape
of Lucretia*. While waiting for the *Grimes* rehearsals to begin he gave
four concerts with Pears in Paris. During the early work on *Lucretia* he
also composed the elaborate 'masque and anti-masque' for a play
(*This Way to the Tomb*: it ran for eighteen months) by the librettist of
Lucretia, Ronald Duncan, as well as the still more extensive music for
Louis MacNeice's *The Dark Tower* (a radio play based on the Childe

Britten and his librettist
Ronald Duncan in
conversation during the
rehearsals of *The Rape of
Lucretia*, Glyndebourne,
July 1946

Roland legend) and a twenty-minute score for an educational film,
Instruments of the Orchestra, which soon achieved independent
existence as one of Britten's most popular concert works, *The Young
Person's Guide to the Orchestra.*

Such fertility is not uncommon among young composers, though
the consistent quality of Britten's music of this year is astonishing.
He maintained this gruelling workload, however, for many years. The
amount of music composed each year eventually began to decrease,
but his concert engagements as pianist and conductor did not. In
addition, he was soon to become the artistic director (not the sole one,
but his was the name held responsible for its successes and failures)
of a major arts festival. Yet the international success of *Peter Grimes*
made him by composers' standards a wealthy man who could easily
have devoted himself to composition alone.

His punishing schedule – it undoubtedly shortened his life – has
been ascribed to a puritan work-ethic, no doubt instilled in him by
his parents. He said that he felt unhappy if a day went by without
composing, and that if forced to break off work on an incomplete

piece he would make himself ill fretting over it. For most of his life, when concerts or other work did not take precedence, he was up by seven in the morning and at his desk soon after. He would compose until lunch, not usually thereafter except when a deadline was pressing. For the rest of the day until dinner he would go on long walks or drives through the Suffolk countryside, play tennis, swim or watch birds, all the time thinking out the music to be written down next day. Friends of his have described his often schoolboyish sense of humour, his pleasure in simple food and his wide knowledge of and interest in the landscapes around his home. Very many of them, often in almost identical words, have said that he was only ever really happy when working.

Aside from the many works that Britten wrote for his concerts with Pears, the two had a wide repertory of music by other composers, especially English song and German Lieder. Most of Britten's folk-song arrangements were also written for his concerts with Pears. They make such inventive use of their traditional melodies that they almost count as original compositions. It is hard for many who first encountered *The Bonny Earl o' Moray* in Britten's arrangement to imagine it without its sombre, bagpipe-inspired drone bass, or *The Ash Grove* without the out-of-key 'blackbird' in the piano part (in fact a distorted echo of the vocal line) which so accurately reflects the pain that the bird's song causes the bereaved singer. The wit of *The Foggy, Foggy Dew* is all the more sly for being so very restrained – the merest hint of a suggestive sidle added to the simple 'walking' accompaniment – while *The Plough Boy* would be a shadow of his insouciant self without his cocksure whistling, provided by Britten as an irresistible piano obbligato.

The Holy Sonnets of John Donne were written in circumstances that can almost be heard in the music. They were begun while he was unwell, perhaps from overwork – in a letter of the period he spoke of being able to sleep only with the aid of drugs – and composition was interrupted by his visit with Menuhin to war-shattered Germany, giving improvised concerts to concentration camp survivors. Britten did not describe the experience in his letters, referring to it only as 'horrific' and 'harrowing' and then hastening on to other matters. On his return he was again ill, with an allergic reaction to the inoculations he had received. The cycle is feverish, obsessive, almost unremittingly

tense, with only one island ('Since she whom I lov'd') of uninterrupted lyricism in the sequence of nine sonnets. Even there the
serenity is shadowed – 'She whom I lov'd hath payd her last debt' – for
the cycle's subject is death, and guilt in the face of it. Its concluding
song, 'Death, be not proud', is all the more nobly confident for its
contrast with what precedes it and for being cast as a Purcellian
chaconne over a five-bar repeated melody in the bass – a 'ground', as
Purcell would have called it.

The Second String Quartet, also a homage to Purcell with its
Chacony finale, is one of Britten's masterpieces. In some ways its first
movement, although worlds away from it expressively, takes a
further step forward from that in the *Sinfonia da Requiem*. Where
the 'Lacrymosa' of the *Sinfonia* had presented two apparently kindred
themes, leaving the shattering demonstration of their incompatibility
until late in the argument, the Quartet's first movement has three
related themes, their close kinship emphasized by them all beginning
with the same rising interval (a tenth) and by their sharing a number
of closely similar phrases. The climactic fusion of all three into a
singing contrapuntal texture is both memorably beautiful and as
ingenious as a conjuring trick. It is at once a demonstration that a
movement can be as satisfying as a conventional sonata form
structure although largely devoid of 'sonata contrasts', and an
expansion of sonata form designed to emphasize harmonious fusion
rather than the reconciliation of opposing forces or the 'victory' of
one over another.

In the hectic central Scherzo the trio section, traditionally a
moment of relief or contrast, is in fact based on the same theme as
the Scherzo proper, thus intensifying its nervous frenzy. The first
movement was in C major, the second in C minor; the third earns
its length (longer than its two predecessors put together) and its
complexity by being so to speak on the very brink of but not in C
major until very near the end. There are twenty-one variations, in
groups exploring the theme's harmonic implications, its striking
rhythm and a more gracious melodic counterpoint to it. The groups
are separated by solo cadenzas for each instrument in turn, the first
violin introducing the three final variations in which the original
theme reasserts itself, more and more emphatically insisting on a
sonorous C major.

'I had never realized, before
I first met Purcell's music, that
words could be set with such
ingenuity, with such colour.'
Both Britten's *Holy Sonnets of
John Donne* and his Second
String Quartet were given
their premières at concerts
marking the 250th anniversary of Purcell's death.

Following page, 'I am
firmly rooted in this glorious
county': Aldeburgh seen
from inland

After the Donne settings and the overt homage of the quartet's final Chacony, Britten's third Purcellian work for the 250th anniversary year was *The Young Person's Guide to the Orchestra*, originally written for a film produced by the government-funded Crown Film Unit, in which the variations were linked by a spoken commentary. It was clearly also intended as an independent concert piece, and was in fact heard in that form before the film appeared. As a didactic piece it works brilliantly: Purcell's theme is presented first by the full orchestra, then by each of its constituent sections. Every instrument in turn is then given prominence in a series of variations, and a concluding fugue brings back the instruments in the order in which they were first introduced, the hubbub crowned by a triumphant return of Purcell's tune. Britten shows great skill in contriving to write so many distinctly characterized variations on the same tune, while ensuring that he never departs so far from it that a young listener will not recognize it as a variant. The whole piece is an example of his frequently restated definition of the composer's function ('to be useful – and to the living').

Meanwhile at Sadler's Wells, despite the success of *Peter Grimes*, the rancour surrounding its première had not subsided. Joan Cross and Eric Crozier wanted the company to build on that success and pioneer the production of new British operas. Other members of the company wanted to concentrate on refurbishing their repertory of

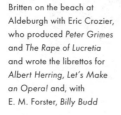

Britten on the beach at Aldeburgh with Eric Crozier, who produced *Peter Grimes* and *The Rape of Lucretia* and wrote the librettos for *Albert Herring, Let's Make an Opera!* and, with E. M. Forster, *Billy Budd*

standard classics, and the divergence between the two groups was so great that in early 1946 *Peter Grimes* was withdrawn from the company's repertory. Cross, Crozier and Pears resigned, and discussions that had already begun about the founding of a new company intensified.

What Britten and the three 'rebels' wanted was a company of modest size, able to mount operas cheaply and to tour them widely, in the hope of building a new audience. It was for this company, as yet no more than an idea, that Britten wrote his second opera *The Rape of Lucretia*. Crozier had the idea that an association with the already successful (and privately funded) Glyndebourne Festival would give the new group a degree of stability. The Festival's general manager Rudolf Bing was enthusiastic, especially after he had heard Britten play the opera at the piano, and recommended that Glyndebourne, which was experiencing difficulties in reopening its own festival in the changed financial climate after the war, make itself responsible for the new company.

The 'Glyndebourne English Opera Company', as the new venture was provisionally called, was risky as well as ambitious. With a repertory so far of only one opera it announced a five-month season, with rehearsals and a fortnight of performances at Glyndebourne itself, followed by a national tour. To make this possible, two casts were engaged, with Kathleen Ferrier and Nancy Evans sharing the title-role. The other members of the company included a high proportion of the best British singers of the period, as well as Pears and one Danish 'visitor', the distinguished tenor Aksel Schiøtz. The conductors were the Swiss Ernest Ansermet, well-known for his advocacy of Stravinsky, and Reginald Goodall, who had conducted the first performances of *Peter Grimes*.

The libretto was by the poet and dramatist Ronald Duncan, who took as his main source a play by André Obey, *Le Viol de Lucrèce*, which had been produced successfully both in Paris and in London. It tells the same story as in Shakespeare's narrative poem (which Obey occasionally quotes) of a group of Roman generals, in camp outside the city, agreeing for a wager to test their wives' fidelity. All but one, Lucretia, the wife of Collatinus, are found wanting. Junius, one of the generals, is maddened by jealousy into challenging Tarquinius, the Etruscan-born Prince of Rome, to prove Lucretia chaste. He does so,

A revival of *The Rape of Lucretia* in 1954, using the sets designed by John Piper for the first performance in 1946

rapes her, and she then sends for her husband to beg his forgiveness before stabbing herself.

The Rape of Lucretia was an attempt to create a new sort of opera, in which not only every singer but every instrumentalist is a soloist: opera as chamber music. It was also formally new, taking over from Obey the device of two narrators, Male and Female Chorus, who not only tell portions of the story but also comment on the plot. At Britten's suggestion Duncan also presented the narrators as specifically Christian commentators upon a pre-Christian story.

After its première the opera was so much abused for this modification and for the occasionally flowery language of Duncan's text that little attention was paid to the ways in which *Lucretia* is an advance on *Grimes*. In its still subtler use of brief germinal motifs, for example: Lucretia's six-note theme (often heard to repetitions of her name) is disturbingly akin, indeed a complement to the four-note idea associated (for example at the words 'Prince of Rome') with her rapist, Tarquinius. A rising scale figure from the recurrent chorale-like theme for the Male and Female Choruses ('[whilst we] as two observers stand') has many progeny throughout the opera, some of them having another parent in the still more pervasive rising theme to which the Choruses sing '[O my God, with what agility does jealousy] jump into a small heart'. Thus Lucretia's maids' joyous greeting to the morning ('O what a lovely day!') as they deck the house with flowers, Lucretia's lament over the flowers' swift fading ('For their beauty is so brief') and the sombre passacaglia that mourns her death and protests against it are all related.

The scoring draws astonishingly varied colour and texture from an ensemble of thirteen players: quintets of wind and strings, harp, percussion and piano. The most celebrated example of Britten's instrumental subtlety in this opera is the slumber music for Lucretia, accompanied by bass flute, bass clarinet, horn and harp harmonics, each contributing to the uniquely evocative, tangibly dark sound.

Duncan's libretto has been much ridiculed, for its poeticisms and for the awkwardness with which the Christian commentary is applied:

Opposite, piano rehearsal in the Organ Room at Glyndebourne for the first production of The Rape of Lucretia: Britten at the keyboard with (left) Ernest Ansermet and (right) Reginald Goodall, conductors of the first and second casts respectively

Virtue assailed by sin
With strength triumphing:
All this is endless
Sorrow and pain for Him,

observe the Male and Female Choruses, as though Lucretia's sorrow
and pain were of less account than His. And yet the libretto was
written to Britten's prescription, he praised it highly, and page after
page of it is memorable and moving in his setting. The disturbing
ambiguity of some of his images (the association of Lucretia's and
Tarquinius's motifs, for example) has parallels in Duncan's own: his
metaphor for the rape:

Now the great river underneath the ground
Flows through Lucretia and Tarquinius is drowned,

is followed almost immediately by

Mary most chaste and pure,
Help us to find your love
Which is His Spirit
Flowing to us from Him.

In fact, far from letting Britten down, Duncan provided him with
exactly what he wanted.

The year 1946 also saw a brief resumption of Britten's work in the
spoken theatre – a simple fanfare for a production of Cocteau's *The
Eagle Has Two Heads* and rather more extended music (the score has
been lost) for a staging of Webster's *The Duchess of Malfi* in New York.
Also during this year, for the opening transmission of BBC radio's
Third Programme, he wrote the *Occasional Overture in C*, and withdrew it after the first performance. It begins with almost pompous
ceremony, develops a folk-like lyrical vein and then effectively
combines the two before a genially noisy conclusion. It is not a piece
of which he need have been so ashamed as to suppress it.

The reviews of *The Rape of Lucretia* were on the whole adverse.
The tour – a week each in Edinburgh, Glasgow, Manchester and
Liverpool, plus a full month in London and a visit to the Holland

Festival – was financially disastrous, with theatres often no more than a quarter full. Glyndebourne's proprietor John Christie, who had disliked both the libretto and the music, honourably and handsomely paid all the bills (the losses – a huge sum for the period – amounted to £14,000), but announced that he would not be financially responsible for the 'sequel' to *Lucretia* that was already being planned. Britten and Crozier therefore took the final step towards founding their own, independent opera company by establishing what they called the English Opera Group and offering to purchase the *Lucretia* sets from Christie. It was this company that at Glyndebourne in the following year, 1947, mounted the première of Britten's new opera *Albert Herring*, as well as a revival of *The Rape of Lucretia*.

'We bring great news to you upon this happy day!': the first performance of *Albert Herring*, Glyndebourne, 20 June 1947. Left to right, Gladys Parr (Florence Pike), Joan Cross (Lady Billows), Margaret Ritchie (Miss Wordsworth), Norman Lumsden (Superintendent Budd), William Parsons (the Vicar, Mr. Gedge), Betsy de la Porte (Mrs. Herring), and Peter Pears (Albert)

Albert Herring was rather better received by the critics than its predecessor, and enjoyed by audiences. The libretto, by Crozier, is an adaptation of Guy de Maupassant's short story 'Madame Husson's May King' to a Suffolk setting. The local grandee Lady Billows, thwarted in her plan to crown a local girl as May Queen (none meet her standards of virtue), chooses Albert Herring as May King instead: he is so simple-minded and downtrodden by his formidable mother that he has never had an opportunity to err. Albert's lemonade at his coronation ceremony, however, is spiked with rum by a pair of local lovers, and under its influence and with the £25 reward for his virtue, he vanishes and is thought dead when his floral head-dress is found crushed by a cart. At the height of the mourning he returns, sober but with a strange new confidence.

There is plenty of room in the plot for a great deal of ingenious but not at all cruel parody: the unctuous Vicar, the pompous Police Superintendent Budd, the overbearing Lady Billows and the vaporous Miss Wordsworth are all sketched with affection as well as wit, and not one of them is overdone. The opera rises above anecdotal comedy in the love music for Sid and Nancy, in the nagging of Albert's Mum and in the shrewd portrayal of Albert himself. Unlike the other characters in the opera he has no defining motif of his own: the chiming 'May King! May King!' and the hymn of praise to his virtue 'Albert the good' are images wished on him by others; in imagining what love might be he can only ruefully quote the music of Sid and Nancy. But slowly, in a series of three monologues, he demonstrates not an unexpected strength of character but a simple creature discovering himself, and not altogether liking what he finds.

As a comedy with a strong element of pathos its highest point is the Threnody over the supposedly dead Albert. It is very moving, indeed some have found it more so than the lament over the dead Lucretia. But the finely sustained tension and genuine emotion of this scene must inevitably be punctured by Albert's return. And in a light comedy we cannot really believe that being thrown out of three public houses and spending three whole pounds on drink can have transformed Albert's character and liberated him from his own timidity. There is, though, a broad hint (until Sid and Nancy intervene to prevent still worse revelations) that Albert did not spend his money only on drink.

The skill and the musical substance of the piece inspire smiles of pleasure at least as often as the plot. It is curious but significant that this apparently most provincially English of comedies, with its allusions to *Hymns Ancient and Modern*, to Elgar (surely: in Lady Billows's music) and to Gilbert and Sullivan, should have proved one of Britten's most popular works in Europe. His adroit reference to Wagner's *Tristan*, the wit and learned skill of his counterpoint (he does not quote Verdi's *Falstaff*, but he obviously knew and loved it) and his sure-footed pacing of a line between farce and pathos are as universal as the details of the plot are parochial.

In 1947 he was asked to write a piece for a concert in memory of the Revd. Dick Sheppard, the founder of the pacifist Peace Pledge Union. Something more substantial than a brief song was clearly called for, and in writing a sort of chamber cantata for voice and piano Britten found a satisfying form that he was to return to several times. He used the word 'canticle' to signify a moderately extended piece for solo voice or voices of more or less spiritual character. For the first of them he chose a poem by Francis Quarles, 'My Beloved is Mine', which describes the soul's relationship to God in terms that echo the secular, indeed sexual imagery of the title's source, the Song of Solomon.

A lilting barcarolle with an ecstatically florid vocal line depicts the lover and the beloved as 'two little bank-divided brooks', the two-part writing beautifully fusing to a single but more richly harmonized line at 'we joined'. Quarles's poem is in six stanzas, with variants of 'My beloved is mine and I am his' recurring at the end of each. To set this strophically could be repetitive, to avoid doing so merely perverse. Britten contrives to do both: the first two verses related and comple-mentary, likewise the fifth and sixth, the third and fourth separate but subtly related 'movements', recitative and dance respectively.

Composed a couple of months later, *A Charm of Lullabies* is an anthology of cradle-songs, from the hypnotic to the malignly threatening, written for Nancy Evans, one of the creators of the role of Lucretia and the first Nancy in *Albert Herring*. After their Glyndebourne performances, both operas were toured to festivals in Holland and Switzerland, and it was this experience that led Pears to suggest a festival of their own. The English Opera Group was, after all, intended to give performances in places where opera would not

Opposite, brochure
announcing the first
Aldeburgh Festival. Of the
founding Executive
Committee, Fidelity
Cranbrook remained
Chairman throughout
Britten's lifetime.

normally be heard, and Aldeburgh had just such a space, though the
Jubilee Hall, seating 300, had only a very small stage. And *Albert
Herring*, set in the fictional Suffolk town of Loxford, would seem far
more at home in Aldeburgh than at Glyndebourne, which in any case
was preparing to resume its own festival.

By now Britten and Pears were themselves 'at home' in Aldeburgh.
Early in 1947 they had moved from the Old Mill at Snape to Crag
House in the centre of the small fishing town where *Peter Grimes* had
been set. Then as now it was an unassuming place, attracting some
summer visitors for the golf and sea-bathing, but with few other
tourist attractions. Its modest buildings, very few of them more than
two storeys high, straggle along three roughly parallel streets set
between a pebbly beach and the low, marshy banks of the River Alde.
It was not, in short, the obvious place for a festival, but at a public
meeting the townspeople were favourable to the idea, local patrons
were found and the Arts Council, enthusiastically promoting the post-
war growth in the number of arts festivals, offered a grant. The first
Aldeburgh Festival, eight days long, took place in June 1948. As soon
became an almost invariable custom it featured the première of a new
work by Britten, the cantata *Saint Nicolas*, commissioned by Lancing
College (where Pears had been a schoolboy) for its centenary; the
College allowed its own performance to be preceded by two at
Aldeburgh. Another tradition, of concentrating each year on one or
two composers other than Britten, was inaugurated with a series of
performances of works by Purcell and Lennox Berkeley, and *Albert
Herring* was successfully restaged in the Jubilee Hall. One local
resident was overheard at the interval saying, 'I took a ticket for this
show because it is local and I felt I had to. I wouldn't part with it now
for ten pounds.'

It was with the foundation of the Aldeburgh Festival that tales of a
'Britten circle' began to circulate, according to some a circle made up
almost exclusively of homosexuals, according to many others a circle
difficult to penetrate and from which the risk of summary expulsion
was ever present. The former allegation is simply untrue. Apart from
Pears, the great majority of Britten's friends and most of his trusted
interpreters were heterosexual, and there were many prominent homosexual composers and performers who were not part of Britten's circle.
His most enduring friendships were with Erwin Stein's daughter

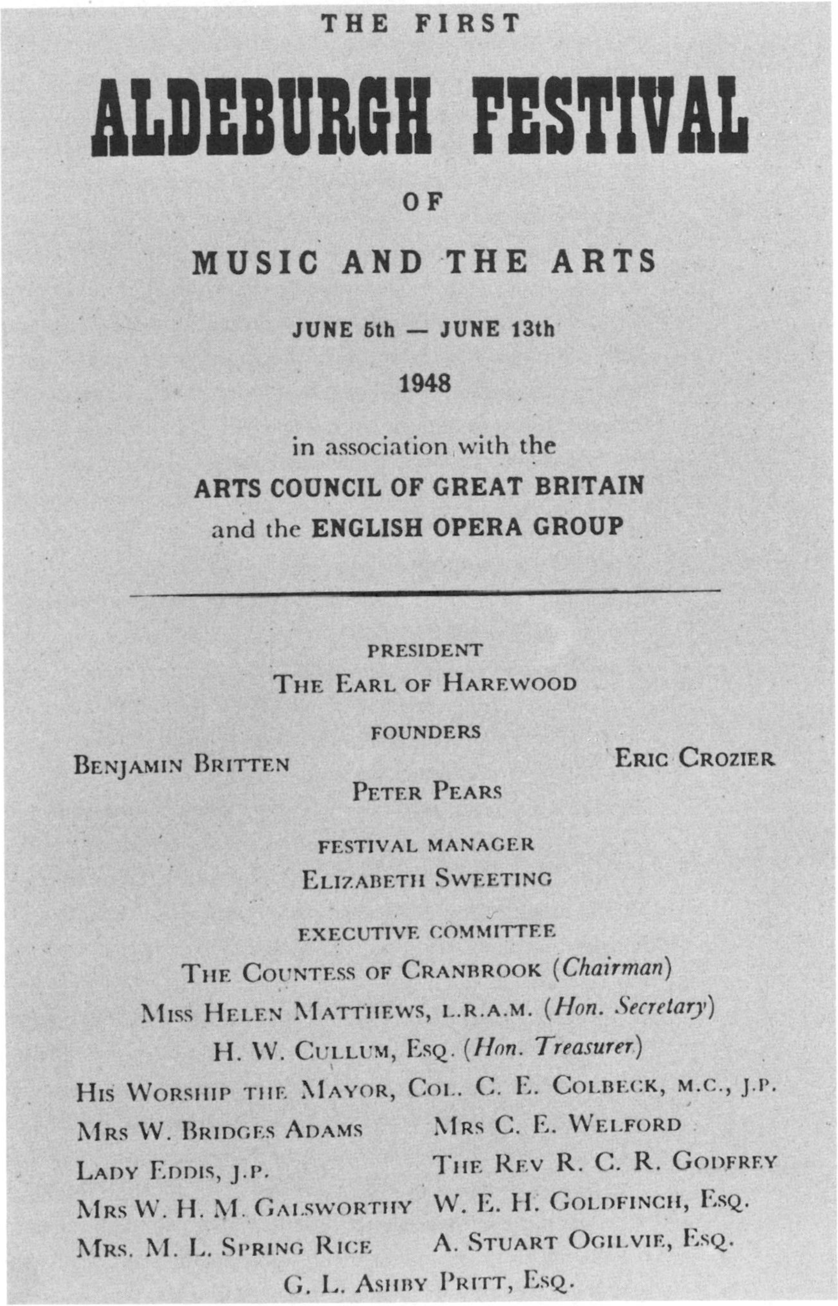

THE FIRST

ALDEBURGH FESTIVAL

OF

MUSIC AND THE ARTS

JUNE 5th — JUNE 13th

1948

in association with the

ARTS COUNCIL OF GREAT BRITAIN
and the ENGLISH OPERA GROUP

PRESIDENT

THE EARL OF HAREWOOD

FOUNDERS

BENJAMIN BRITTEN   ERIC CROZIER

PETER PEARS

FESTIVAL MANAGER

ELIZABETH SWEETING

EXECUTIVE COMMITTEE

THE COUNTESS OF CRANBROOK (*Chairman*)

MISS HELEN MATTHEWS, L.R.A.M. (*Hon. Secretary*)

H. W. CULLUM, ESQ. (*Hon. Treasurer*)

HIS WORSHIP THE MAYOR, COL. C. E. COLBECK, M.C., J.P.

MRS W. BRIDGES ADAMS   MRS C. E. WELFORD

LADY EDDIS, J.P.   THE REV R. C. R. GODFREY

MRS W. H. M. GALSWORTHY W. E. H. GOLDFINCH, ESQ.

MRS. M. L. SPRING RICE   A. STUART OGILVIE, ESQ.

G. L. ASHBY PRITT, ESQ.

Marion (later Lady Harewood, later still Mrs Jeremy Thorpe), with
John and Myfanwy Piper, with his musical assistant Imogen Holst,
with sympathetic neighbours like the artist Mary Potter, and with
performers whom he admired and trusted. The latter were sometimes
first welcomed to the circle, later abruptly and distressingly excluded
from it. In some cases this was because the artist in question was no
longer useful to Britten, in others because of some real or imagined
slight. They were called Britten's 'corpses', and over the years there
were many of them. After the problems with the libretto of *Peter
Grimes*, for example, Britten never expressed an interest in working
with Montagu Slater again, and although he and Ronald Duncan
remained friends and collaborated occasionally after *The Rape of
Lucretia*, it was to be their last opera together. Some have found these
exclusions from favour, often without a word of explanation, callously
cruel; others no more than the necessary ruthlessness of a creative
artist whose first priority was always the work in hand. It inevitably
increased the gossip about Britten and, if he heard about it (which he
surely must have), his sensitivity to criticism and adverse comment.

Saint Nicolas, which requires six professional musicians as well as
amateur forces consisting of a mixed choir (girls' as well as
boys' voices), string orchestra, piano duet, organ and percussion, is
nevertheless a work 'for children'. Nicolas's birth is evoked in the
sort of tune that children love singing rather loudly, but which adults
are apt to deprecate as naïve or 'childish'. The two quite long tenor
solos, on the other hand, are in Britten's most developed operatic
manner (they were written for Pears). The juxtaposition of the two,
together with choral music carefully written with the abilities of
amateurs in mind, plus two well-known hymns (spiced with simple
but agreeable dissonances) for the entire audience to sing, is a lesson
in 'musical appreciation' of a high order for its period. Britten was
greatly to refine this combination of skilled and less-skilled performers
in later works, but the structure of *Saint Nicolas* is ingenious and
satisfying, its 'simplicity' (Nicolas's growth to manhood symbolized by
the treble's voice giving way to that of the tenor; the heart-stopping
sweetness of Nicolas's death) at times both moving and inspired.

It was decided immediately that the festival should be an annual
event, and for the rest of his life it was a central factor in Britten's
existence. He not only planned each festival with meticulous care, but

composed many of his works with the scale and circumstances of the festival and of the English Opera Group in mind. It did not, however, until late in his life put an end to his writing music for other places and occasions, especially since Aldeburgh could not accommodate full-scale opera nor concerts involving anything but a very small orchestra. In the three years immediately following the move to Crag House, aside from works for the Festival or for the English Opera Group, he composed an opera on a larger scale even than *Peter Grimes* and responded to another commission from Koussevitzky for the Boston Symphony Orchestra.

The two 'domestic' works were the 'entertainment for young people' *Let's Make an Opera!* and an elaborate 'realization' of John Gay's *The Beggar's Opera*. Britten devoted enormous trouble to this edition, but in an age much concerned with fidelity to the authentic text it is now rarely performed. Quite apart from deserving to be heard as an original work of Britten's own, it is worth recalling that Britten's was the first modern edition of the ballad opera to use nearly all of the original songs (the Frederic Austin/Nigel Playfair edition, which had a famous production in 1921, omitted about a third of them). Britten also attempted to recapture something of the raffish-ness and the satiric edge of the original. He and the stage director Tyrone Guthrie turned the work into an opera mounted by beggars and thieves, in a rough-and-ready low-life setting (an abandoned laundry), with all necessary set changes carried out by the cast, in view of the audience while the action and the music continued. They therefore also recaptured something of the sheer speed that so captivated eighteenth-century spectators, with brief songs, salty dialogue and dramatic confrontations succeeding each other at a pace that would have made the Italian operas of the day (themselves satirized by Gay and his musical colleague Pepusch) seem tediously slow.

Unlike his numerous 'realizations' of Purcell, Britten gave his version of *The Beggar's Opera* an opus number (43), no doubt to acknowledge that it contains a great deal of recomposition. He aimed to restore the 'strange and severe ... toughness' that he felt earlier arrangements had understated. Even his 'straightest' settings of the original airs are reharmonized, given new accompaniments or (a favourite device) with instrumental detail interspersed between lines

'I must have women! There is nothing unbends the mind like them': *The Beggar's Opera*, 1948, Peter Pears as Macheath

or phrases that in the original were continuous. Many of the airs
are reworked into much more elaborate 'arias', often with choral
commentary; in others two or more of the original melodies are
combined; in yet others Britten has composed elaborate preludes or
postludes to accompany spoken dialogue. Macheath's scene in prison,
where the original score gives fragments only of no fewer than ten
melodies, is worked into an ingenious multi-section aria, brilliantly
unified by using Britten's own bass-line to the last of them (a version
of *Greensleeves*) as a ground, thus turning the entire sequence into a
Purcellian chaconne. And yet the melodies themselves are treated with
such scrupulous respect that it would be going too far to suggest that
the work be listened to as an opera by Britten 'suggested by' Gay's
and Pepusch's, like Brecht's and Weill's *Threepenny Opera*. It is a rare
example of posthumous collaboration, like Mozart's edition of
Handel's *Messiah*, and has a similar fascination.

The major opera that he began working on not long after the move
to Crag House was *Billy Budd*; it was eventually commissioned by
the Arts Council for the Festival of Britain in 1951. E. M. Forster, the
enthusiast for Crabbe who had first drawn Britten's attention to the
subject of Peter Grimes, had become a friend and was soon a regular
visitor to the Aldeburgh Festival. He and Crozier had talked about
collaborating on a libretto for Britten but it was the composer himself
who proposed Herman Melville's story.

Although Forster was widely honoured as one of the finest English
novelists of the century, he had not published a novel since *A Passage
to India* in 1924. His reason, as he admitted to friends and to his diary,
was 'weariness of the only subject that I both can and may treat – the
love of men for women and vice-versa'. He wanted, in short, to write
about homosexual love, and that being legally impossible until late in
his life he chose instead not to write fiction at all, save for a few overtly homosexual short stories that he circulated among friends. The
homosexual undertones of Melville's story were as obvious to him as
they must have been to the composer. 'I want *passion*,' Forster wrote,
in a letter almost dictating the sort of monologue he wanted Britten
to write for the evil Claggart, whose jealousy of Billy Budd's beauty
and goodness leads him to plot his destruction: 'love constricted,
perverted, poisoned, but nevertheless *flowing* down its agonising
channel; a sexual discharge gone evil.'

The libretto took a long time to write, Forster having no experience of writing for music and professing himself incapable of writing
verse (even at this period *Billy Budd* was unusual among librettos in
being almost entirely in prose). During 1949 five successive drafts were
prepared, and Britten spent most of 1950 writing the music.

He used Koussevitzky's commission, received two years earlier in
1947, as a pretext for something he had wanted to write for some time,
his first large-scale choral work with orchestra. It was to a skilfully
planned anthology of verses by a dozen English writers from the
seventeenth century to Auden that he composed the *Spring Symphony*
while work on the libretto for *Billy Budd* continued. The Holland
Festival, which since the war had been very receptive to Britten's
music, expressed an interest, and again Koussevitzky did not insist on
giving the première himself. That took place in Amsterdam in July
1949, the first American performance, at Tanglewood, a month later.

It is one of Britten's serenest works, a sunlit counterpart to all his
broodings on evening, night and unquiet dreams. Even the nocturnal
Auden setting, a memory of war, is a reminder of conflict, not an
account of it, and it takes place in an English garden, in starlight;
all the more jolting, therefore, the brief savagery of its final verse.
Although the title *Spring Symphony* was scoffed at by some it was well
chosen, no doubt by reference to Mahler's fusion of symphony and
song-cycle in such a work as *Das Lied von der Erde*. It is divided
into four 'movements', though composed of three times that many
individual songs. In the first, frozen winter prays for the warmth of
spring, which arrives in four joyous evocations of the season's
pleasures. A more reflective 'slow movement' culminating in the
Auden setting is followed by a scherzo of love and youth in May-time.
The finale uses only a single text, lines from Beaumont and Fletcher's
The Knight of the Burning Pestle ('London, to thee I do present the
merry month of May'), but develops it into an elaborate three-part
structure culminating in a boys' choir (reinforced for the sake of
audibility above the jubilant tumult by four horns) vociferously inton-
ing the ancient 'Sumer is i-cumen in'.

It is an ingenious work (in the way that each of its twelve sections
is quite differently scored, for example) and a lovable one, but it is
hard to suppress a feeling that it is overextended. The slow
introduction to the 'first movement' is a satisfyingly structured first

movement in itself. The slow movement is beautifully balanced, the delicate variations of its first section (Herrick's 'Welcome, Maids of Honour') and the exquisite evocation in the second (Vaughan's 'Waters Above') of rain as a welcome, blessed thing reaching a satisfying conclusion with Auden's dark saying. But, albeit appropriately in a symphony about the joys of spring, this slow movement is surrounded by an excess of scherzo material. Few who love the work are wholly satisfied with it; few could bear to have much of it omitted.

After a recital tour of North America with Pears in the late autumn and early winter of 1949, Britten broke off work on *Billy Budd* only to write a handful of short pieces, all prompted by affection or duty: incidental music for another play by Ronald Duncan, an anthem (to words by Duncan) for the wedding of his publisher Erwin Stein's daughter Marion to the Earl of Harewood, the *Five Flower Songs*, a twenty-fifth wedding anniversary present for two other friends, and *Lachrymae*, 'reflections on a song of Dowland', designed for a visit to the 1950 Aldeburgh Festival by the great violist William Primrose. The anthem and the *Flower Songs* both have eloquence as well as charm, but *Lachrymae* is a much more substantial piece than either, a small masterpiece of the art of variation writing. The melancholy of Dowland's theme ('If my complaints could passions move') is intensified by using only its first eight bars, so each variation ends mournfully, as that opening phrase does. Another sad Dowland song, 'Flow, my tears', is quoted in the sixth variation, prefiguring the masterly conclusion where the closing bars of 'If my complaints' are heard at last, in Dowland's original harmonization.

During 1951, after the completion of *Billy Budd* but before its première, Britten worked on a 'realization' of Purcell's *Dido and Aeneas* which the English Opera Group added to its repertory for the Festival of Britain. Britten's realizations all stem from a desire to see Purcell's music more widely performed and appreciated. Most of his editions of isolated songs were made for his concerts with Pears. The originals were for voice with accompaniment of harpsichord (or organ) with cello or bass viol, these 'continuo' parts, as they are called, written as a single line of notes with numerals ('figured bass') to represent harmonic in-filling; it was Purcell's intention that the players would embellish this outline according to their own taste and skill. Britten's realizations take account not only of this convention

but of the fact that the piano is of a quite different nature to the
harpsichord. They are therefore very free, and a fascinating indication
of Britten's attitude to a composer who influenced him greatly. They
and his editions of *Dido and Aeneas* and *The Fairy Queen* have tended
to fall out of use as the attractions of 'authentic' Purcell have become
more manifest. But Britten's editions made this music accessible at a
time when it would otherwise have remained unperformed, and they
played an important part in the revaluation of a great composer much
of whose music was then little known.

Only two other compositions date from 1951, the first a seemingly
occasional *jeu d'esprit* which has nevertheless survived as a central
work in the repertory of oboists, the second an expansion of the form
of the Canticle to become the seed of a new sort of musical drama.
The *Six Metamorphoses after Ovid* were written for the oboist Joy
Boughton to play at that year's Aldeburgh Festival. The première was
given from a punt on a nearby lake; during it the manuscript blew
into the water and had to be hastily rescued and dried. Since each
movement depicts a transformation, each is taken as a pretext for a
virtuoso exercise in the 'metamorphosis' of the brief figure which
opens each piece: the serene image of Narcissus reflected in the water
turning into the more fragile, tremulous likeness of a flower,
and so on.

The Second Canticle, *Abraham and Isaac*, is perhaps the most
moving of what eventually became a sequence of five. The subject,
the sacrifice of a child, would have been likely to appeal to Britten. As
Isaac pleads for his life to be spared ('for I am but a child') there is a
poignant recollection of 'O dear white children, casual as birds' in the
Hymn to Saint Cecilia and surely also of Britten's diary reference as a
teenager to an Alfred Stevens drawing of a dead boy: quite apart from
his sexuality, pity for children was one of Britten's deepest feelings.
The utter simplicity of Isaac's submission to his father's will and
God's ('Father, do with me as you will') is moving at least as much
for this reason as for its deliberate foreshadowing of Christ's words
on Gethsemane.

It was written, to a text from the Chester cycle of mystery plays, for
Pears and Kathleen Ferrier, but the part of Isaac has often been sung
by a boy alto. The Canticle's most striking device, however, the use of
both voices in unison or octaves to represent the voice of God (it so

struck Stravinsky that he copied it), works rather better with two adult voices. Not the least of the work's subtleties is its opposition of two remote keys, E flat and A, the E flat music for Abraham's decision to obey God's will reappearing in A, quite transformed into gracious serenity at the end. Unlike the First Canticle it is dramatic (it could easily be staged) and in this it foreshadows *Noye's Fludde* (also to a text from the Chester cycle) of five years later, and its successors, the three 'parables for church performance'.

Billy Budd is even more of a challenge to the musical dramatist than *Peter Grimes*. Far more than the absence of female voices (the opera is set on a British naval ship in 1797), the need to present a personification of virtue and beauty on the one hand (Billy Budd), of pure evil on the other (John Claggart, the ship's master-at-arms) is one that Verdi himself might have baulked at. The historical, political element (the ship from which Billy is press-ganged is called *Rights o' Man*) adds to the potential difficulty, with Captain Vere referring to himself as 'King of this fragment of Earth, of this floating monarchy' in contrast to the 'floating republic' of Spithead and the Nore, recent naval rebellions whose implications terrify him and his officers.

Despite the symbolic nature of the plot the drama grips powerfully, largely because Britten and his librettists understood how Melville's stylizations could be transformed into operatic ones. That a crew of ill-paid, downtrodden men should burst into a chorus of loving praise for their Captain is improbable, but 'Starry Vere, God bless you!' is an effective image of the willing submission to authority without which this system would not have worked, and it is thrillingly stirring music, perfectly timed and placed in the sweep of the drama. Alas, in Britten's revision of the opera this scene was removed (though a later reference to it survives), the only major casualty of an otherwise skilful intensi-fication of the opera's dramatic thrust.

Any choral scene is a stylization, but Britten's choruses in *Billy Budd* never merely register the presence of a crowd. To the officers, hearing a shanty below decks, it is an image of the reliable *esprit de corps* of their men. But as the focus shifts and we move from the officers' quarters to the men's, it first asserts their identity as a group, then changes into the more individualistic form of a round, from which Dansker's loneliness, Billy's affectionate generosity and the

'I've sighted a sail in the storm, the far-shining sail that's not Fate, and I'm contented': Theodor Uppmann as Billy Budd, Covent Garden, 1 December 1951

wretched Apprentice's betrayal emerge naturally. The exquisite dawn lullaby of 'Billy in the Darbies' as he awakes on the morning of his execution is moving because of its stylized unreality, as Billy is overtly compared to Christ. But it has been preceded by the boldest stylization of all, the sequence of thirty-four major chords which follow the drum-head court's verdict and 'depict' Vere's communication of the sentence to Budd.

The opera is more tightly constructed than *Grimes*; dramatically and in thematic organization it is formidably concentrated. It is also orchestrally still more resourceful. It has to be: low voices are less able to penetrate orchestral textures than high ones, and the particular colour of the opera is partly due to Britten's many skilful solutions to this problem. But above all, the more remarkable because of the darkness of the subject as well as the vocal timbres, it is a powerfully exciting work, masterly in its handling of big scenes: the battle, the three crucial 'arias' for Vere, Claggart and Budd, the moment of near-mutiny after the execution. In choosing a subject with few parallels in earlier opera, Britten relies less obviously on previous models:

Shostakovich, Verdi and Mussorgsky are still present, as is Mahler, but the greatest moments in *Billy Budd* are Britten's own.

The opera was given its première at Covent Garden in December 1951, and was recognized as a work of major importance. There were some reservations: about the libretto (which the otherwise impressed Philip Hope-Wallace in the *Manchester Guardian* thought held the opera back from being a true masterpiece) and about the drama's inevitable but almost unprecedented reliance on male voices. Not unexpectedly, there were still those who thought the work merely 'clever'. There was also among some composers an understandable jealousy of Britten's success, of what must have seemed his favoured status. If only a fraction of this found its way back to Britten himself (that, for example, people were calling *Billy Budd* 'The Bugger's Opera' – a phrase attributed by some gossips to William Walton – or that Sir Thomas Beecham had renamed it 'The Twilight of the Sods') it would explain both his intensified resentment of adverse criticism, which dates from around this time, and his tendency to retreat within a protective circle of chosen friends, interpreters and admirers.

Britten's sensitivity, to criticism and to anything else that might undermine his self-confidence, was extreme. A story that, some years later, he found himself unable to work for weeks after overhearing in Aldeburgh some ill-natured reference to 'his' festival, is well attested. He suffered acutely from performance nerves, being unable to keep down any solid food for as long as forty-eight hours before a concert. The closed circle surrounding Aldeburgh was largely established by loving and concerned friends who realized how thin-skinned Britten was and determined to enable him to work undisturbed and to shield him from shocks that might undermine his creativity. But it may also have cut him off from a realization that beyond the small world of critics and the musical profession there was a much larger one of listeners who were excited and moved by each new work that he wrote, and both admired and loved him.

7

John Piper's costume design
for Flora in the original
production of *The Turn of the
Screw*, 1954

Don't help on the big chariot;
You will only make yourself dusty.
Don't think about the sorrows of the world;
You will only make yourself wretched.

The Book of Songs (trans. Arthur Waley)

The Big Chariot 1952-60

The year 1952 was crucial in Britten's life, a trough as well as a peak. He was now widely regarded as the most important of living British composers (though Vaughan Williams, at eighty, had another six years to live). On a skiing holiday in March, he, Pears and the Harewoods discussed the nature of 'national' music and the possibility of writing an opera to mark the coronation of Queen Elizabeth II, who had just succeeded to the throne on the death of her father George VI. A subject was proposed, the life of her ancestress Elizabeth I, and Harewood, the Queen's cousin, obtained her permission to go ahead. Thus it was Britten, not the Master of the Queen's Music Sir Arnold Bax nor Britten's senior William Walton, who effectively received a 'commission' to compose a coronation opera, the first time such a thing had happened in British history.

He had scarcely begun the opera when the first comprehensive study of his music appeared, a symposium called *Benjamin Britten: a Commentary on his Works from a Group of Specialists*, edited by Donald Mitchell and Hans Keller. Apart from the editors themselves, the contributors included Harewood (a brief biographical sketch), Pears (on the solo vocal music), Georges Auric, Lennox Berkeley, Norman Del Mar, Imogen Holst, George Malcolm, Boyd Neel, Hans Redlich and Erwin Stein.

The book was received with hostility, partly due to Keller's use of the language of Freudian psychology and his comparisons of Britten to Mozart, partly to exasperation at the impudence, as some saw it, of devoting a 400-page survey to a composer not yet forty, of gifts that were not universally acknowledged. That many of the 'specialists' were close associates of Britten, including his publisher and his newly appointed musical assistant (Imogen Holst) did not go unnoticed. In fact the book still makes bracing, occasionally aggressive reading, but the storm that surrounded it was as nothing to that which greeted *Gloriana*, as Britten's coronation opera was called.

A coronation gala, before an audience consisting mainly of diplomats and 'high society', was hardly an ideal première for an opera which concerned itself less with the glories of the Elizabethan age (of which some newspapers were confidently predicting a renaissance, ushered in by the new Queen's coronation) than with the private conflicts and sorrows that were their background. The opera was described as an insult to the new Queen and a slight on the reputation of her predecessor. Others grumbled at the expense of staging such an opera in a country still recovering from post-war austerity. Some critics defended the work, but few with real warmth.

It is hard to avoid the impression that the viciousness of the attacks was prompted by resentment at Britten's apparently favoured status. The new monarch herself cannot have helped by appointing Britten a Companion of Honour in the Coronation Honours List a week before the première, a distinction awarded to very few composers, and to none of Britten's age. A feeling that ever since *Peter Grimes* he had

Queen Elizabeth II attending the Coronation gala première of *Gloriana*, 8 June 1953, with (left to right) the Crown Princess and Crown Prince of Norway, the Duke of Edinburgh and Queen Elizabeth the Queen Mother

Britten at a rehearsal,
with his musical assistant
Imogen Holst

been riding for a fall would not have been surprising. The words of
Essex and Mountjoy, rivals in the opera for Elizabeth's favour, perhaps
tempted providence:

I curse him for his impudence
And some day I will hurl him down.

Although apparently well liked by the public (there were nine
well attended performances after the gala première, and a revival the
following season), *Gloriana* soon fell from the repertory and was not
staged again for another dozen years; alone of Britten's operas it was
not recorded in his lifetime.

It is a 'number opera', and the score, which gives an individual
title to each number, emphasizes this. With its frequent changes of
location and its discontinuities of narrative it has been described
as more of a pageant than an opera, and even sympathetic critics
have seen its relatively loose structure as a step backwards from the
close motivic working and the symphonic thinking of *Billy Budd*. It
contains a good deal of pageantry, but it is seldom pageantry unrelieved or for its own sake. The masque at Norwich that begins Act II
is punctuated by insights into the Queen's character and Essex's, and
the court ball that ends the act provides both a spectacular finale and
further illumination of the characters of the Queen and her rashly
ambitious favourite.

Recurring themes are relatively few, though memorable. Brief ideas represent Essex's self-serving 'love' for the ageing monarch ('Queen of my life!') and his touchiness: a motif first heard as he sneers at his rival Mountjoy 'a favour now for every fool' and is with disturbing irony transformed into the music of his disastrous appointment as Lord Deputy in Ireland. There are others for the Queen's nagging responsibilities (the 'cares of state' motif, constantly recurring), her love (Essex's second lute song 'Happy were he' is used more to evoke her nostalgia for love than his insincere expression of it) and the more dependable relationship with her people: the haunting chorus 'Green leaves are we, red rose our golden Queen'.

Two of the opera's devices have been criticized. The first is the extensive use of what it is surely over-simplifying to call historical pastiche. Britten's range of historical reference is wide, from the literal quotation of a phrase from a madrigal by Elizabeth's contemporary John Wilbye back in time to an austerely harmonized chant-like

Peter Pears (Lord Essex), Jennifer Vyvyan (Penelope Rich) and Britten during a rehearsal of *Gloriana*

theme (the Queen's prayer) and forward to Purcell. Yet all are stylizations rather than pastiches, sometimes so far from their originals
(the mere hints of a madrigalian manner in the choral dances of the
Act II masque) as to constitute an almost entirely imaginary 'neo-
Elizabethan' music, at others purposefully distorting the originals (the
sequence of courtly dances) to dramatic effect.

That the opera ends not with a great aria or ensemble but with
speech has also been the subject of dissatisfaction, and the fact that
Britten revised this final scene more than once suggests that he had
his own doubts about it. Or, perhaps, was determined to perfect its
balance between speech, orchestral gesture, the three phrases (only) in
which Elizabeth rises from speech to song, and the concluding off-
stage choral reprise of 'Green leaves are we'. The soprano who has just
sung Britten's most demanding female role must now demonstrate
herself to be a powerful speaking actress as well, but when finely cast
and staged this nightmarish résumé of Elizabeth's life after the fall of
Essex and her approach to death can be intensely moving.

Britten's recorded reactions to the reception of *Gloriana* were
stoical, but combined with the reviews of the symposium they must
have depressed him. It cannot be coincidental that apart from another
and a very different opera for which he had already accepted a commission, his only major works of the succeeding three years were a
set of songs and a third Canticle in which a new austerity of manner
was obvious.

Winter Words is described on the title page not as a song-cycle but
as 'Lyrics and Ballads' by Thomas Hardy. Hardy's lyrics are in several
ways ideal song texts: they are brief, of varied but firm metre, they
often proceed from a mundane detail to a deep thought and frequently refer to some crucial sound that a composer may imitate or
parallel. Whether or not they answered to Britten's mood in the aftermath of *Gloriana*, they drew from him a pared-down economy of
manner that looks forward to his next opera and to the works of his
last period. There are few big gestures, little vocal display, but among
them are some of the greatest songs in the English language.

'The Choirmaster's Burial' matches both Hardy's irony, in its
characterization of the pompous cleric who will not allow old-
fashioned string-band music at the choirmaster's funeral, and his
visionary description of an angelic host welcoming the old man with

Winter Words

The first edition of Britten's
Winter Words, incorporating
a drawing by the poet,
Thomas Hardy

his favourite tune. Again and again Britten finds a perfect musical
analogue for the homely sound or image that is Hardy's starting point
(a distant engine whistle, a creaking table), and uses it not as a mere
sound effect but, as Hardy does, as a seed from which an eloquent
meditation grows. In the final song, 'Before Life and After', Britten
finds phrases as simple and memorable, yet as darkly pessimistic, as
Hardy's own in a song of bitter nostalgia for irrecoverable innocence.

Winter Words had its première at Harewood House in October 1953
as part of the Leeds Festival. It is dedicated to John Piper, who had
designed all Britten's operas since *The Rape of Lucretia*, and to his
wife Myfanwy, who was by then already working on the libretto of an
opera. It was she who had suggested Henry James's story *The Turn of*

the Screw; Britten asked her to draft an outline, which it was then his intention to hand over to William Plomer, the librettist of *Gloriana*, to expand and develop. He was evidently so impressed by Mrs Piper's draft that he asked her to continue the work.

It is some measure of Britten's assurance, even if his confidence had been shaken by reactions to *Gloriana* and to the Mitchell/ Keller symposium, that with the première of *The Turn of the Screw* already fixed for September 1954 (it was commissioned for the Venice Biennale of that year) he did not start work on it until February. The earlier stages of composition were hampered by his having to write with his left hand due to an attack of bursitis in his right shoulder. Even so, he wrote so fast that Imogen Holst, who was preparing the vocal score for rehearsal and publication, had difficulty in keeping up with him. She was amazed that he was so sure of what

Venice: a picnic during rehearsals of *The Turn of the Screw*. Clockwise from left: John Piper (set designer), Britten, Peter Pears (Quint), Edward Piper, Basil Douglas (manager of the English Opera Group), Clarissa Piper and Myfanwy Piper (librettist)

he was doing that he would send the first part of a scene to his publisher before he had written the end of it.

James's story is not an obvious one for musical setting. Two of its principal characters – the ghosts – do not speak; the story is also very short. The solution to the first problem – to characterize the ghosts elaborately, and to give them extended singing roles – also solved the second, but simultaneously raised three more. One of these, the invention of dialogue without any basis in James that would at once retain the ghosts' mystery and explore their influence over the children, was solved by Piper with subtle ingenuity. She gives the ghosts words that are poised between the enigmatic and the explicit, extravagant yet poetic, corrupt yet potentially alluring to an imaginative child. Indeed her libretto is the finest that Britten ever set, the addition of a single line from Yeats, 'The ceremony of innocence is drowned', a masterstroke.

'Wonderfully impressive, but terribly eerie and scary': Henry James, whose *The Turn of the Screw* Britten had greatly admired since his student years

The second problem, that making the ghosts 'real', removes the central ambiguity from James's story – which can be read as though the ghosts were products of the Governess's obsessive, unhealthy imagination – is perhaps inevitable, but Britten's and Piper's own ambiguities are so delicate that it is possible to read even those scenes between the children and the ghosts in which the Governess takes no part as projections of her obsession – imaginings of what the children are doing when she is not watching; even, more horrifyingly still, that it is she who corrupts the children, drawing them into the fantasies of a sick mind.

Britten's finest stroke, though, was his solution to the third problem, the risk that expanding the ghosts into full-scale singing characters would hold up the inexorable progress towards catastrophe that James so grippingly conveys and to which his title refers. The solution was to divide the opera into a prologue and fifteen scenes, not separated but linked and intensified by sixteen instrumental interludes that together form a theme and fifteen variations.

The theme uses all twelve notes of the chromatic scale, but in a far from Schoenbergian manner. Its essential shape (Britten disguises this by the device of octave transposition) is an alternation of fourths and fifths: back and forth, back and forth, but inexorably rising, a powerful musical metaphor for a turning screw. The peaks of this shape and its troughs both outline a scale of whole tones; neither scale, in short, is unequivocally major or minor. One of them incorporates the note A, the key-note of the theme itself and of the opera as a whole, but the other does not, replacing it with A flat. This instability – A flat is the key associated with the ghosts – haunts the opera as insidiously as Peter Quint and Miss Jessel haunt the lonely manor house of Bly. The theme and seven variations that form the interludes in Act I start from A and seem destined to return to it. But at the last moment, the moment at which it becomes obvious not only that Miles has seen the ghosts but is in active collusion with them, the music sidesteps to A flat. The second act reverses the process, starting from A flat but achieving A only, so to speak, by brute force: A, now firmly associated with the Governess, drowns out Quint's A flat, but destroys Miles in the process. Over a held A he cannot sing but only scream in agony, 'Peter Quint, you devil!' It remains ambiguous to the end whether this cry is addressed to Quint or to the Governess who has torn the secret from him.

The ingenuity of this structure has not trapped Britten into rigid austerity. On the contrary it allowed him within its formality to exercise his fantasy, his sense of atmosphere, his ability to use instrumental colour to evoke place and mood with extraordinary freedom and richness. The hypnotic strangeness of Quint's vocalises, the essential part in the opera's colour played by celesta, harp and bells, the parodies of flashy piano étude, of children's games and psalm-chanting – all these are immediately striking, but are given inexorable momentum by the always audible web of relationships which links them to the pervasive 'screw' theme and to the firm architecture of the opera as a whole. The score of *The Turn of the Screw* is also notable for a strange echo or prediction: the music associated with Quint's appearances is reminiscent both in sound (the celesta, Quint's 'own' instrument) and in texture of gamelan.

The Turn of the Screw was rehearsed in Aldeburgh and given its première in Venice in September 1954. It was reviewed by a much wider range of international critics than was the case with *Gloriana*, and their generally admiring tone must have been heartening to Britten, not only after the débâcle of the earlier opera but because many of the reviews recognized the work's firm structure and rigorous economy. One prominent French critic, however, stated in a crude over-simplification that the subject of the opera was homosexuality.

This seems to have been the first time that the word had been used in print in discussing Britten, and it would be interesting to know whether he saw this review. At the time his affection for David Hemmings, the boy soprano singing the role of Miles, was so obvious that some of his friends were alarmed by it. It was only a year earlier that a notorious prosecution for 'gross indecency' had led to the police interviewing several well-known English homosexuals, Britten among them. Hemmings himself, who later became a well-known film actor, said that he was perfectly aware of the nature of Britten's affection for him, felt quite unthreatened by it and counted his friendship with the composer as one of the most enriching of his life.

The English Opera Group's production of *The Turn of the Screw* was immediately repeated in London before a national tour and a visit to Holland. Since 1960 the work has never been out of the international repertoire, with often as many as three or four different productions being mounted somewhere in the world every year.

The only other important work of 1954 was Canticle III, written for a memorial concert for the young and gifted pianist Noël Mewton-Wood, who had committed suicide after the death of a close friend. It was another restatement of Britten's pacifism, a setting of a poem by Edith Sitwell whose full title is 'Still Falls the Rain (The Raids, 1940. Night and Dawn)'. It is closely related to *The Turn of the Screw*, in its tension between opposing keys, its use of a twelve-note theme and its structure of alternating 'scenes' (in this case recitatives) and variations on that theme. Each of the tenor's recitatives begins with a haunting 'motto' (to the words 'Still falls the rain'); each of the variations, mostly baleful or sinister, are for horn and piano. The recitatives intensify after each variation, the last of them breaking into Schoenbergian 'speech-song' (*Sprechgesang*) where Sitwell quotes an agonized line from Faustus's death scene in Marlowe's tragedy. It is an austerely eloquent work, achieving a drained quiet and simplicity in its final bars.

After each of the preceding years had been largely filled with work on three operas, Britten composed very little in 1955, though in the earlier part of the year he gave a series of concerts in Europe with Pears, before a skiing holiday in Switzerland to which he invited his former librettist Ronald Duncan. Towards the end of the holiday he asked Duncan to draft the text for an oratorio suitable for perform-

'At last one could get away from the immediate impact of the war and write about it': Dame Edith Sitwell, whose 'Still Falls the Rain' Britten set as his Canticle III

ance in York Minster. Duncan responded with a poem on the life and martyrdom of St Peter, to whom the Minster is dedicated, but to his irritation Britten never used it. The invitation was probably the first stirring of a desire to write a full-evening choral work, an ambition that would not be realized for another six years.

After the 1955 Aldeburgh Festival and a recording of *The Turn of the Screw* that Britten conducted later that summer, he and Pears left in November for a world tour lasting four months. This was more of a holiday than a professional engagement, though a number of concerts were given. With their friends the Prince and Princess of Hesse as travelling companions for much of the way (the Prince was a generous patron of the Aldeburgh Festival and, under the pseudo-nym of Ludwig Landgraf, prepared the German translations of several of Britten's works), Pears and Britten visited Turkey, Singapore, Indonesia, Japan, Hong Kong, Thailand, Bali, India and Ceylon. From Britten's point of view the most important incidents of the trip were his first 'live' encounter with gamelan music and his experience in Japan of Noh theatre.

He was deeply excited by his rediscovery of gamelan music, describing it as '*fantastically* rich' and reporting to Imogen Holst that he was 'beginning to catch on to the technique – but it's about as complicated as Schoenberg.' Its effect was immediately audible in the first major work he undertook after his return, the ballet *The Prince of the Pagodas*, but it was to be no passing enthusiasm, and Britten's personal reinterpretation of gamelan music continued to develop.

Britten admired the work of the choreographer John Cranko, and was enthusiastic about the prospect of working with him on a full-length ballet, but he was quite uncharacteristically late in finishing the score: the première had to be postponed from September 1956 to January 1957. This may partly have been due to working in an unfa-miliar medium – it would have been the first time that he had had to trust someone else's sense of stage timing – but the episodic nature of the fairy-tale plot may also have given him problems. The scenario was revised to take account of Britten's wish to use recurring themes to unify the score and give it momentum and continuity, but in its original form the ballet has insufficient dramatic interest to sustain three acts. Although the music was well received the ballet itself was not and, like *Gloriana*, it fell from the repertory for many years.

Pears, Prince Ludwig and
Princess Margaret of Hesse
and Britten in traditional
Balinese costume,
January 1956

The Prince of the Pagodas is a homage to the great full-length ballets
of Tchaikovsky, Delibes and Prokofiev and to Stravinsky's early and
neo-classical dance scores, and it sometimes pays them the sincerest
form of flattery by imitating them. Handsome prince, good princess,
wicked princess, doddering old king, clownish fool – there is little
room here for subtlety of characterization, let alone character
development, and to many at the time it seemed a strange thing for
Britten to undertake after *The Turn of the Screw*. Yet his use of
recurring themes does at least allow the 'good' princess Belle Rose to
be shown as reticent and wistful as well as joyous, and her music gains
in confidence and serenity as the ballet proceeds. The prince, too, has
more than one dimension: he is an ideal which Belle Rose seeks,
guided by the prince himself, magically transformed into a
salamander. He has, inevitably, two themes, both appearing in
different guises until he and Belle Rose finally triumph over her evil
sister Belle Épine. The flashing imperiousness of Belle Épine's

magnificent string theme, the skill with which her father is sketched, hardly with a theme at all, but with limping rhythms, narrow intervals and the somehow vulnerable sound of the alto saxophone are brilliantly devised for their purpose, as are the exotic variations for the four suitors and the mysterious gamelan music for the Kingdom of the Pagodas.

When the ballet was revived in 1989, with new choreography by Kenneth Macmillan and a revised scenario by Colin Thubron, Britten's music seemed to gain in depth and resonance. It had not changed, of course, but until the revival it had been wedded to a plot that was a good deal less subtle than it was. It is no more episodic than the great ballets of the past that are its models, and it is so prodigal of invention that it ranks as one of his richest scores. The strain of writing it, however, together with the adverse critical reaction left deep scars. After recording the ballet (with some cuts) he seems to have wanted to forget it; no score was published until long after his death,

Noye's Fludde: the first
production, 17 June 1958,
with Owen Brannigan as
Noye; Jaffet (right) is played
by Michael Crawford, sub-
sequently a well-known actor.

and for many years he would not even sanction the preparation of a concert suite from it, thus hampering its circulation still further.

For a composer who, between 1945 and 1954, had written an opera almost every year, it would have seemed in 1957 that a new one was overdue. It would have been understandable, however, if *Gloriana* had given him a distaste for working in 'grand' opera houses, while *The Turn of the Screw* pointed a more difficult direction forward. More and more, from this point, Britten's major works were conceived for performance at Aldeburgh, where the tiny stage at the Jubilee Hall made operatic production of any complexity impossible. His principal works of 1957, therefore, were a new song cycle for Pears, the first for which any accompanist but himself was envisaged (the *Songs from the Chinese*, for voice and guitar) and an opera for children, *Noye's Fludde*, much more sophisticated than *Let's Make an Opera*, and intended not for performance in a theatre but in a church.

The *Songs from the Chinese*, like *Winter Words* – a collection rather than a cycle – are much less often heard than the Hardy settings, though they are scarcely their inferior. The unique sound-world of these songs is due to a minute exploration of the potentialities of the guitar, aided by the virtuosity and musicianship of the player for whom they were written, Julian Bream. The unfamiliar instrument gave him a range of new sonorities and figurations which challenged his inventiveness in a way analogous to his explorations of the sounds, stresses and prosody of languages other than his own.

Nothing could be simpler than 'The Big Chariot': a plain vocal line, acutely responsive to the words, accompanied by simple chords from the guitar, which also adds a tracery of comment. Yet by the end the contrast between the 'big chariot' of public life and the misery of private despair that it brings is poignant. Subtler still, 'The Autumn Wind' sets brief vocal phrases against a single line in the guitar, the line returning ever and again to the bass register, the 'sad thoughts' of 'Youth's years how few, age how sure!' which obsess the poet. The essence of 'Depression' lies in the mournful sound of the guitar's glissando: the directness of the plucked chord, the immediate, wailing ascent or descent from it. The vocal line is simple, cast in brief phrases; the last and longest of them, 'Though my limbs are old, my heart is older yet,' gains its eloquence from the fact that it is prompted by grief at the death of a boy. Even the final 'Dance Song', a depiction of a hunt, is a lament at the destruction of beauty.

Noye's Fludde, begun immediately after finishing the Chinese songs and completed in less than two months, is the pinnacle of Britten's writing for children and an important step forward in the development of his musical language. It is scored to provide opportunities for as many children, with as wide a range of musical experience, as possible and takes great care not to give all the most interesting music to the more accomplished ones. Three of the principal singing parts are taken by adults; the solo string quartet, piano duet, organ and timpani need experienced players, but the main orchestra of strings and recorders is of children, some of them beginners, and Britten has also written simple but welcomingly idiomatic music for handbell players, buglers and a percussion band which includes the celebrated 'slung mugs', china mugs and teacups hung in pitch order on a string and played (with wooden spoons) to suggest the pattering rain that begins the flood. It is, in short, a work for an entire community to perform, and for some listeners the most stirring moments are the three great hymn tunes in which that community is united. The setting of 'The spacious firmament on high' to the melody of Tallis's Canon is especially memorable for the ingenuity with which the accompaniment to each verse illustrates it, culminating in the apotheosis of the gamelan, each instrumental group doing its own characteristic thing as a richly-woven background to Tallis's melody, now a grandiose eight-part round sung by every available voice. But to others the most abiding memory the work leaves behind are the blaring bugles that summon the animals, the strangely but intensely moving use of handbells to evoke the rainbow and God's covenant or the extraordinarily rich and complex storm passacaglia, crowned to sublime effect by John Bacchus Dykes's hymn 'Eternal Father, strong to save'.

Noye's Fludde retains its impact on repeated hearing – and not only for children – because all of Britten's skills are used in it. It is simple, yet complex, yet comprehensibly complex, and as it was intended for an entire community, so it can appeal to a whole community of musical tastes. It is the most genially and affectingly approachable of Britten's masterpieces.

Noye's Fludde was the first work that Britten completed after moving house again. The appeal of Crag House had been its view over the beach to the sea; now its appeal for many curious visitors was the view from the beach into Britten's and Pears's drawing-room. Their move to the seclusion of the Red House, set in a substantial garden on a private road, but without any view of Britten's beloved North Sea, suggests that an awareness of prying eyes was rather more than a minor irritation to him.

In his first summer at the Red House, after the première of *Noye's Fludde*, Britten worked on yet another song cycle for Pears, this time with orchestra, in effect a sequel to the *Serenade*. This was the *Nocturne*, in which the single solo instrument of the earlier work is replaced by seven. Here the theme is wholly nocturnal, not a progress from sunset to night: a sequence of evocations of sleep, dreams and nightmares. Unlike the *Serenade*, it plays uninterruptedly, unified by a dreamy rocking in the strings: a 'sleep theme' from which all eight songs emerge, but its oscillations sketch a tonal conflict, between C and D flat, that adds urgency as well as unity. Not all the songs quite live up to the promise of this long-term plan. The bassoon obbligato to Tennyson's 'The Kraken' is an adroitly handled idea, but the submarine beast is not as formidable as it might have been if Britten had not saved the solo horn for the charming but mere onomatopoeia of Middleton's 'Midnight Bell'. The tonal uncertainty, present even here, becomes a slippery slope of instability in the superb central setting, of terrified words from Wordsworth's 'The Prelude', and it is put to rest in the concluding Shakespeare sonnet, whose noble line rises to great eloquence.

It seems to have needed another of Britten's explorations of a foreign language for him to continue the line of development already opened up by *Winter Words* and *Songs from the Chinese*. The *Sechs Hölderlin-Fragmente* (so titled, in German) were written as a fiftieth-birthday present for Prince Ludwig of Hesse, and have never achieved the popularity of Britten's English songs, though he thought them his 'best vocal work so far'. They have an epigrammatic quality, appropriate to their texts, and they are barer than the Hardy or the Chinese songs. They look forward to the spareness of his late work, and include at least two great songs: the poignantly weary setting of 'Hälfte des Lebens' and the grave 'reply' to it, 'Die Linien des Lebens'.

In the earlier part of 1959 Britten worked on two commissions that evidently gave him pleasure to accept. For George Malcolm's

The Red House, Aldeburgh,
Britten's home from 1957.

retirement as organist and choirmaster at Westminster Cathedral he wrote a miniature masterpiece, the *Missa Brevis*, which like the Hölderlin cycle looks to the future, this time to the *War Requiem*. The other commission, for the *Cantata Academica, Carmen Basiliense*, was from Paul Sacher, generous patron of new music and founder of the Basel Chamber Orchestra, to commemorate the 500th anniversary of his city's university.

At last in the autumn of 1959 Britten began a new opera, his first for five years. The pretext was not a commission but the long overdue refurbishment of the Jubilee Hall in Aldeburgh. There was no time for the detailed planning that would have been needed for an entirely original libretto. Even so, Britten was over-simplifying a little when he said that it was only shortage of time that led him to Shakespeare's *A Midsummer Night's Dream*. Since the Nocturne in the Auden cycle *On This Island* twenty-two years before, he had returned again and again to the imagery of night and dreams, and had further prepared himself for Shakespeare's play by his exploration of the supernatural in *The Turn of the Screw*. With Pears's help he reduced the play's text to manageable length (only six 'inauthentic' words needed adding) and completed the entire opera, words and music, in seven months.

This amazing swiftness is due in part to Britten's by now comprehensive mastery of techniques for building large-scale structures. His lifelong exploration of the tension between adjacent notes and keys is combined with his more recent investigation of the uses to which a tonal composer could put Schoenberg's rigorous use of all twelve notes of the chromatic scale. This expanded language, together with experience of an opera as symphonically planned as *Billy Budd*, of a ballet necessarily divided into many short numbers and of another opera, *The Turn of the Screw*, in many sections but powerfully unified by sophisticated use of variation technique, enabled him in *A Midsummer Night's Dream* to write an opera of which each act is firmly structured, but in a quite different way. Act I, which introduces the opera's three 'worlds' (humans, fairies and mechanicals) does so in a symmetrical sequence of five scenes, linked and framed by a prelude, interludes and postlude of 'forest music'. Act II, where the three worlds interact, is more flexibly divided but again unified by a refrain, in the form of variations on a sequence of 'magic chords'. Act III, the return to normality after the midsummer night's encounters,

uses brief scenes in which each of the three 'worlds' react to what
has happened to them as upbeats to the reconciliation at Theseus's
court, the mechanicals' grotesque play of Pyramus and Thisbe, and a
concluding epilogue for the fairies.

Because of the enlargement of the Jubilee Hall (and the probability
of later performances in larger theatres: *A Midsummer Night's Dream*
was soon transferred to Covent Garden) Britten was able to use a
compromise between a chamber orchestra and a symphony orchestra,
and thus to give each of the opera's worlds its own instrumental
colour: 'normal' strings and woodwind for the humans, a delicate
ensemble of two harps, harpsichord, celesta and percussion for the
fairies (with trumpet and drum for Puck), bassoon, brass and lower
strings for the rustics. The fairies' magic is intensified by the piping
sound of children's voices, by Tytania's high coloratura and the casting
of a counter-tenor as Oberon. Britten's un-Schoenbergian use of
Schoenberg's techniques also contributes to the opera's atmosphere.
The 'forest music' consists of a sequence of common chords, rendered
strangely uncommon by the slow slides between them, and by the fact
that each is rooted on a different note of the chromatic scale. This

The Jubilee Hall renovated:
Britten rehearses children
in the cast of *A Midsummer
Night's Dream*,
Aldeburgh, 1960.

strongly conjures up a sense of things not being what they appear, of
the unexpected waiting to happen. Similarly, the 'magic chords' of Act
II convey the strangeness of the fairy world because they too use
all twelve notes, arranged as four chords each of a totally different
sonority despite their very close relationship.

The 'magic chords' or 'sleep chords' return at the climax of the
sensuously beautiful love-duet between Tytania and Bottom, to
explain or excuse its lusciousness. Lysander and Hermia range through
all twelve keys in their love-duet (each is overacting a little, and daring
the other to do likewise). But these subtleties are always audible,
not merely visible to the score-reader. And they have not driven out
Britten's vein of haunting simplicity. It was the presence of the great
counter-tenor and great Purcellian Alfred Deller in the first cast that
led him to write the exquisite 'I know a bank', Purcellian in its florid
opening declamation, yet Purcell distilled to a subtle essence in its

Britten and Rostropovich
rehearsing the Cello Sonata,
with members of the English
Chamber Orchestra as its
first audience

continuation. 'Forest music' and 'magic chords' and their derivations
evaporate as the opera returns to normality in Act III, yet simplicity
here finds room both for the broad humour and parody of the
rustics' play, and the magical simplicity of the epilogue: a hypnotically
lulling theme enriched with high, clear counterpoints, a spell that is
eventually broken by trumpet, drum and the voice of Puck: 'Give
me your hands if we be friends, and Robin will restore amends.'

Shortly after the highly successful première of his Shakespeare
opera (it was soon taken up by many opera houses worldwide) Britten
produced a revised version, in two acts and slightly cut, of *Billy Budd*.
He himself prepared and conducted a BBC studio broadcast of the
revision in the autumn of 1960. By then one of the most momentous
meetings of his life had taken place. As one who had admired
Shostakovich since his student days, and learned from him, he was in
the audience for the Western première of Shostakovich's First Cello
Concerto. The two composers met, and Britten was also introduced
to the concerto's soloist and dedicatee, Mstislav Rostropovich. Neither
spoke the other's language, and their differences of character and
manner were extreme. But a friendship between them was struck up
almost immediately, based on deep mutual admiration, a shared but
imperfect knowledge of German (the *patois* that they devised, and
in which they soon conversed fluently, although incomprehensible to
German-speakers, became known as 'Aldeburgh-Deutsch') and, at
their first proper meeting the day after the concert and on many occasions thereafter, the drinking of copious quantities of whisky. It is no
exaggeration to say that the meeting with Rostropovich and, later,
with his wife, the soprano Galina Vishnevskaya, was to give Britten a
new lease of creative life.

Shostakovich, the exuberant and brilliantly gifted youthful prodigy
of the early Soviet years, had been turned by decades of conflict
with the Russian authorities into an anxious, withdrawn, oppressed
figure. In photographs he is almost never seen to smile or even to look
relaxed: he is watchful, nervously frowning. His battles with the
Soviet regime, his works often attacked or suppressed, some remaining
unperformed for many years, are audible in the music itself. Many
would even say that his works illustrate these struggles, and were heard
by some Russians as cryptic messages. Britten's admiration for him
was reciprocated. Shostakovich later described the *War Requiem* as the

greatest masterpiece of his time, and on one occasion when Britten praised a passage in one of his works the Russian was overheard, in the smattering of English that he had now acquired, saying 'No, no: you great composer; I little composer.' Between the two shy and reticent composers a warm friendship developed. Rostropovich's character was so different as to be almost Shostakovich's opposite: demonstratively emotional (no one who has ever been embraced by Mstislav Rostropovich will ever forget the experience), impulsive, endearingly flamboyant and eccentric, his personality is as closely reflected in Britten's music for him as the virtuosity and intense expressiveness of his playing.

One of the reasons that Britten resented criticism so much, with its harping on his 'cleverness' and facility, may perhaps have been that he feared that there was some truth in it. He had already, during his twenties and thirties, withdrawn a number of works or suppressed them before they could be performed. In some pieces from the late 1950s and 1960s he seems to be doing what his critics had always accused him of: allowing efficiency and flawless technique to stand in for inspiration. In some of these it could be argued that he was (indeed 'efficiently') entering into the spirit of the occasion or the commission. To have celebrated Basel University's anniversary with a challenging masterpiece would have been over-reacting, as well as wasting effort on an 'occasional' piece that might not survive its occasion. In any case, to expect a composer to explore new ground in an uninterrupted series of masterpieces is absurd. But in the works written for Rostropovich there is a sense of urgent response to the challenge of a new medium and to the musicianship of a new friend that contrasts strongly with some of the slighter works between them.

Opposite, '"Have you ever sung in English?" "No, of course not, only in Italian." "Then I'll write your part in Latin. Do you know Latin?" "Yes!", I exclaimed, and joyfully threw my arms around his neck': Britten with Galina Vishnevskaya

The first of the Rostropovich pieces, the Sonata in C for cello and piano, already contains arresting 'new' sounds, idiomatically used: a virtuoso use of guitar-like pizzicato, for example. But Britten's acquisition of a musical partner upon whose technique and musical sympathy he could rely absolutely is more profoundly felt in the Sonata's further explorations of tonal ambiguity and thematic economy. The latter is most obvious in the first movement, where both the turbulent first theme and the more lyrical second are both derived from the introduction, in which a fragment of rising scale in the piano evokes anxious cries, single notes or pairs of them, from the

cello. The pairs are sometimes a whole tone, sometimes a semitone, and Britten's examination of the expressive difference between them leads him several times in this work to reorder the steps of the scale; hence the Sonata's tonal ambiguity. He must have known that such 'artificial' scales had been widely used in Russian music since Glinka. It can also be no accident that there seem to be sidelong glances towards Shostakovich in the sinister little March of the fourth movement and the rapid mood changes of the final Moto Perpetuo. The work continues the barer, more epigrammatic manner of the *Songs from the Chinese* and the *Hölderlin-Fragmente* but has also the sense of two musicians meeting and immediately recognizing each other that is conveyed by the photographs of Britten and Rostropovich together at this time.

The Sonata was completed in February 1960 and a copy sent to Rostropovich in Moscow. It was given its première at the Aldeburgh Festival, in a recital with Britten that also included sonatas by Schubert and Debussy. Rostropovich also played the Schumann Cello Concerto in a concert conducted by Britten, and himself acted as his wife's accompanist in a concert of operatic arias and German and Russian songs. After it Britten told Vishnevskaya that he was writing a *War Requiem* and had now decided to include a part in it for her.

8

Britten in Coventry Cathedral
during a rehearsal for
the *War Requiem*; in the
background is the engraved
glass entrance screen by
John Hutton.

Why do you disturb me?
What do you mean, tedious whispers?
Is it the day I have wasted
Reproaching me or murmuring?
What do you want from me?

Alexander Pushkin (trans. D. M. Thomas)

My Subject is War 1961–71

Where texts by Auden and Ronald Duncan had failed to stimulate
Britten's ambition to write a full-length choral work, an invitation to
commemorate the rebuilding of Coventry Cathedral succeeded. Sir
Basil Spence's design for the new cathedral incorporated the burnt-out
remains of the old, which had been bombed during World War II.
The prospect of a first performance in a large space in which groups
of performers could be spatially separated prompted one train of
thought, the symbolic significance of the new building rising beside
the ruin of the old another, and for the bold plan that resulted Britten
needed neither an Auden nor a Duncan.

The idea was a threnody for the dead of all wars, taking place on
three planes: a setting of the Latin Requiem Mass for soprano, chorus
and orchestra; a sequence of settings, for male soloists and a chamber
orchestra of twelve players, of poems by Wilfred Owen, a victim of
World War I and one of the most famous of English war poets; and as
a timeless background to both these, an image of innocence unstained
by war, a separate choir of boys' voices.

Wilfred Owen: 'All a poet
can do today is warn.'

Britten spent most of 1961 writing the *War Requiem*, which was
first performed at the end of May 1962 to unprecedented critical and
public acclaim. It was recorded eight months after the première, and
within five months the recording had sold 200,000 copies, powerful
evidence of how the Requiem seized the public imagination at a time
when the Cuban missile crisis and the intensification of American
involvement in Indo-China had made the outbreak of a third world
war seem perilously possible.

The choral settings of the Mass are a culmination of Britten's
symphonic writing, the Owen settings his most extensive orchestral
song-cycle. The work is a synthesis of two of the most important
strands in his output, and an attempt to weave a climactic statement
from them. The correspondences Britten draws between the Owen
poems and the text of the Mass are powerful, the source of much of
the Requiem's impact. The most vivid of these, the juxtaposition of

Owen's retelling of the story of Abraham and Isaac and the Mass's reference to God's promise to 'Abraham and his seed', is one of the few points where the two worlds of liturgy and front-line reportage share musical material. The theme of Britten's fugal setting of the promise to Abraham is taken up by the tenor and baritone soloists; the two voices unite, as in Britten's earlier treatment of the subject in the Second Canticle, when an angel releases Abraham from his promise to sacrifice his son to God. To the words 'Offer the Ram of Pride instead of him', however, Owen's poem has the rejoinder, set to a variant of the fugal promise:

But the old man would not so, but slew his son,
And half the seed of Europe, one by one.

The 'reply' to this is the sound of boys voices praying 'Lord, let them pass from death to life, as Thou didst promise Abraham and his seed' against which the main choir repeats its earlier fugue, now in a shocked undertone.

Britten (who conducted the chamber orchestra, on the right) and his co-conductor Meredith Davies conferring at a rehearsal of the *War Requiem*

Elsewhere, however, Britten allows the two worlds to remain parallel but separate, linked only by their common exploration of a notoriously unstable interval, the tritone (described in the middle ages as *diabolus in musica* – 'the devil in music'). The division is emphasized spatially: the male soloists and their chamber group, with a separate conductor, are placed in front and to one side of the main orchestra. In the wake of the *War Requiem*'s huge public success, perhaps even because of it, this 'failure' of the two worlds to relate musically was criticized. The divisions between the Mass settings and the Owen songs are in fact shrewdly varied and powerfully dramatic. The reference in the Mass to the last trumpet is an obvious cue for Owen's 'Bugles sang', mere hints of the massed brass of the 'Dies irae'

The new Coventry Cathedral rising amid the bombed ruins of the old: the setting for which Britten wrote the *War Requiem*

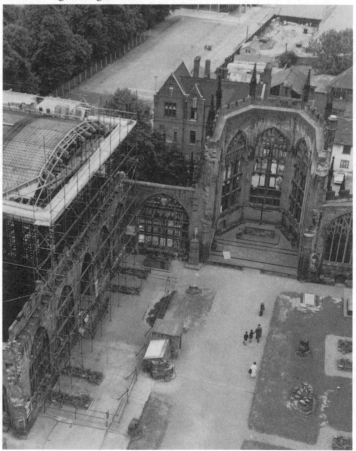

underlining Owen's insistence on the poignancy of bugle calls as heralds of death. A more abrupt conjunction is heard when soprano and chorus, singing of God 'the King of awful majesty', are interrupted by the tenor and baritone evoking another King:

Oh, Death was never enemy of ours!
We laughed at him, we leagued with him, old chum.
No soldier's paid to kick against his powers.

The agonizing of the choral 'Recordare Jesu pie':

Suppliant and bowed I pray,
My heart turned to ashes in contrition,
Help me in my last hour

receives a horrifying answer in the baritone's description of a great cannon:

Be slowly lifted up, thou long black arm...
But when thy spell be cast complete and whole,
May God curse thee, and cut thee from our soul!

at which the chorus despairingly return to their account of the Day of Judgement.

The huge range of these juxtapositions demands a weighty conclusion. The emotional crux of the *War Requiem* lies in its shortest and simplest section, the Agnus Dei, where a mournful tread and a poignant melody serve for both the Latin and the English texts, the one a prayer for peace, the other a meditation on a mutilated crucifix found amidst the devastation of battle:

One ever hangs where shelled roads part.
In this war He too lost a limb.

Britten then combines the final section of the Requiem Mass, the 'Libera me', with Owen's 'Strange Meeting': in some limbo after death a British soldier meets a German who tells him, 'I am the enemy you killed, my friend.' At the first performance the extreme poignancy of

Following page, Britten conducts a performance of the War Requiem at the Abbey Church of Ottobeuren in Bavaria; again Dietrich Fischer-Dieskau and Peter Pears are the male-voice soloists.

this setting was intensified by the fact that while Pears took the part of
the British soldier, that of the German was taken by the great baritone
Dietrich Fischer-Dieskau; he has related how he was so overcome by
the emotion of the music that he had to be helped from the platform.
The 'Libera me' takes up images of violence and horror from earlier
in the work, screwing them to still greater intensity, after which the
hushed setting of the Owen poem seems numb and motionless. Only
when the baritone enters does the music grow warmer until the voices
join in repetitions of 'Let us sleep now'. Boys' voices then sing the 'In
Paradisum', whose swelling fullness of sound as the main chorus and
soprano soloist enter is twice checked and then concluded by memories of passing bells and prayers for peace. The resigned rather than
tranquil ending recalls Owen's preface to his poems:

*My subject is War, and the pity of War. The Poetry is in the pity ... All
a poet can do today is warn.*

By now Britten was approaching fifty (his birthday fell in
November 1963), and the celebrations left no doubt of the respect in
which he was held. Apart from his stature as a composer, he was
widely recognized as a superb pianist, not only in performing his own
music. The great Russian pianist Sviatoslav Richter, famously shy of
appearing in public and notorious for cancelling engagements, was
delighted to play at Aldeburgh, for and with Britten, because of his
deep admiration for him as performer as well as creator. Britten was
no less respected as a conductor, his gifts acknowledged by orchestral
musicians, generally shrewder than critics in their judgements of
conductors. He had already become a frequent visitor to the recording
studio, and by the time of his death most of his major works had been
recorded under his direction.

A year before this birthday he had been made an Honorary
Freeman of Aldeburgh. He found public speaking painful, and his
audience would no doubt have been content with a eulogy of the
town and news of future plans for its festival. He did indeed speak
of how important it was for him to feel part of a community, and of
how attached he was to that one in particular, but he used this as a
preliminary to an attack on artists who do not have such a direct
contact with the public. He blamed them for much of the 'obscurity'

Britten conducting a
Promenade Concert at the
Royal Albert Hall on
12 September 1963; the
programme, to mark his
fiftieth birthday two months
later, consisted of his *Spring
Symphony* and *Sinfonia
da Requiem* and the British
première of the *Cantata
Misericordium*.

and 'impracticality' of some modern art. He thought it necessary to make this point 'because there are audiences who are not discriminating about it. They think that everything new is good; that if it is shocking it is important.'

This was a reaction to the polarization of British music at the time, when for example the BBC, after decades of conservatism, was making an effort to introduce audiences not only to the new music of the 1960s but to the classics of the preceding decades which had been unheard or uncomprehended in Britain until then. A new generation of composers was growing up, excited by the music of Schoenberg and his followers. Peter Maxwell Davies, Harrison Birtwistle and Alexander Goehr (known at the time as the 'Manchester School', since all three had studied there) were the most radical of these, but Richard Rodney Bennett, Malcolm Williamson, Thea Musgrave and others were all writing music much more 'advanced' than Britten was. Some of the most talented of them were, if not antagonistic, no less woundingly indifferent to him.

So the celebrations of his birthday – many concerts, a television profile, a Festschrift with over forty contributors – were clouded slightly by the pronouncements of Britten himself. In the Aldeburgh speech he expressed sentiments which could be read as defensively conservative, in an article to mark his birthday he denied that with so many works behind him he had at last acquired confidence ('It is not so at all'), regretted that he had still not achieved the simplicity he sought and was grieved that he had not come up to the technical standards that Frank Bridge had set him.

The works that follow the *War Requiem* seem to reflect this self-questioning and a conscious attempt to find a new style. Britten perhaps felt that the *War Requiem* had 'drained' him in more than one sense: it had exhausted him, and in its effort to make a great public statement from elements of his earlier music had exhausted those elements also.

The *Cantata Misericordium* is an occasional work (for the centenary of the Red Cross) and a quietly restrained one in which Britten's striving for simplicity is audible. But it was immediately preceded by the second of his works for Rostropovich, the Symphony for Cello and Orchestra, his first major work for orchestra without voices for over twenty years. It is long (forty minutes) and fully scored, yet the impression it leaves is of a great step forward in Britten's search for economy. Most of its ideas, even the wonderfully confident trumpet melody in D that opens the final passacaglia, are derived from close scrutiny of a few simple intervals. The orchestral sonorities, too, are new. Britten, absorbedly studying the potentialities of the cello, used an uncommon richness of dark, deep sounds against which the cello's line can stand in relief: bass clarinet, contrabassoon, tuba, gongs, percussion and double basses. There is much turbulence in the Cello Symphony, much darkness (an eerily shadowy scherzo), and in the elegiac slow movement a tragic eloquence. Yet the passacaglia finale is one of Britten's most joyous statements, which can be heard as a response to Rostropovich's exuberant personality and as an expression of Britten's relief at being able to renew his musical language after the *War Requiem.*

He was delighted, too, by the Symphony's first performances, in Moscow (where the last movement was encored) and Leningrad. The students in the audience were especially enthusiastic – one of their teachers told a visiting critic that no new work had excited them so much in years – and at the Conservatoire in Leningrad Britten was impressed by a student performance of parts of the *War Requiem*, a work as yet disapproved of in Russia because of its religious content.

Britten's new, sparer style, together with the experience of *Noye's Fludde* and memories of the music and drama of Japan, led to the composition of *Curlew River* and the invention of a new musical-dramatic form, the 'parable for church performance'. There were to be three of them, written in 1964, 1966 and 1968, and during that decade Britten wrote no other major dramatic works. It was as though he had found not an alternative to opera but a replacement for it.

The Noh play *Sumidagawa* had impressed him with its ritualistic slowness and economy of style and its formalized use of an all-male cast. In search of a way of transforming it into a musical drama, he sought the advice of the poet and novelist William Plomer, who had written the libretto of *Gloriana* and had lived in Japan. Plomer was dubious, and the work progressed slowly, but he and Britten gradually found parallels between Noh and the medieval mystery plays and Britten himself suggested a Christian retelling of the story of *Sumidagawa* by a group of monks in a fenland monastery (Noh plays were first performed in temples).

The first two Church Parables: *right*, Peter Pears as the Madwoman in *Curlew River; opposite*, dress rehearsal for the première of *The Burning Fiery Furnace*

Curlew River was followed by *The Burning Fiery Furnace*, on the Old Testament subject of Nebuchadnezzar, and by the New Testament parable of *The Prodigal Son*. Each begins with the singers and instrumentalists, all in monks' robes, entering in procession while singing a plainchant melody; these melodies are used throughout each work as a reservoir of thematic ideas. Noh plays are traditionally accompanied by a very small group of instruments: a flute and three drums. For each of his parables Britten uses a basic ensemble of flute, horn, viola, double bass, harp, percussion and a small organ. *Curlew River* is the story of a woman (sung by a tenor: Pears at the first performance) driven mad by grief at the loss of her son, who finds only his grave but receives comfort and healing from the appearance of his ghost. Here the flute takes a solo role, reflecting the woman's distracted state. In *The Burning Fiery Furnace* an alto trombone is added to express the exotic magnificence of Nebuchadnezzar's court and temple. In *The Prodigal Son* the flute becomes an alto flute to portray the pastoral scenes that the Son abandons, while a trumpet represents the temptations that beset him.

Each parable is conceived as chamber music, and no conductor is used, players and singers taking cues from each other. Britten takes advantage of this to write passages of free, unmeasured declamation (that is without bar-lines), and no less free textures, in which phrases are repeated without precise synchronization (a development of his preoccupation with gamelan). A consequence of this was his invention of a new musical notation, the 'curlew mark', indicating that a player or singer must hold a note or repeat a given phrase until an audible cue from another performer. Another innovation in the church parables is the use in the chamber organ part of chords that slur into one another, one note changing at a time. This is an echo of the *sho*, an instrument Britten had heard in Japan and which so attracted him

that he bought one and tried to teach himself to play it. It is a cluster of seventeen bamboo pipes arranged in a circular column, played through a single mouthpiece. In Japanese music it plays only chords, and the gradual shift from one chord to another is characteristic of court music or *gagaku*. The other instruments of Britten's diminutive 'orchestra' are used no less resourcefully. In the church parables he acquired a whole repertory of new sonorities as well as intensifying the expression of each note and phrase by a rigorous economy of means. In all three works Britten's quarrying of thematic material from the opening plainchant seems inexhaustible.

He began work on *Curlew River* in Venice, a city that he was to visit regularly for the rest of his life. He made slow progress to begin with, feeling very tired (and Venice was bitterly cold). The city exerted a spell, however, and so did his visits to S. Giorgio Maggiore, where he heard Mass sung in plainchant, the monks entering in procession and ritually donning ecclesiastical vestments. Britten adopted both procession and robing ritual in *Curlew River* and its successors. Before completing the church parable he travelled to Moscow for the first performance of the Cello Symphony. There was a visit to Budapest after the completion of *Curlew River*, during which Britten was evidently much taken with the talent and charming persistence of Zoltán and Gabriel Jeney, twelve-year-old twins who played respectively the flute and the violin, and both of them the piano. According to Britten he thought he had escaped their importunacy by agreeing to write a piece for them only if they wrote him a detailed letter about themselves in English. Within a short while, however, they did reply, in an English so 'vivid and idiomatic' that he felt he had no alternative but to write what he called the *Gemini Variations*, for two players at three instruments. A sequence of attractive character studies, it has one or two variations that reflect his preoccupation at this time with structural economy, in particular two beautiful and rather Bachian exercises in 'mirror' canon.

Far more resourceful, a little earlier in date, is the *Nocturnal after John Dowland*, a set of variations on Dowland's song 'Come, heavy sleep' that makes still more comprehensive use of guitar technique than the *Songs from the Chinese*, and is a more searching exploration of Dowland's melancholy than *Lachrymae*. Written for Julian Bream, it ranks as one of the masterpieces of the instrument's repertory.

At around this time also, Britten was asked to write a test piece for the Leeds Piano Competition. *Night Piece* is a quiet, Bartókian nocturne, much more demanding of the contestants' musicianship than their virtuosity; it is Britten's only solo work for his own instrument other than the early *Holiday Diary*.

Curlew River had its première at the Aldeburgh Festival in June 1964, Britten proving that he occasionally lacked confidence to a painful degree by repeatedly revising its closing pages at rehearsal. The Cello Symphony, again with Rostropovich as soloist, had its British première six days later, some critics recognizing that in it Britten was moving forward in a fruitful new direction.

He had been told in May that he was to be the first recipient of the Aspen Award, newly established by Robert Anderson of the Institute of Humanistic Studies at Aspen, Colorado. He was chosen from over a hundred nominations as 'the individual anywhere in the world judged to have made the greatest contribution to the advancement of the humanities', and was awarded $30,000 (he gave the money to a fund to help young musicians). Britten travelled to Aspen in July 1963 to receive the award, and before an audience of 1500 gave a speech which is the most considered formulation of his views on the role of the artist in society. One passage was read by some as an attack on the recording industry, which had served him better than almost any living composer. He deplored the fact that great masterpieces were available at the flick of a switch 'to any loud roomful of cocktail drinkers', and argued that it was the essence of the musical experience that the listener should take some trouble over it, ideally 'as much effort on the listener's part as the other two corners of the triangle, this holy triangle of composer, performer and listener'.

By now Britten had presumably been offered a knighthood and refused it, perhaps as an honour as often awarded for 'political services' as for genuine distinction. Early in 1965 he was awarded the highest distinction that a British sovereign can bestow, arguably higher even than a peerage since the number of holders of the Order of Merit at any time is limited to a maximum of twenty-four. Only two musicians before him had received it, Elgar and Vaughan Williams, and only one since, Sir Michael Tippett. Some will have seen his acceptance as an erstwhile radical's capitulation to the establishment. The distinguished American composer and critic Virgil Thomson (who listed 'Anglophobia' among his relaxations in *Who's Who*) was more publicly forthright than many in his assertion that part of Britten's success was due to friendships with 'royalty' (by which he meant Lord Harewood, the Queen's cousin), but others whispered what Thomson wrote.

Britten's response to gossip, criticism and jealousy was to withdraw more and more to Aldeburgh. Most of his major works for the remainder of his life were written for the festival, although it still lacked a theatre and an adequate concert hall (the church parables and other larger pieces were performed in such relatively ample buildings as Blythburgh Parish Church). It was in 1965, however, that he and Pears began to talk of converting a disused building at Snape into an adaptable concert hall that could also be used for stage productions.

This massively built structure, once used for the malting of barley for beer, was not far from the Old Mill which had been Britten's first home in the district. It is some measure of his and Aldeburgh's prestige that the money necessary for the conversion of The Maltings, £175,000, was raised without difficulty. The hall, seating 800, was opened within two years of the original suggestion. Its acoustic was immediately recognized as one of the finest in the country, and it rapidly became not only the festival's principal auditorium but a hall in use throughout much of the year for a variety of events and for recording. Many of Britten's own later and larger works were recorded or filmed there.

Meanwhile, apart from another occasional work and a curiously pallid one (an anthem, *Voices for Today*, for the twentieth anniversary of the United Nations – it received simultaneous premières in New York, Paris and London in October 1965), he had written his first song cycle for eight years, and his first true cycle for over a quarter of a century for any voice other than Pears's. The *Songs and Proverbs of William Blake*, written for Dietrich Fischer-Dieskau (the great German baritone who had sung in the première of the *War Requiem*), were first performed by him and Britten at the Aldeburgh Festival in June 1965, at which the *Gemini Variations* and the First Cello Suite also received their premières. Formally the Blake cycle is related to the First Cello Suite, in that its seven 'songs' are framed and separated by much shorter 'proverbs'. The latter are based on elements from a theme of twelve notes, heard in its entirety only in the final proverb.

The relationship of the songs to the twelve-note theme becomes more apparent as the cycle proceeds. The agitated piano scales underlying the setting of 'London' ('I wander thro' each charter'd street') resolve each time on a different note of the chromatic scale, giving a sense of restless unease. 'The Chimney-Sweeper' conveys pathos with childlike simplicity of means, but the terrible 'A Poison Tree' seems to be a response to the sufferings of the little sweep ('... because I am happy and dance and sing/They think they have done me no injury'). A dark melody using all twelve notes leads via knotted, almost atonal textures to a cry of triumphant evil, all the more horrible for its emergence in an unequivocal E major. From 'Tyger! Tyger!' (suggesting, with its repetitions and tigerish but repressed activity, that the creature's 'fearful symmetry' is chained and caged) to the austere final song it continues in an unbroken span of almost unrelieved stoical pessimism. For that reason perhaps, although it is one of Britten's finest and most unified song-cycles, it has never proved widely popular.

The *Gemini Variations* were based on a theme by the 83-year-old Zoltán Kodály, who joined the Jeney twins, Fischer-Dieskau, Rostropovich and Vishnevskaya at that year's festival. It was not untypical. During the twenty-five years of Britten's directorship, the festival drew not only old friends but new associates and admirers from all over the world. By the time that the Maltings was ready, Britten had little need to travel beyond his doorstep. The world came to him, including many of its composers, from abroad notably Poulenc, Copland and Henze. Yet he continued to travel widely, partly because Pears's career demanded it, partly from a sense of duty, but now also because he had new and dear friends in Russia who could not visit him as often as they would have wished.

After the 1965 festival Britten and Pears flew to Armenia, as guests of the Soviet Union of Composers, an invitation manœuvred by Rostropovich and Vishnevskaya, who joined them in what was styled a 'Composers' Home for Creative Work'. The holiday was by all accounts joyous and hospitably bibulous; it was also productive. Britten was no doubt glad of the hint provided by the name of the place where he was staying, and of course realized how delighted his hosts would be if a work for them were the outcome of the trip. On the flight he read a paperback selection of Pushkin's poems in English translation. He selected a group for possible setting and asked

Rostropovich and Vishnevskaya to read them to him in Russian while he jotted down a rough phonetic transcription. Within a fortnight he had written four songs and by the end of the month had completed a set of six, which he called *The Poet's Echo*. Vishnevskaya sang two of them at a festival of Britten's music held in Yerevan, the capital of Soviet Armenia, shortly afterwards, and gave the première of the complete set in Moscow in December.

It is not a true song-cycle, but it does have an overriding 'theme', suggested in the title, that although all sounds in nature receive back an echo, the poet's song does not. Britten's image for this 'silent echo', an answer that the artist longs for but never receives, is the interval of a falling seventh. *The Poet's Echo* is as pessimistic as the Blake cycle, but Britten's ear for the Russian language and for the amplitude of Vishnevskaya's very Russian soprano voice bring qualities of Tchaikovskian grace to the music as well. 'The Nightingale and the Rose' is one of his loveliest songs, and the concluding 'Lines Written during a Sleepless Night' one of his most memorable. The falling seventh becomes the ticking of a clock as the poet seeks a meaning in the quiet sounds of the night. Musical images from the title-song and from the nightingale's unheeded outpourings recur, but there is no answer. Britten himself suffered from insomnia, and has uncannily evoked it.

Britten returned to England to write yet another work for Rostropovich, a Suite for unaccompanied cello which was to be the first of three. Its six movements are comparable to those of a Bach solo suite, but they are framed and punctuated by four varied recurrences of a noble 'Canto', motifs from which provide the material for all of the movements that it separates. In them he shows that his 'new style' can incorporate wit (the impassioned middle section of the Marcia has a flamboyance that is perhaps a good-natured portrait of Rostropovich) as well as expressive intensity.

By the end of 1965 Britten was at work on his second church parable, *The Burning Fiery Furnace*. Rostropovich and Vishnevskaya spent Christmas at the Red House, enjoying his hospitality as much as he had appreciated theirs. Not long afterwards he was taken ill with a stomach ailment, diverticulitis, which required surgery and a spell in hospital, but the new church parable was completed in time for the 1966 festival. Britten was well enough before then to give recitals with

Pears in Austria and to attend the Russian première of the
War Requiem.

Following a successful concert revival of *Gloriana* on his fiftieth
birthday, the Sadler's Wells Opera now announced a staged production
and Britten made a number of slight revisions to the score.
His other works of 1966 were relatively minor: a miniature concert
opera requested by the Vienna Boys' Choir, *The Golden Vanity*, and
an arrangement of an English folk dance, *Hankin Booby*, commissioned by the Greater London Council for the opening of the Queen
Elizabeth Hall, newly built on the south bank of the Thames.
Immediately after this Britten and Pears made yet another visit to
Russia, to spend Christmas and the New Year with the Rostropoviches.

Britten returned to conduct the première of *Hankin Booby* and most
of the rest of the Queen Elizabeth Hall's inaugural concert, and to prepare for the opening of the Maltings. The 1967 Aldeburgh Festival was

Britten in his studio at the
Red House, the window
overlooking the garden;
his dachshund Clytie stands
by the piano.

expanded to three weeks to mark the occasion. For the opening by the Queen, Britten conducted his new *The Building of the House*, an orchestral overture with optional (but highly desirable) chorus, based on a metrical psalm-tune and including some passages of gamelan-inspired simultaneous rhythms. The Vienna Boys' Choir's performance of *The Golden Vanity* was immediately encored in its entirety. The acoustic of the Maltings was enthusiastically praised, and its suitability for opera demonstrated by a new production of *A Midsummer Night's Dream*.

Immediately after the festival Britten completed a second Cello Suite for Rostropovich, and then in rapid succession visited the Edinburgh Festival (where, together with Schubert, he was the year's 'featured composer') and gave a performance in the Maltings of Bach's *Christmas Oratorio* which was filmed by the BBC for more seasonal transmission. Later in the autumn he accompanied the English Opera Group on a visit to Canada before embarking with Pears on an extensive recital tour of North and South America.

He was now also acquiring the habit of re-examining his early unpublished works, revising and publishing those that he found of interest. In this way the charming *Sweet was the Song the Virgin Sung,*

Britten shows Queen Elizabeth II around the newly converted Maltings at Snape.

for unaccompanied women's voices, was revised for performance at the 1966 Aldeburgh Festival, thirty-five years after it had been written. The still earlier *The Sycamore Tree* and *A Wealden Trio* were more thoroughly rewritten in 1967 and some settings of Walter de la Mare, mostly dating from his schooldays, appeared in 1968.

Early that year he paid another visit to Venice, to begin work on the third church parable, *The Prodigal Son*, but while there he became seriously ill with bacterial endocarditis, an inflammatory infection of the inner tissues of the heart. As usual, he managed nevertheless to finish the parable for that year's festival which, with the Maltings as its new centrepiece, was especially rich: the premières of *The Prodigal Son* and the Second Cello Suite, as well as the two recently rewritten early choral pieces and performances of the Sadler's Wells production of *Gloriana*. Apart from *The Prodigal Son*, though, the only original composition completed during 1968 was *The Children's Crusade*, like *The Golden Vanity* a miniature 'concert opera', written for the fiftieth anniversary of the Save the Children Fund. It is Britten's most austere work for children's voices, much of it written in a recitative that reflects the matter-of-fact quality of the text, by Bertolt Brecht. It makes elaborate use of Britten's by now habitual 'twelve-note' patterning and of a large percussion ensemble but echoes Brecht, for some tastes too successfully, in eschewing all but a brief passage of lyrical expansiveness.

Britten's life was saved, early in 1968, by skilled nursing and antibiotics, but bacterial endocarditis is a grave illness (Mahler, without the aid of modern medicine, died of it) and there is little doubt that it precipitated the more serious heart condition that he suffered not long afterwards. The events of 1969 and 1970 would have put a man of much more placid temperament under great strain.

As long before as 1966 the BBC had commissioned a television opera. For many years Britten had wanted to make an operatic version of Henry James's story *Owen Wingrave*, with its pacifist, anti-militarist theme, and had already discussed the idea with Myfanwy Piper, the librettist of his other James opera, *The Turn of the Screw*. The urgency of the subject matter was no doubt intensified by contemporary events, including growing opposition to the war in Vietnam and widespread outrage at the Russian invasion of Czechoslovakia (Britten was reluctant to add his name to letters of protest at this because of his

The Maltings, Snape: Britten assesses the acoustics of the new building as one of the carpenters working on it, Len Edwards, plays the violin.

numerous friendships with Russians and his fear that such action might sever cultural links between East and West). Dramatizing James's story was not easy – it is a good deal shorter and its characters less rounded than those of *The Turn of the Screw* – and composition of the opera was interrupted by other work (including a brief, charming Suite for harp, written for the Welsh harpist Osian Ellis), by illness and by a fire which completely gutted the Maltings barely two years after it had been opened.

The fire took place during the night after the opening concert of the 1969 festival. Britten and Pears were deeply involved in the effort to ensure that every single planned event took place as advertised, even the production of Mozart's *Idomeneo* which had been designed for the facilities of the Maltings. Most of these, including a much modified *Idomeneo*, were moved to Blythburgh Parish Church. After the festival, although the hall was insured, there were many financial problems to sort out, and a brave promise was made that the Maltings would be rebuilt for the 1970 festival. It is scarcely surprising that in photographs taken amid the ruins of the hall and shortly thereafter in the USA where they gave recitals to raise money for the rebuilding fund, both Britten and Pears look markedly older and under strain.

For all that the Red House was removed from the bustle of the centre of Aldeburgh during festival time, it had become not only a home but the headquarters of a substantial 'Britten industry', receiving many necessary but distracting visitors; it was also much disturbed by aircraft noise. In 1970 Britten and Pears bought a house at Horham, nearly twenty miles inland from Aldeburgh, as a retreat. Most of Britten's later works were written there.

There were more recitals in New Zealand in the spring, and an English Opera Group tour of Australia. Understandably, the 1970 Aldeburgh Festival did not feature a Britten première, though he conducted the first performance outside Russia of Shostakovich's Fourteenth Symphony, which is both dedicated to Britten and shows his influence. All this time Britten was working on an opera conceived for a medium of which he had little experience, for which the casting had been fixed before he wrote a note of music.

James's story, of a sensitive young man who rebels against his family's military traditions, was bound to appeal to Britten, but its plot is slight: disinherited by his family and rejected by his fiancée,

Owen tries to prove that he is not motivated by cowardice by spending a night in a haunted room; in the morning he is found dead. Not all Myfanwy Piper's skill can turn the Wingrave family, barely sketched by James, into much more than a collection of grotesques. Kate, the fiancée, necessarily more fully developed than the others, is acutely unsympathetic. More troubling still, Owen himself is shallow, a personification of rebellion and pacifism but little more. After its television transmission in May 1971 (within the space of a week it was shown in thirteen countries) it was staged at Covent Garden two years later but had to wait over twenty years for another production.

Janet Baker and Benjamin Luxon in Britten's *Owen Wingrave*

The opera's dramatic weaknesses are the reasons for this neglect, all the more regrettably since the score is strong. It continues Britten's exploration of ideas that use all twelve notes of the chromatic scale, but does so with a mastery of instrumental colour that is the product of what he had learned from the church parables. Caricatures though they are, all the principal characters are portrayed graphically, and the construction of the score from a restricted range of intervals has intensified rather than reduced both its sense of relentless progress towards the dénouement and the variety of types of scene that contribute to that progress. In the Prelude, for example, Britten brilliantly combines his 'serial' preoccupations with a perception of what the medium of television could offer. Piano, harp and percussion begin with a series of aggressively clashing chords: an image of the Wingraves as a family whose ancestral profession is war. The camera then focuses on a series of family portraits, each represented by a cadenza, usually for a solo instrument, each in turn adding a single note to a chord that is held throughout. By the time the portrait of Owen's dead father is reached that chord contains eleven notes, but at Owen's appearance the chord is not 'completed' but withdrawn entirely, the missing note becoming the starting point for a horn melody representing Owen himself. The whole brief scene is a musical and dramatic exposition of great originality and effectiveness: nearly all the opera's melodic and harmonic material has by now been stated, as has the drama's essential conflict.

Several other scenes make ingenious use of the possibilities of television: one at a dinner party, for example, in which the music as well as the camera 'cross-cuts' between the whole group making awkward conversation and close-ups on their inner, unspoken monologues. The use of an off-stage ballad-singer to unify Act II, on paper a curious device, in fact works superbly, since Owen's own theme was the ballad in embryo; it is also heard, half-formed, in the magical orchestral interlude during which we first see the Wingraves's family home, Paramore, symbol of their past and of Owen's fate. It is sad that an opera of such subtlety should contain no character capable of arousing our sympathy; Owen's weakness and his inexplicable attachment to the nagging, intolerant Kate are simply irritating.

The filming sessions of *Owen Wingrave* were unhappy, with tension between Britten and the production team, culminating in his insistence that several scenes be re-shot. He was still unwell, and found the complexity of the filming process both annoying and exhausting. The opera reached a wider audience than any of his other works but very shortly afterwards he made it clear that he had no desire to return to the medium of television. Shortly before filming began, he told Myfanwy Piper that he had decided on the subject for a new opera, and that he wanted her to write the libretto. The subject was Thomas Mann's *Death in Venice*. Her first reaction was that it was impossible. Dining with the painter Sidney Nolan not very long afterwards Pears said, 'Ben is writing an evil opera, and it's killing him.'

9

Baron Britten of Aldeburgh:
Britten on 12 June 1976,
the day that his Life Peerage
was announced

But this is beauty, Phaedrus,
Discovered through the senses
And senses lead to passion, Phaedrus,
And passion to the abyss.

Myfanwy Piper (after Plato):
Death in Venice (libretto)

Aschenbach 1971–6

Britten's state of health was causing his friends anxiety, but in 1971
he showed few signs of giving in to the weakness that he visibly felt.
He completed a fourth Canticle in January, a third Cello Suite barely
a month later, working at the same time on a new song-cycle for
Pears and himself. After another visit to Russia for performances in
Leningrad and Moscow as part of a British Week, he began sketching
Death in Venice. After the televising of *Owen Wingrave* and the 1971
Aldeburgh Festival (at which Britten conducted Elgar's *The Dream of
Gerontius*) there was a further 'festival' to prepare for, the first of what
was to become a regular autumn annexe to the Aldeburgh Festival
proper: in September 1971 Britten supervised performances of all
three of the church parables. It was only then that he could return to
Venice, with Pears and the Pipers, to continue work on the opera.

   The Fourth Canticle, *The Journey of the Magi*, is a setting for three
voices (counter-tenor, tenor and bass) and piano of a poem by T. S.
Eliot describing the rigours of the wise men's journey to Bethlehem
('A cold coming we had of it') and by analogy the harshness of the
truths revealed by the birth of Christ. This is reflected in the angular,
stumbling keyboard part and the gruffness of the word-setting, which
also involves a large amount of chant-like word-repetition. At Eliot's
dry climactic line 'It was (you may say) satisfactory', the voices'
repetitions of 'satisfactory' begin to outline the plainchant melody
'Magi videntes stellam' ('The wise men, seeing the star...').

   The third and last Cello Suite was written in early 1971 but not
heard until 1974. Rostropovich had offended the Soviet authorities by
speaking in defence of the dissident novelist Aleksandr Solzhenitsyn,
and he was not allowed to leave Russia. Britten gave him the manuscript in April 1971, but it was neither published nor performed
until Rostropovich was once again able to visit Britain. It is in nine
movements, still more unified than the ten-movement First Suite
by being based on four Russian melodies that are only stated in their
original form in the concluding passacaglia. Three are folk-songs,

T. S. Eliot, whose poetry
Britten chose for the last two
of his Canticles

from a collection arranged by Tchaikovsky; the fourth is the
Orthodox *Kontakion,* or Prayer for the Departed ('With the Saints
you will find peace'). It is the most eloquent of all the Cello Suites,
sounding like an anxious message to Rostropovich in the troubles
he was experiencing. He has said that he could not play it without
weeping, and since Britten's death he has not felt able to play it at all.

The new song-cycle, Britten's last for himself and Pears, sets twelve
poems by the Scottish writer William Soutar (1898–1943), four in
English, eight in Scots. In one way, then, this continues Britten's habit
of spurring his imagination with a study of the sounds of a 'foreign'
tongue; he was prompted to do so by the circumstances of the cycle's
commission (for the 700th concert in a series mounted by the
National Gallery of Scotland). The poem that gives the cycle its title,
'Who Are These Children?', demonstrates what close affinities
Britten found in Soutar, who was little known in England. The poem
was inspired, as a marginal note on the manuscript makes clear, by
a photograph printed in the *Times Literary Supplement* in 1941 of
a group of huntsmen, some in military uniform, riding through a
bombed village, watched by perplexed children:

Who are these children gathered here
Out of the fire and smoke
That with remembering faces stare
Upon the foxing folk?

The four poems in English are all songs of protest, the eight in
Scots are what Soutar called 'Bairn-Rhymes', and Britten's juxtapositions of the two give the cycle a compelling unity. Thus the third
song, 'Nightmare', a vision of a tree as a human creature, bleeding
under the axe, has a grim reply in the concluding 'The Auld Aik':

The auld aik's doun;
The auld aik's doun;
Twa hunna year it stüde or mair,
But noo it's doun, doun.

The eloquent denunciation of 'Slaughter', another of the English
poems, resonates into the enigmatic Scots riddle that follows it;

'Who Are These Children? itself is given poignant or ironic context both by the poems of childhood that surround it and by its relationship to the penultimate song, 'The Children', perhaps the most deeply felt of all Britten's pitying elegies for destroyed innocents:

A wound which everywhere
Corrupts the hearts of men:
The blood of children corrupts the hearts of men.

His next concentrated period of work on *Death in Venice* was in March 1972, at Schloss Wolfsgarten, the home of the Hesses. He returned to Aldeburgh for the Festival, where he conducted not only a production of his own *The Turn of the Screw* but a performance of Schumann's *Scenes from Goethe's 'Faust'* which was widely recognized as a revelation of a neglected masterpiece. In the autumn he recorded it, but was by then so weak that he needed frequent rests between short recording sessions. His left arm was painful whenever he raised it to conduct. Doctors diagnosed this as a symptom of a seriously defective heart valve and urged an operation to replace it. Britten hoped to finish the opera and conduct its first performance before undergoing surgery, but after completing the composition sketch in December 1972 he realized that he would not have the strength to conduct it.

By now he found walking difficult and climbing stairs almost impossible. He nevertheless insisted on finishing the full score of *Death in Venice*, and on not disappointing the Princess of Hesse by missing her birthday celebrations at Schloss Wolfsgarten in March. Only after his return and the completion of the opera in April did he undergo surgery on 8 May.

Although he left hospital three weeks later he was exhausted by the journey back to Horham, disturbed by the partial paralysis of his right arm caused by a stroke during the operation, and far too ill to attend the first performance of *Death in Venice* on 16 June. Even the live broadcast a few days later was too much for him: alarmed by an unexpected noise (stage machinery, in fact) he switched the radio off after a few moments. Not until September, when the cast put on a private performance for him, did he hear or see the complete work. By October, when it was produced at Covent Garden, he was well enough to attend, although very frail and looking much older than his

fifty-nine years. His sixtieth birthday in November was marked
world wide, with relief as well as affection, but he took no part in
the celebrations.

Mann's *novella* is the story of a fatal obsession, of the elderly writer
Aschenbach for a radiantly beautiful twelve-year-old boy in cholera-
stricken Venice. It was written under the impact of the death in 1911 of
Gustav Mahler, and Mann uses the story to explore the dichotomies
between life and art, between reason and the senses, health and sickness, order and corruption that were a central theme of his fiction.
Britten depicts Aschenbach's feverish and hopeless pursuit of the boy
Tadzio with an ingenuity of motivic cross-reference that is a brilliant
analogue of obsession. A single motif, first heard to Aschenbach's very
first words ('My mind beats on'), is expanded into a series
of very closely related ideas, used exhaustively but with great
subtlety throughout the opera to signify the allure of Venice and the

Thomas Mann, the author of
Death in Venice, who knew
Britten's music and thought
that he would have been
the ideal composer for an
opera based on his novel
Doktor Faustus

corruption of the plague. Aschenbach's music and that of the seven
fateful figures (sung by the same bass-baritone singer) who seduce or
compel him towards his fate is saturated in manifestations of this
protean motif. Tadzio is not corrupt, but a vision of chaste, classical
beauty, of the ideals of Aschenbach's art. For him, his family and
friends (their play ritualized into the danced Games of Apollo which
conclude Act I), Britten devised almost a second musical language.
Melodically it is based on an ambiguous six-note scale, almost but not
quite definable as A major; it is coloured by gamelan-like percussion
and, most crucially, by the cool, penetrating sound of the vibraphone.

It is an almost painfully personal opera, given added poignancy
by the taxing demands it made of, and the boundless confidence it
expressed in Peter Pears. Aschenbach is on stage almost uninterruptedly, his monologues given a bare piano accompaniment. Yet
these are no dry recitatives, but intensely expressive and revealing
of character; most of them are 'unmeasured', without bar-lines or
notated rhythms, leaving their precise phrasing to the taste and
sensitivity of the singer. Tadzio is a silent role, and Britten cast him as
a dancer. A twelve-year-old child could hardly sustain the role, and
it is normally taken by a young adult, which can explicitly overstate
the homoerotic element of Mann's plot. Yet the danced Games of
Apollo are the trigger for the ensuing nightmare in which Aschenbach
realizes the conflict within him between an Apollonian love of beauty
and a Dionysiac sensual passion, and that in its turn is the catalyst for
the scene of his deepest humiliation, when he allows the insinuating
hotel barber to dye his hair and rouge his cheeks in a vain attempt
at rejuvenation. The dance sequence is thus essential as the turning-
point of Aschenbach's tragedy, and future solutions to it may well
concentrate on genuine children's games rather than a choreographer's
balletic fantasy on them. Aschenbach's final, self-realizing and
intensely moving aria to beauty:

What if all were dead
And only we two left alive?
...Does beauty lead to wisdom, Phaedrus?
Yes, but through the senses.

needs to refer back to the vision of sensual beauty that Britten's music for the Games of Apollo demands from any staging of the opera.

For all the centrality of Aschenbach's obsession, the details of *Death in Venice* are no less beautifully painted. The sounds, even the smell of Venice, the lapping of water, the omnipresent bells, the acoustic of St Mark's, the cries of gondoliers and street vendors, Aschenbach's inner turmoil before his avowal of 'I love you' have a graphic quality that is surely, including the last of these, 'taken from life'.

For some while after the operation Britten could not compose. He had no confidence in his ideas or his critical faculty, and this distressed him. Early in 1974 he revised his early String Quartet in D and was persuaded to look again at the almost forgotten *Paul Bunyan*. Three songs from it were sung at that year's Aldeburgh Festival, and Britten went on to prepare a revised edition of the work. This seems to have given him back his confidence, and although still so weak that he could only work for an hour each day he was able to begin composing again by the summer of 1974, fourteen months after the operation.

The new work was a fifth Canticle, written for Pears and the harpist Osian Ellis. Britten was very concerned at not being able to accompany Pears any more, encouraging him to continue giving recitals with Ellis and with the young American pianist Murray Perahia. Pears was now sixty-four but seemed vocally ageless, meeting the huge demands of the role of Aschenbach in *Death in Venice* with apparently no strain. His performance in the New York première of the opera late in 1974 meant a separation of nearly three months, an experience that was harder for Britten than for Pears. Yet it was during that separation that Britten began another work for Pears, performance of which would inevitably separate them again. This was the sequence of part-songs on old English texts *Sacred and Profane*, intended for Pears's madrigal group the Wilbye Consort. It was just before starting this work that Britten heard a broadcast recording of Pears singing *Winter Words* and wrote to him (in a letter ending 'I love you, I love you, I love you') that he had to switch the radio off after the cycle because he could not bear to hear anything after 'How long, how long?', the last words of the Hardy cycle, from a poem that had given the *Suite on English Folk Tunes* its subtitle, 'A time there was'.

The Fifth Canticle, *The Death of Saint Narcissus,* sets one of the most obscure of T. S. Eliot's poems, a parable of the difficulty of religious or artistic fulfilment. The vocal line is lyrical but spare; despite its length (seven minutes) the whole work has the quality of an austerely beautiful but enigmatic epigram. The *Suite on English Folk Tunes* had its origin in the setting for wind and drums of the folk dance *Hankin Booby* that Britten had made for the opening of the Queen Elizabeth Hall eight years earlier. He now added four more movements, each based, like *Hankin Booby*, on two traditional melodies. At the time of its première *Hankin Booby* seemed a robust celebratory clamour for a special occasion. Heard in its final context an enigmatic shadow is also perceptible, and these two moods are picked up in the outer movements, the first bold and robust, the fourth a lively evocation of folk fiddle playing, but the pastoral second has a nostalgic quality, almost an ache to it; the final and longest movement is subdued, dark and desolate, with something of protest to its climax.

Sacred and Profane, completed early in 1975, was followed by another set of songs for Pears and Osian Ellis, seven poems by Robert Burns requested by the Queen as a seventy-fifth birthday present for her mother. Britten's health had now temporarily improved as a result of a change in his medication, and both works suggest it. The Burns settings are mostly agreeable trifles, some in what might disrespectfully be termed a 'wrong-note folk-song' style, but the exquisite 'My Early Walk', with its florid vocal twinings, is one of the finest of Britten's late songs. In *Sacred and Profane* he recaptures not only his characteristic lyricism, but brilliantly and sometimes disturbingly catches the robust, unsentimental directness of his chosen texts. The most striking of the songs, especially from someone so close to death, is the last of them, a catalogue of the physical manifestations of mortality which Britten sets with almost jovial relish. None of the eight settings suggests a composer in anything but total command of his craft and his material.

Indeed he was well enough after composing these part-songs to go on a brief holiday on a narrow-boat owned by the singer John Shirley-Quirk. By now he had a nurse, Rita Thomson, in constant attendance. The 1975 Aldeburgh Festival reassured his admirers: as well as a revival of *Death in Venice* there were three Britten premières, of the revised String Quartet in D, the Fifth Canticle and the *Suite on English Folk Tunes*. There was also a performance of Berlioz's cycle

Robert Burns, whose poems were chosen for a set of songs to honour the Scottish-born Queen Elizabeth the Queen Mother

Nuits d'été by Janet Baker, after which Britten told her that he would like to write a similar piece for her. Some years earlier he had considered writing an opera based on Racine's *Phèdre*; now he selected passages from Robert Lowell's verse translation of the play and wove them into a solo cantata in the manner of Handel, a prologue and two arias separated by recitatives accompanied by harpsichord and cello.

It is a masterly score, with a characteristic, pervasive motto phrase echoing through it. *Phaedra* has an operatic amplitude of gesture, from the declamatory first aria, culminating in the heroine's confesion of her incestuous love for her stepson, to the huge phrase, tragic and even proud, in which she confesses to her husband. Again there is no hint of a fatally ill composer husbanding his resources, rather of one eagerly responding to new stimuli: the sequences of opaque ten-part string chords in the second aria, clearing each time to a poignant recollection, are a new sound in Britten's music. So is the remarkable coda, in which fleeting recollections of Phaedra's passion, madness and death fade out over a long-held octave C in the basses.

Only a year before, when working on the *Suite on English Folk Tunes*, he had jokingly said that the flutes and piccolos 'tended to get left out' because of the painful difficulty he experienced in moving his right arm over a page of full score. *Phaedra*, for strings and continuo only, was easier, but by now he was so weak that he wrote the work slowly into full score, lacking the energy to write a preliminary draft and then a fair copy. He had mentioned his difficulties with a large page of score to the writer on music Hans Keller, to whom he had promised that he would one day write another string quartet. Keller only half-jokingly replied that four staves would be easier, and in October 1975 Britten began another quartet, completing the sketch in November, on a last visit to Venice.

The Third String Quartet has the sublimity of a work that its composer must have realized might be his last. It is somehow deeply moving to hear in it also a faint but unmistakable smile. Keller had always been dismissive of quartets that to him denied the essence of quartet-writing by retreating to textures of three parts or less. Britten's opening movement, surely a gesture to Keller (the work's dedicatee), is called 'Duets' and almost throughout conspicuously avoids four-part writing. Its successor, 'Ostinato', vigorously makes satisfyingly economic use of two bluntly brief motifs, while the third movement,

'Solo', must have proved even to Keller that single lines have a place even in a quartet. It is in this movement, moving from note to note with slow precision, that Britten perhaps reveals how painful the act of writing was by this stage. Yet the music itself is not painful but intense, concentrated and ethereal. The scherzo, 'Burlesque', seems like a homage to Shostakovich, whose death, which grieved Britten deeply, was announced two months before work on the quartet began. Yet it is no lament, but a brusque, almost savage stamping dance, with a trio rendered ghostly by the sound of violins using the wood of the bow and the viola producing unearthly whistlings by playing on the wrong side of the bridge.

It seems that at one stage Britten was thinking of not calling the work a quartet at all, but a divertimento. It is the finale, a recitative and passacaglia entitled 'Serenissima', which proves that his final choice was the right one. Most affectingly, it takes up elements from *Death in Venice*, presents them in a new context, and provides them with an alternative conclusion, resigned but not tragic. Instead of a final statement of the pensive passacaglia theme, the violin climbs quietly to a high D, like a last avowal, the recurrent bass is heard once more, the upper strings' last chord is in conflict with the cello's held D, but the conflict is not resolved. The D is held after the chord ceases, and is marked both 'dying away' and 'long'.

Britten's health had now deteriorated shockingly. His doctors, realizing that the valve replacement had failed, discussed the possibility of a further operation but concluded that he was too weak to survive it. Realizing that he had little time to live, Britten made a new will in March 1976. He received visitors, but only for very brief periods, saving what little energy he had for what little work he could still do. He fulfilled a promise to the violist Cecil Aronowitz to arrange the piano accompaniment of his *Lachrymae* for a small string orchestra (in fact he virtually recomposed the piece, deepening and darkening it considerably). He made a group of folk song arrangements for voice and harp to expand Pears's and Osian Ellis's recital repertory. At that year's Aldeburgh Festival the première of *Phaedra* abundantly demonstrated that his imaginative powers were undiminished, and he must also have been pleased by the success of the first stage production for many years of *Paul Bunyan* and the revival after long neglect of his early song cycle *Our Hunting Fathers*.

During the Festival it was announced in the Queen's Birthday
Honours list that a life peerage had been conferred on him. Some of
his friends were disconcerted by his acceptance of the honour. Britten
joked that it would save him energy since he would now be able to
sign letters 'Britten'.

Spurred by these events, perhaps, he began work later that year
on two further pieces. The first was a *Welcome Ode* for local school-
children to sing and play during a visit to the area by the Queen as
part of her Silver Jubilee celebrations. This he wrote with the
assistance of the young composer Colin Matthews, who had been
helping Britten by playing his sketches to him, since the semi-paralysis
of his right arm made it impossible for him to play the piano to his
own satisfaction. For the *Welcome Ode* he asked Matthews to prepare a
score from his sketches, himself supervising every detail of the work.
The task was eased by the relative simplicity of the music, and the
result was so successful, a return to the robust tunefulness of his earlier
music for children, that Britten planned to use the same method for
a cantata setting a poem by Edith Sitwell that she had written many
years before, dedicating it to him and hoping that one day he would

Britten working on *Phaedra*
with Janet Baker; his musical
assistant, the composer
Colin Matthews, is on
the left.

set it. Rostropovich had been appointed Musical Director of the National Symphony Orchestra of Washington DC, and Britten intended it for his opening concert. Its title was to be *Praise We Great Men*, and he began work on it during a brief summer holiday in Norway in August.

On his return, after putting the finishing touches to the *Welcome Ode*, the Amadeus Quartet came to the Red House for two days to work on the Third String Quartet with him. He resumed work on *Praise We Great Men* early in November, and arranged a working session with Colin Matthews on the opening section of it for the ninth of that month. Before the meeting could take place, however, he realized that he would never finish the work. Urgent messages were sent to Pears, who was teaching and giving recitals in the USA and Canada. By 22 November Britten was so ill that he needed oxygen, but insisted on champagne being served to celebrate his birthday, and on having a few words with each of those who came to congratulate him. Six days later, when Rostropovich called, Britten gave him the sketch – amounting to about five minutes in all – of 'his' cantata. Colin Matthews's performing edition of the sketch reveals that even at this stage Britten's physical exhaustion was not accompanied by any enfeeblement of his imaginative powers: it incorporates a striking further development of his 'gamelan style' and a last, serene solo for Pears. By now even speech was a great effort. He died in Pears's arms

Britten in the last summer of his life, with Mstislav Rostropovich

Britten with Pears on the terrace outside the Red House library; in nearly all the late photographs he supports or covers his partly paralysed right hand.

very early in the morning of 4 December 1976, twelve days after his sixty-third birthday.

He was buried in the graveyard of Aldeburgh Parish Church. Pears outlived him by ten years, continuing his singing career until the age of seventy and his teaching until the day before he died. The gross value of Britten's estate was considerable, £1,664,000, but about two-thirds of this sum was accounted for by the value of his manuscripts. On Pears's death his estate and Britten's were merged as the Britten-Pears Foundation which, greatly enriched by the royalties from Britten's compositions, supports the continuing Aldeburgh Festival, maintains the Britten-Pears Library at the Red House as a centre of research and sponsors young composers by means of a biennial competition and a triennial Britten Award.

During his last days he said several times that he had been forgotten, that because he was no longer seen outside the Aldeburgh circle no one remembered him. In the aftermath of his death, while obituaries sought to assess his achievement and his permanent place in musical history, doubts were expressed whether some of his works would find any such place, since they were written with such deep responsiveness to a chosen group of interpreters that other performers would be repelled by them. Indeed, to begin with, tenors were slow to take on some of the operatic roles that had become, so to speak, Pears's property. The later songs, whether written for him, for Fischer-Dieskau or for Vishnevskaya, have been very rarely sung in the years since Britten's death.

But the fear that much of his work would not long survive him has proved ill-founded. Since his death the idea that modernism, essentially descending from Schoenberg and his pupils, is the central musical language of our time, a language to which Britten's music made no contribution and is therefore irrelevant, has become less and less tenable. Music in the 1990s rejoices in diversity and an absence of dogmatism, and in that climate Britten's music has largely escaped even the temporary eclipse that so often ensues after a great creator's death.

Britten correcting a fair copy of the Third String Quartet, 24 September 1976, six weeks before his death

He insisted that he did not write for posterity but for 'the living'. In his speech accepting the Aspen Award he said, 'That is what we should aim at – pleasing people today as seriously as we can, and letting the future look after itself.' Much of his music does precisely that, and demonstrates that 'pleasing ... as seriously as we can' is no contradiction. But his greatest music has deeper qualities too, expressing a personality that felt deep pain as well as exuberant joy in the exercise of his craft. There is a haunted poignancy, an awareness of mortality, a horror at cruelty and a tragic sense of the lost and unregainable paradise of childhood. If these qualities mean anything to the posterity that he took no thought of, then Rostropovich's prediction, congratulating Britten on one of his birthdays and foreseeing celebrations of his 150th and 200th anniversaries, will prove an accurate one.

Classified List of Works

Britten's list of published works runs to Op. 95, with only a small group of compositions not given opus numbers. The following catalogue contains well over twice that many entries, not including the transcriptions of folk-songs or Britten's editions of music by other composers. With the exception of most of his juvenilia (roughly defined as works written before he began studying at the Royal College of Music) an attempt has been made to list all of his completed compositions. This is partly because a substantial amount of his music was written for films, radio and the theatre, and to omit these scores would give a misleading impression of his astonishing fertility. Their importance in developing his fluency and his flair for dramatic music can hardly be overstated. Some of these works (suitably edited for concert performance) and others forgotten or withdrawn by the composer, have been released for publication by his estate since his death.

Dates in brackets are those of composition unless otherwise stated. The abbreviation 'fp' denotes first performance, and details are given where known.

Stage Works

(extracts, suites etc. prepared or authorized by Britten himself are listed after the main entries)

Plymouth Town, ballet score for small orchestra, scenario by Violet Alford (1931). Unperformed and unpublished

Paul Bunyan, Op. 17, operetta in a prologue and two acts, libretto by W. H. Auden (1940–41; revised 1974). fp New York, 5 May 1941

Peter Grimes, Op. 33, opera in a prologue and three acts, libretto by Montagu Slater after George Crabbe's poem *The Borough* (1944–5). fp London, 7 June 1945 [*Four Sea Interludes from Peter Grimes*, Op. 33a; *Passacaglia from Peter Grimes*, Op. 33b; 'Old Joe has gone fishing' and 'Song of the Fishermen' for mixed chorus and piano; *Three Arias from Peter Grimes*, for soprano, tenor and piano (or orchestra)]

The Rape of Lucretia, Op. 37, opera in two acts, libretto by Ronald Duncan after André Obey's play *Le Viol de Lucrèce* (1945–6; revised 1947). fp Glyndebourne, 12 July 1946 [*Three Arias from The Rape of Lucretia*, for mezzo-soprano, contralto, tenor and piano (or orchestra)]

Albert Herring, Op. 39, comic opera in three acts, libretto by Eric Crozier freely adapted from Guy de Maupassant's story *Le Rosier de Madame Husson* (1947). fp Glyndebourne, 20 June 1947

The Little Sweep, Op. 45, children's opera in three scenes, libretto by Eric Crozier, forming 2nd part of *Let's Make an Opera!* (1949). fp Aldeburgh, 14 June 1949

Billy Budd, Op. 50, opera in two acts (originally four), libretto by E. M. Forster and Eric Crozier after Herman Melville's story (1950–51; revised 1960). fp London, 1 December 1951

Gloriana, Op. 53, opera in three acts, libretto by William Plomer (1952–3; revised 1966). fp London, 8 June 1953 [Symphonic Suite 'Gloriana', Op. 53a, for orchestra with optional tenor solo; *Six Choral Dances from Gloriana*, for mixed voices; *Morris Dance from Gloriana*, for two descant recorders]

The Turn of the Screw, Op. 54, opera in a prologue and two acts, libretto by Myfanwy Piper after Henry James's story (1954). fp Venice, 14 September 1954

The Prince of the Pagodas, Op. 57, ballet in three acts, scenario by John Cranko (1956). fp London, 1 January 1957 [*Pas de Six* from *The Prince of the Pagodas*, Op. 57a]

Noye's Fludde, Op. 59, the Chester Miracle Play set for adult and child performers in one act (1957). fp Orford, 18 June 1958

A Midsummer Night's Dream, Op. 64, opera in three acts, libretto by Benjamin Britten and Peter Pears adapted from Shakespeare's play (1959–60). fp Aldeburgh, 11 June 1960 [*Bottom's Dream* from *A Midsummer Night's Dream*, for bass-baritone and orchestra (or piano)]

Curlew River, Op. 71, parable for church performance, libretto by William Plomer, adapted from the Japanese Noh play *Sumidagawa* (1964). fp Orford, 12 June 1964

The Burning Fiery Furnace, Op. 77, parable for church performance, libretto by William Plomer, after the Bible (1966). fp Orford, 9 June 1966

The Prodigal Son, Op. 81, parable for church performance, librctto by William Plomer, after the Bible (1968). fp Orford, 10 June 1968

Owen Wingrave, Op. 85, opera in two acts, libretto by Myfanwy Piper after Henry James's story (1970). fp (television) 16 May 1971; (stage) London, 10 May 1973

Death in Venice, Op. 88, opera in two acts, libretto by Myfanwy Piper after novella by Thomas Mann (1971–3). fp Snape, 16 June 1973

Orchestral

Sinfonietta, Op. 1, for chamber orchestra (1932). fp London, 31 January 1933

Simple Symphony, Op. 4, for string orchestra (1933–4). fp Norwich, 6 March 1934

Soirées Musicales, Op. 9; based on Rossini arrangements made in 1935 for animated film *The Tocher* (1936). fp (radio) 16 January 1937; (concert) London, 10 August 1937

Russian Funeral, march for brass and percussion (1936). Posthumously published. fp London, 8 March 1936

Variations on a Theme of Frank Bridge, Op. 10, for string orchestra (1937). fp Salzburg, 27 August 1937

Mont Juic, Op. 12; Catalan dances arranged by Britten and Lennox Berkeley (1937). fp (radio) 8 January 1938

Piano Concerto in D, Op. 13 (1938; revised 1945). fp London, 18 August 1938

Violin Concerto, Op. 15 (1939; revised 1950). fp New York, 28 March 1940

Young Apollo, Op. 16, for piano, string quartet and string orchestra (1939). fp Toronto, 2 August 1939

Canadian Carnival (*Kermesse Canadienne*), Op. 19 (1939). fp (radio) 6 June 1940; (concert) Cheltenham, 13 June 1945

Sinfonia da Requiem, Op. 20 (1940). fp New York, 30 March 1941

Diversions, Op. 21, for piano (left hand) and orchestra (1940; revised 1950). fp Philadelphia, 16 January 1942

Matinées Musicales, Op. 24; suite after Rossini (1941). Commissioned by the American Ballet Company to form, with *Soirées Musicales*, a ballet with choreography by George Balanchine. fp Rio de Janeiro, 27 June 1941

Scottish Ballad, Op. 26, for two pianos and orchestra (1941). fp Cincinnati, 28 November 1941

An American Overture, Op. 27 (1941). Commissioned by the Cleveland Orchestra and given the title *Occasional Overture*; unperformed until 1983, then retitled to avoid confusion with Op. 38. Posthumously published. fp Birmingham, 1983

Prelude and Fugue, Op. 29, for eighteen-part string orchestra (1943). fp London, 23 June 1943

The Young Person's Guide to the Orchestra (*Variations and Fugue on a Theme of Henry Purcell*), Op. 34, for orchestra with optional narrator (1946). Originally written for a film, *The Instruments of the Orchestra*. fp Liverpool, 15 October 1946.

Occasional Overture in C, Op. 38 (1946). Withdrawn after a single performance; posthumously published. fp (radio) 29 September 1946.

Variations on an Elizabethan Theme (Sellenger's Round) (1953). Composed by six English composers to celebrate the coronation of Elizabeth II. Britten's variation is no. 4; the others are by Arthur Oldham, Michael Tippett, Lennox Berkeley, Humphrey Searle and William Walton. fp Aldeburgh, 20 June 1953.

Symphony for Cello and Orchestra, Op. 68 (1962–3). fp Moscow, 12 March 1964

The Building of the House, Op. 79, overture for orchestra with optional chorus, text based on a metrical version of Psalm 127 (1967). fp Snape, 2 June 1967

Suite on English Folk Tunes: 'A Time There Was …', Op. 90 (1974). fp Snape, 13 June 1975 (première of third movement, *Hankin Booby*: London, 1 March 1967)

Lachrymae, Op. 48a, for viola and small string orchestra (1976); arrangement of *Lachrymae*, for viola and piano (1950). fp Recklinghausen, Germany, 3 May 1977.

Choral

A Wealden Trio: The Song of the Women, carol for women's voices, text by Ford Madox Ford (1929; revised 1967). fp (revised version) Aldeburgh, 19 June 1968

A Hymn to the Virgin, anthem for mixed voices, anonymous text from c. 1300 (1930; revised 1934). fp Lowestoft, 5 January 1931

I Saw Three Ships, carol for mixed voices, traditional text (1930; revised 1967 as *The Sycamore Tree*). fp (revised version) Aldeburgh, June 1968

Two Part-Songs, for women's voices and piano, text by Wilfred Scawen Blunt and Walter de la Mare (1931). Unpublished

Two Madrigals, for mixed voices, texts by Robert Herrick and anonymous (1931). Unpublished

Two Psalms, for chorus, brass, percussion and strings, texts from the Bible (Psalms 130 and 150) (1931). Unpublished

O Lord, Forsake Me Not, motet for double chorus, text from the Book of Psalms (1931). Unpublished

Variations on a French Carol, for women's voices, violin, viola and piano (1931). Unpublished

Thy King's Birthday, Christmas suite for chorus with solo soprano, texts by Robert Southwell and from the Bible (1931). Posthumously published as *Christ's Nativity*. fp Aldeburgh, 12 June 1966 (one section rewritten 1966 as *Sweet was the Song the Virgin Sung*)

Three Two-part Songs, for boys' or women's voices and piano, texts by Walter de la Mare (1932). fp London, 12 December 1932

A Boy was Born, Op. 3, choral variations for mixed choir (with optional organ), texts by Christina Rossetti, Thomas Tusser, Francis Quarles and anonymous (1932–3; revised 1955). fp (radio) 23 February 1934; (concert) London, 17 December 1934 [*Corpus Christi Carol* from *A Boy was Born*, arranged (1961) for treble solo or unison voices and organ]

Two Part-songs, for mixed chorus and piano, texts by George Wither and Robert Graves (1933). fp London, 11 December 1933

Friday Afternoons, Op. 7, for children's voices and piano, texts by Thackeray, Jane Taylor, Nicholas Udall, Izaak Walton, Eleanor Farjeon and anonymous (1933–5). The fourteen songs were written over three years for the pupils of Clive House School, Prestatyn, of which Britten's brother Robert was headmaster. *A New Year's Carol* from *Friday Afternoons* arranged (1971) for women's voices and piano. *Lone Dog*, rejected song from *Friday Afternoons*, posthumously published.

May, unison song with piano, anonymous text (1934)

Te Deum in C, for chorus and organ (or strings, with harp or piano), text from Book of Common Prayer (1934). fp London 27 January 1936

Jubilate Deo, for chorus and organ, text from Book of Common Prayer (1934). Posthumously published

Pacifist March, for chorus and orchestra, text by Ronald Duncan (1937)

Advance Democracy, for eight-part chorus, text by Randall Swingler (1938). There is no connection between this secular motet and Britten's music for a 1939 film of the same title.

Ballad of Heroes, Op. 14, for tenor or soprano, chorus and orchestra, texts by Randall Swingler and W. H. Auden (1939). fp London, 5 April 1939

A. M. D. G., for mixed chorus, text by Gerard Manley Hopkins (1939); withdrawn by Britten, its opus number (17) reassigned to *Paul Bunyan*. Unperformed during Britten's lifetime, posthumously published

Hymn to St Cecilia, Op. 27, for five-part chorus, text by W. H. Auden (1942). fp London, 22 November 1942

A Ceremony of Carols, Op. 28, for treble voices and harp, texts by James, John and Robert Wedderburn, Robert Southwell, William Cornish and anonymous (1942). fp Norwich, 5 December 1942

Rejoice in the Lamb (Jubilate Agno), Op. 30, festival cantata for mixed chorus and organ, text by Christopher Smart (1943). fp Northampton, 21 September 1943

The Ballad of Little Musgrave and Lady Barnard, for male voices and piano, anonymous text (1943). fp Eichstätt, Germany (prisoner-of-war camp), February 1944

Festival Te Deum, Op. 32, for mixed chorus and organ, text from Book of Common Prayer (1944). fp Swindon, 24 April 1945

A Shepherd's Carol, for mixed voices, text by W. H. Auden (1944). fp (radio, as part of a feature, *Poet's Christmas*) 1944; (concert) London, 17 October 1962

Chorale after an Old French Carol, for mixed voices, text by W. H. Auden (1944). Posthumously published. fp (radio, as part of a feature, *Poet's Christmas*) 1944

Saint Nicolas, Op. 42, cantata for tenor, chorus, string orchestra, piano duet, percussion and organ, text by Eric Crozier (1948). fp Aldeburgh, 5 June 1948

Spring Symphony, Op. 44, for soloists, chorus, boys' choir and orchestra, texts by Edmund Spenser, Thomas Nashe, George Peele, John Clare, John Milton, Robert Herrick, Henry Vaughan, Richard Barnefield, William Blake, Beaumont and Fletcher, W. H. Auden and anonymous (1949). fp Amsterdam, 9 July 1949

A Wedding Anthem (Amo ergo sum), Op. 46, for soloists, mixed chorus and organ, text by Ronald Duncan (1949). fp London, 29 September 1949

Five Flower Songs, for mixed voices, texts by Robert Herrick, George Crabbe, John Clare and anonymous (1950). fp (radio) 24 May 1951; (concert) London, June 1951

Hymn to St Peter, Op. 56a, for mixed chorus and organ, text from Gradual of the Feast of Saints Peter and Paul (1955). fp Norwich, 1955

Antiphon, Op. 56b, for mixed chorus and organ, text by George Herbert (1956). fp Tenbury, 1956

Einladung zur Martinsgans, eight-part canon for voices and piano; composed for the sixtieth birthday of Martin Hürlimann (1958). Unpublished

Cantata Academica, Carmen Basiliense, Op. 62, for soloists, chorus and orchestra, Latin text compiled by Bernhard Wyss (1959). fp Basel, 1 July 1960

Missa Brevis in D, Op. 63, for boys' voices and organ, Latin text from the Roman Missal (1959). fp London, 22 July 1959

War Requiem, Op. 66, for soloists, chorus, boys' choir, orchestra, chamber orchestra and organ, texts from Latin Requiem Mass and the poems of Wilfred Owen (1961). fp Coventry, 30 May 1962

Jubilate Deo, for mixed chorus and organ, text from the Book of Common Prayer (1961). fp Leeds, 8 October 1961

Fancie, for unison voices and piano, text by Shakespeare (1961)

A Hymn of St Columba (Regis regum rectissimi), for mixed chorus and organ, text attributed to St Columba (1962). fp (on a pre-recorded tape) Garton, Co. Donegal, 2 June 1963

Psalm 150, Op. 67, for children's voices and instruments (any available selection of treble, bass, percussion and keyboard), text from the Bible (1962). Written for the centenary of Britten's preparatory school in Lowestoft and first performed there in July 1962. fp (concert) Aldeburgh, 24 June 1963

The Twelve Apostles, for solo voice, unison chorus and piano, traditional text (1962). Posthumously published

Cantata Misericordium, Op. 69, for soloists, small chorus, string quartet, string orchestra, piano, harp and timpani, Latin text by Patrick Wilkinson (1963). fp Geneva, 1 September 1963

Voices for Today, Op. 75, anthem for men's, women's and children's voices and optional organ, Latin texts from Virgil and English texts from thirteen different authors (1965). fp New York, Paris and London (simultaneously), 24 October 1965

The Golden Vanity, Op. 78, vaudeville for boys' voices and piano, text by Colin Graham after a traditional ballad (1966). fp Snape, 3 June 1967

The Oxen, carol for women's voices and piano, text by Thomas Hardy (1967)

Children's Crusade (Kinderkreuzzug), Op. 82, ballad for children's voices, percussion, two pianos and organ, German words by Bertolt Brecht, English translation by Hans Keller (1968). fp London, 19 May 1969

Alleluia, for voices; three-part canon on the plainchant 'Alleluia' used in *A Ceremony of Carols*; composed for the eightieth birthday of Alec Robertson (1972)

Sacred and Profane, Op. 91, eight medieval lyrics for five-part chorus, anonymous text (1974–5). fp Snape, 30 December 1977

Welcome Ode, Op. 95, for young people's choir and orchestra, text by Thomas Dekker, John Ford, Fielding and anonymous (1976). fp Ipswich, 11 July 1977

Praise We Great Men, for soloists, chorus and orchestra, text by Edith Sitwell (1976). Unfinished; sketch orchestrated and edited by Colin Matthews. fp Snape, 11 August 1985

Solo Vocal

'Beware' and two other songs, for medium voice and piano, texts by Burns, Longfellow and Herbert Asquith (1922–6). Posthumously published

Quatre Chansons françaises, for high voice and orchestra, French texts by Victor Hugo and Paul Verlaine (1928). Posthumously published. fp (radio) 30 March 1980; (concert) Snape, 10 June 1980

Tit for Tat, five songs for voice and piano, text by Walter de la Mare (1929–31; rewritten 1968). fp (revised version) Aldeburgh, 23 June 1969

The Birds, song for voice and piano, text by Hilaire Belloc (1929; revised 1934). fp (BBC broadcast) 13 March 1936

Autumn, for voice and string quartet, text by Walter de la Mare (1931). Unpublished

Three Small Songs, for soprano and small orchestra, texts by Samuel Daniel and John Fletcher (1931). fp Snape, 6 October 1986. Unpublished

Elizabeth Ann, song for voice and piano, text by John Drinkwater (1932). Unpublished

A Poison Tree, song for voice and piano, text by William Blake (1935). fp London, 22 November 1986

When You're Feeling Like Expressing Your Affection, song for voice and piano, text by W. H. Auden? (1935 or 36). Posthumously published. fp Blythburgh, 15 June 1992

Our Hunting Fathers, Op. 8, symphonic cycle for high voice and orchestra, texts by W. H. Auden, Thomas Ravenscroft and anonymous, devised by Auden (1936). fp Norwich, 25 September 1936

Two Ballads, for two voices and piano, texts by Montagu Slater and W. H. Auden (1936). fp London, 15 December 1936

Not Even Summer Yet, song for voice and piano, text by Peter Burra (1937). Posthumously published. fp 1937

On This Island, Op. 11, five songs for high voice and piano, texts by W. H. Auden (1937). fp (radio) 19 November 1937

Fish in the Unruffled Lakes, song for high voice and piano, text by W. H. Auden (1937)

Four Cabaret Songs, for contralto and piano, texts by W. H. Auden (1937–9). Two or more other 'cabaret songs' written at this period have been lost.

The Red Cockatoo, song for voice and piano, text by Arthur Waley, after Po Chü-i (1938). Posthumously published. fp Snape, 17 June 1991

Les Illuminations, Op. 18, for high voice and string orchestra, French words by Arthur Rimbaud (1939). fp London, 30 January 1940 (nos. 5 and 7 performed separately, Birmingham, 1939)

Seven Sonnets of Michelangelo, Op. 22, for tenor and piano, Italian words by Michelangelo Buonarroti (1940). fp London, 23 September 1942

Cradle Song, for voice and piano, text by Louis MacNeice (1942). Posthumously published. fp Blythburgh, 15 June 1992

Two Songs, for voice and piano, texts by Thomas Lovell Beddoes (1942). Posthumously published. fp Blythburgh, 15 June 1992

Serenade, Op. 31, for tenor, horn and string orchestra, texts by Charles Cotton, Tennyson, Blake, Jonson, Keats and anonymous (1943). fp London, 15 October 1943

The Holy Sonnets of John Donne, Op. 35, for high voice and piano, texts by John Donne (1945). fp London, 22 November 1945

Birthday Song for Erwin, song for voice and piano, text by Ronald Duncan (1945). Posthumously published. fp (private, at a sixtieth birthday party for Erwin Stein) London, 7 November 1945; (public) London, 22 November 1988

Canticle I: *My Beloved is Mine*, Op. 40, for high voice and piano, text by Francis Quarles (1947). fp London, 1 November 1947

A Charm of Lullabies, Op. 41, for mezzo-soprano and piano, texts by Blake, Burns, Robert Greene, Thomas Randolph and John Philip (1947). fp The Hague, 3 January 1948

Canticle II: *Abraham and Isaac*, Op. 51, for alto, tenor and piano, text from the Chester Miracle Play (1952). fp Nottingham, 21 January 1952

Winter Words, Op. 52, for high voice and piano, text by Thomas Hardy (1953). fp Leeds, 8 October 1953

Canticle III: *Still Falls the Rain*, Op. 55, for tenor, horn and piano, text by Edith Sitwell (1954). fp London, 28 January 1955

Farfield (1928–30), song for voice and piano, text by John Lydgate (1955); contributed by Britten to an edition of *Grasshopper*, the school magazine of his public school, Gresham's, to mark the 400th anniversary of its foundation

Songs from the Chinese, Op. 58, for high voice and guitar, texts by Chinese poets, translated by Arthur Waley (1957). fp Great Glemham, Suffolk, 17 June 1958

Nocturne, Op. 60, for tenor, seven obbligato instruments and string orchestra, texts by Shelley, Tennyson, Coleridge, Thomas Middleton, Wordsworth, Wilfred Owen, Keats and Shakespeare (1958). fp Leeds, 16 October 1958

Sechs Hölderlin-Fragmente, Op. 61, for voice and piano, German words by Friedrich Hölderlin (1958). fp (radio) 14 November 1958; (concert) London, 1 February 1960

Um Mitternacht, song for voice and piano, German words by Goethe (1959). Posthumously published. fp Blythburgh, 15 June 1992

Songs and Proverbs of William Blake, Op. 74, for baritone and piano, words by Blake compiled by Peter Pears (1965). fp Aldeburgh, 24 June 1965

The Poet's Echo, Op. 76, for high voice and piano, Russian words by Pushkin, English version by Peter Pears (1965). fp Moscow, 2 December 1965

Who are these children?, Op. 84, lyrics, rhymes and riddles for tenor and piano, texts by William Soutar (1969). fp Edinburgh, 4 May 1971 (nos. 1, 2, 3, 4, 7, 9 and 12 given their premières separately: Cardiff, 7 March 1971)

Canticle IV: *The Journey of the Magi*, Op. 86, for counter-tenor, tenor, baritone and piano, text by T. S. Eliot (1971). fp Snape, 26 June 1971

Canticle V: *The Death of St Narcissus*, Op. 89, for tenor and harp, text by T. S. Eliot (1974). fp Schloss Elmau, Germany, 15 January 1975

A Birthday Hansel, Op. 92, for tenor and harp, text by Robert Burns (1975). fp (private, for Queen Elizabeth the Queen Mother's seventy-fifth birthday) 4 August 1975; (public) Cardiff, 19 March 1976 [Four of these songs also published as *Four Burns Songs* for voice and piano; piano arrangement by Colin Matthews]

Phaedra, Op. 93, dramatic cantata for mezzo-soprano and small orchestra, text by Racine translated by Robert Lowell (1975). fp Snape, 16 June 1976

Chamber/Instrumental

Five Walztes (sic), for piano (1923–5; rewritten 1969)

Rhapsody, for string quartet (1929). Posthumously published

Bagatelle, for piano trio (1929–30). Unpublished. fp Holt, Norfolk (Gresham's, Britten's public school), 1 March 1930.

Quartettino, for string quartet (1930). Posthumously published

Three Character Pieces, for piano (1930). Posthumously published. fp Chester, 28 July 1989

Elegy, for solo viola (1930). Posthumously published

String Quartet in D (1931; revised 1974). fp Snape, 7 June 1975

Two Pieces, for violin and piano (1931). Unpublished and unperformed

Twelve Variations, for piano (1931). Posthumously published. fp Snape, 22 June 1986

Phantasy, for string quintet (1932). Posthumously published. fp London, 12 December 1932

Introduction and Allegro (formerly titled Phantasy-Scherzo), for piano trio (1932). Unpublished. fp London, 22 November 1986

Phantasy, Op. 2, for oboe and string trio (1932). fp (radio) 6 August 1933; (concert) Florence, 5 April 1934

Alla quartetto serioso: 'Go play, boy, play', three movements from unfinished suite for string quartet (1933; revised 1936 as Three Divertimenti). One movement from 1st version of the suite, *Alla Marcia*, posthumously published. fp London, 11 December 1933; (revised version) London, 25 February 1936

Holiday Diary, Op. 5, for piano (1934). fp London, 30 November 1934

Suite, Op. 6, for violin and piano (1934–5). fp (radio) 6 March 1936; (concert) Barcelona, 21 April 1936 (three movements performed separately: London, 17 December 1934)

Two Insect Pieces, for oboe and piano (1935). fp Manchester, 7 March 1979. Posthumously published

Temporal Variations, for oboe and piano (1936). fp London, 15 December 1936

Lullaby for a Retired Colonel, for two pianos (1936). Posthumously published. fp (privately, for a BBC audition) London, 19 March 1936; (concert) Snape, 22 June 1988

Lullaby, for two pianos (1936). Posthumously published. fp Snape, 22 June 1988.

Reveille, concert study for violin and piano (1937). Posthumously published. fp London, 12 April, 1937

Sonatina Romantica, for piano (1940). Two movements, Moderato and Nocturne, posthumously published. fp Aldeburgh, 16 June 1983

Introduction and Rondo alla Burlesca, Op. 23, No. 1, for two pianos (1940). fp New York, 5 January 1941

Mazurka Elegiaca, Op. 23, No. 2, for two pianos (1941). fp New York, 9 December 1941

String Quartet No. 1 in D, Op. 25 (1941). fp Los Angeles, 21 September 1941

String Quartet No. 2 in C, Op. 36 (1945). fp London, 21 November 1945

Prelude and Fugue on a Theme of Vittoria, for organ (1946). fp Northampton, 21 September 1946

Lachrymae, Op. 48, reflections on a song of John Dowland for viola and piano (1950). fp Aldeburgh, 20 June 1950

Six Metamorphoses after Ovid, Op. 49, for solo oboe (1951). fp Thorpeness, 14 June 1951

Timpani Piece for Jimmy, for timpani and piano (1955). Unpublished

Alpine Suite, for three recorders (1955). Written to amuse a friend, the artist Mary Potter, during her convalescence after a skiing accident

Scherzo, for recorder quartet (1955). fp Aldeburgh, 1955?

Fanfare for St Edmundsbury, for three trumpets (1959). fp Bury St Edmunds, June 1959

Fanfare for SS Oriana (1960). fp (at launching of ship) 3 November 1960

Sonata in C, Op. 65, for cello and piano (1961).
fp Aldeburgh, 7 July 1961

Night Piece (Notturno), for piano (1963); written for
Leeds International Piano Competition. fp Leeds, 1963

Nocturnal after John Dowland, Op. 70, for solo guitar
(1963). fp Aldeburgh, 12 June 1964

Suite, Op. 72, for solo cello (1964). fp Aldeburgh,
27 June 1965

Gemini Variations, Op. 73: twelve variations and fugue
on an epigram of Kodály, 'quartet for two players'
(flute, violin and piano duet; also playable by four
players) (1965). fp Aldeburgh, 19 June 1965

Hankin Booby, folk dance for wind and drums (1966).
fp London, 1 March 1967 [Subsequently incorporated
into Suite on English Folk Tunes: 'A Time There Was...'
(1974)]

Second Suite, Op. 80, for solo cello (1967). fp Snape,
17 June 1968

Suite, Op. 83, for harp (1969). fp Aldeburgh,
24 June 1969

Third Suite, Op. 87, for solo cello (1971). fp Snape,
21 December 1974

String Quartet No. 3, Op. 94 (1975). fp Snape,
19 December 1976

Tema ... Sacher, for solo cello (1976); written as the
theme for a set of variations by seven other composers
to celebrate the seventieth birthday of Paul Sacher.
fp Zürich, 2 May 1976

Music for Film, Radio and Theatre

For GPO Film Unit (1935):
The King's Stamp
Coal Face (with W. H. Auden)
The Tocher (silhouette film produced by Lotte Reiniger;
music based on Rossini)
Telegram Abstract
C. T. O.
Conquering Space
How the Dial Works (music by Britten, John Foulds and
Victor Yates)
Sorting Office
The Savings Bank
The New Operator
Negroes (released as God's Chillun)

For Gas Association (1935):
Men Behind the Meters
Dinner Hour
How Gas is Made

Theatre (1935):
Timon of Athens, Group Theatre production of play by
Shakespeare. fp London, November 1935
Easter 1916, music (lost) for Left Theatre production of
play by Montagu Slater. fp London, 1935

For GPO Film Unit (1936):
Night Mail (text by W. H. Auden)
Peace of Britain
Calendar of the Year
Men of the Alps (including music by Rossini, arranged
by Britten and Walter Leigh)
The Saving of Bill Blewett
Line to the Tschierva Hut
Message from Geneva
Four Barriers

For Travel and Industrial Development Association
(1936):
Around the Village Green

For Trafalgar Films (1936):
Love from a Stranger

For Strand Films (1936):
The Way to the Sea (with W. H. Auden)

Theatre (1936):
Stay Down Miner, Left Theatre production of Montagu
Slater's play. fp London, 10 May 1936
Agamemnon, Group Theatre production of Aeschylus's
play (translated by Louis MacNeice). fp London,
November 1936

Radio (1937):
King Arthur, radio feature by D. G. Bridson; suite
arranged by Paul Hindmarsh. Posthumously published
Up the Garden Path, feature (with W. H. Auden)
The Company of Heaven, eleven musical numbers, for
soloists, chorus and orchestra, for a feature interspersing
music with prose and verse readings. Posthumously
published. fp (radio) 29 September 1937; (concert)
Aldeburgh, 10 June 1989
Hadrian's Wall, feature (with W. H. Auden)

Theatre (1937):
Pageant of Empire, revue sketch by Montagu Slater.
fp London, 28 February 1937
The Ascent of F6, Group Theatre production of play by
W. H. Auden and Christopher Isherwood. fp London,
26 February 1937
Out of the Picture, Group Theatre production of play by
Louis MacNeice. fp December 1937

Radio (1938):
Lines on the Map, feature series
The Chartists' March, feature
The World of the Spirit, feature by J. H. Miller

Theatre (1938):
Old Spain, puppet play by Montagu Slater
The Seven Ages of Man, puppet play by Montagu Slater
On the Frontier, play by W. H. Auden and Christopher
Isherwood. fp Cambridge, 4 November 1938
Johnson over Jordan, play by J. B. Priestley.
Posthumously published as independent
orchestral score. fp 22 February 1939 (revised for
subsequent radio adaptations in 1951 and 1955)
They Walk Alone, play by Max Catto

For GPO Film Unit (1938):
Mony a Pickle (in collaboration with John Foulds and
Victor Yates)

For Realist Film Unit (1938):
Advance Democracy

For GPO Film Unit (1939):
H.P.O. or 6d Telegram
God's Chillun (see *Negroes*, 1935)

Radio (1939):
The Sword in the Stone, dramatization of T. H. White's
novel. Suite posthumously published
The Dark Valley, radio play by W. H. Auden (CBS,
New York)

Radio (1940):
The Dynasts, radio adaptation of Thomas Hardy's
dramatic poem (CBS, New York)

Radio (1941):
The Rocking Horse Winner, radio adaptation (by W. H.
Auden and James Stern) of D. H. Lawrence's story
(CBS, New York)

Radio (1942):
Appointment, feature by Norman Corwin
An American in England, six features broadcast live to
the USA
Lumberjacks of America (CBS, New York)
The Man Born to be King, radio drama by
Dorothy L. Sayers
Britain to America, three programmes (with Louis
MacNeice) (joint BBC and NBC, New York)
The Four Freedoms: No. 1, Pericles (with Louis
MacNeice)

Theatre (1942):
An Agreement of the People (later called *Over to You*),
pageant by Montagu Slater

Radio (1943):
The Rescue, radio drama (after Homer's *Odyssey*) by
Edward Sackville-West; posthumously published;
concert version entitled *The Rescue of Penelope*
A Poet's Christmas, three contributions to a feature by
W. H. Auden

Theatre (1945):
This Way to the Tomb, masque by Ronald Duncan.
Three of its songs, *Morning, Evening, Night*,
posthumously published. fp London 11 October 1945

For Crown Film Unit (1946):
Instruments of the Orchestra. Score subsequently
published as *The Young Person's Guide to the Orchestra
(Variations and Fugue on a Theme of Henry Purcell)*

Theatre (1946):
The Eagle has Two Heads, play by Jean Cocteau,
translated by Ronald Duncan. fp London,
September 1946
The Duchess of Malfi, play by John Webster.
fp New York, 1946

Radio (1947):
Men of Goodwill, Christmas radio feature; variations on
the carol 'God rest ye merry gentlemen'. Posthumously
published as an independent orchestral work

Theatre (1949):
Stratton, play by Ronald Duncan. fp Brighton,
October 1949

Transcriptions

Folk songs
(dates are those of publication)

Volume 1 (British) (1943), for high or medium voice
and piano: The Salley Gardens*+; Little Sir William+;
The Bonny Earl o' Moray+; O can ye sew cushions?+;
The Trees they grow so high; The Ash Grove; Oliver
Cromwell*+.
(* also unison voices and piano; + also arranged for
orchestra)

Volume 2 (French) (1946), for high or medium voice
and piano: *La Noël passé*+; *Voici le printemps, Fileuse; Le
roi s'en va-t'en chasse*+; *La belle est au jardin d'amour; Il
est quelqu'un sur terre, Eho! Eho! ... Quand j'étais chez
mon père*+.
(+ also arranged for orchestra)

Volume 3 (British) (1947), for high or medium voice
and piano: The Plough Boy+; There's none to soothe;
Sweet Polly Oliver; The Miller of Dee; The Foggy
Foggy dew; O Waly, waly+; Come you not from
Newcastle?+
(+ also arranged for orchestra)

Volume 4 (Irish) (1960), for voice and piano: Avenging
and bright; Sail on, sail on; How sweet the answer; The
Minstrel Boy; At the mid hour of night; Rich and rare;
Dear harp of my country; Oft in the stilly night; The
Last Rose of summer; O the sight entrancing.

Volume 5 (British) (1961), for voice and piano: The
brisk young widow; Sally in our alley; The Lincolnshire
poacher; Early one morning; Ca' the yowes.

Volume 6 (1961), for voice and guitar: I will give my
love an apple; Sailor-boy; Master Kilby; The Soldier
and the sailor; Bonny at morn; The shooting of his
dear.

Eight Folk Song Arrangements (1976), for voice and
harp or piano: Lord, I married me a wife; She's like the
swallow; Lemady; Bonny at morn; I was lonely and
forlorn; David of the white rock; The False Knight;
Bird Scarer's Song.

The Holly and the Ivy (1957), arranged for mixed chorus

King Herod and the Cock (1965), arranged for unison
voices and piano

Arrangements of Works by Other Composers

Bach, Johann Sebastian: *Five Spiritual Songs (Geistliche Lieder)* (1969), for high voice and piano: *Gedenke doch, mein Geist*; *Komm, Seelen, dieser Tag*; *Liebster Herr Jesu**; *Komm, süsser Tod**; *Bist du bei mir*
(* also arranged for mixed voices)
fp Blythburgh, 18 June 1969

Chopin, Frédéric: *Les Sylphides* (Britten rescored the ballet for small orchestra for Ballet Theatre, New York, in 1940; transcription lost)

Gay, John: *The Beggar's Opera*, Op. 43, ballad opera realized by Britten from the original airs (1948; prelude to Act III added 1963). fp Cambridge, 24 May 1948

Haydn, Joseph: Cello Concerto in C, cadenzas by Britten (1964). fp Blythburgh, 18 June 1964

Mahler, Gustav: 'What the Wild Flowers Tell Me'; second movement of Symphony No. 3, transcribed for small orchestra by Britten (1941)

Mozart, Wolfgang Amadeus: Piano Concerto in E flat, K 482, cadenzas by Britten (1966). fp July 1966

Purcell, Henry: *Dido and Aeneas*, realized and edited by Britten and Imogen Holst. fp London, 1 May 1951

—*The Fairy Queen*, realized and edited by Britten and Imogen Holst, shortened and the numbers rearranged for concert performance by Peter Pears, harpsichord part realized by Philip Ledger. fp Aldeburgh, 25 June 1967

—*When Night her Purple Veil had softly spread*, realization of secular cantata

—*Chacony in G minor*, transcribed for string quartet or string orchestra

—*The Golden Sonata*, transcribed for piano and string trio

—*Orpheus Britannicus*, three volumes of songs transcribed for voice and piano, with Peter Pears

—Six Duets, transcribed for high and low voices and piano, with Peter Pears

—Suite of Songs, transcribed for high voice and orchestra, with Peter Pears

—Three Songs, transcribed for high voice and orchestra, with Peter Pears

—*Harmonia Sacra*, nine sacred songs transcribed for voices and piano

—*Odes and Elegies: The Queen's Epicedium*, transcribed for high voice and piano

Rossini, Gioacchino: see *Soirées musicales* (1936) and *Matinées musicales* (1941) and *The Tocher* (1935)

The National Anthem: arrangements by Britten for mixed chorus and orchestra (1961), the same with reduced orchestra (1967) and for orchestra alone (1971)

Further Reading

Blyth, A. (ed.) *Remembering Britten* (London, Hutchinson, 1981)
Memories of Britten by friends and colleagues interviewed by the editor. Affection and admiration are seasoned by a few more critical judgments of his personality and of the 'Aldeburgh circle' that surrounded him.

Britten, B. *On Receiving the First Aspen Award* (London, Faber and Faber, 1964)
Britten was reluctant to express himself in words, and rarely did so at any length. His formal speech accepting the Aspen Award is his most considered statement of an aesthetic position and of his view of the composer's function in society.

Britten, B[eth]. *My Brother Benjamin* (Bourne End, The Kensal Press, 1986)
An affectionate memoir of Britten's childhood, family background and youth by his younger sister, who remained close to him (they shared lodgings for some years) until he set up home with Peter Pears.

Carpenter, H. *Benjamin Britten: A Biography* (London, Faber and Faber, 1992)
The first full-scale biography, written with the co-operation of the Britten-Pears Foundation and based on detailed interviews with many of Britten's friends and colleagues. It contains a fuller discussion than had been possible before of Britten's sexuality and the more difficult aspects of his personality, but in covering these areas it tends to over-emphasize them and the result, though sympathetic, is somewhat unbalanced.

Duncan, R. *Working with Britten: A Personal Memoir* (Welcombe, The Rebel Press, 1981)
A memoir by the librettist of *The Rape of Lucretia* and Britten's collaborator on numerous other projects, some of them unrealized. Not always factually reliable, and the author has been hampered by the Britten-Pears Foundation's decree that letters from Britten to Duncan in the latter's possession are the Foundation's copyright, not to be printed without their permission (the author does not say whether he was refused this permission or himself refused to ask for it). Valuable with some reserve for its affectionate but at times hurt and critical insights into Britten's personality.

Evans, J., P. Reed and P. Wilson (compiled)
A Britten Source Book (Aldershot, Scolar Press, 1987)
Aptly described by its title, this book consists of a lengthy chronological table of Britten's life and compositions, a valuable and very detailed listing of his music for films, theatre and radio, and the first attempt at a comprehensive Britten bibliography.

Evans, P. *The Music of Benjamin Britten* (Oxford, Oxford University Press, revised edition, 1996)
The most detailed and scholarly discussion of Britten's music so far published and an invaluable source. Inevitably 'technical' in its language, but not excessively so for any reader who can read music reasonably fluently.

Headington, C. *Peter Pears: A Biography* (London, Faber and Faber, 1992)
The 'standard' biography, written with great affection and insight by an admiring friend.

Kennedy, M. *Britten* (Oxford, Oxford University Press, revised edition, 1993)
A well-balanced and judicious study, following the house style of this series by presenting a biographical narrative and a chronological discussion of Britten's works separately.

Mitchell, D. *Britten and Auden in the Thirties: The Year 1936* (London, Faber and Faber, 1981)
A brief but detailed examination of Britten's collaborations with Auden, based on Mitchell's 1979 Eliot Memorial Lectures at the University of Kent.

Mitchell, D. and J. Evans (eds.) *Pictures from a Life: Benjamin Britten 1913–76* (London, Faber and Faber, 1978)
440 photographs arranged in chronological order, annotated in sufficient detail to form a pictorial biography.

Mitchell, D. and H. Keller (eds.) *Benjamin Britten: a Commentary on his works from a group of specialists* (London, Rockliff, 1952)
Many of the essays in this pioneering symposium still make enlightening reading.

Mitchell, D. and P. Reed (eds.) *Letters from a Life: the Selected Letters and Diaries of Benjamin Britten 1913-76*, Vol. 1: 1923-39; Vol. 2: 1939–45 (London, Faber and Faber, 1991)
The first two volumes of a projected series, so voluminously annotated with footnotes as to constitute a biography, though one that is hard to read chronologically.

Palmer, C. (ed.) *The Britten Companion* (London, Faber and Faber, 1984)
A successor to the Mitchell/Keller symposium, usefully supplementing new essays with reprinted ones that would otherwise be hard to find.

Pears. P. *Travel Diaries 1936–78*, edited by P. Reed (Woodbridge, Boydell Press/Aldeburgh, Britten-Pears Library, 1995)
Peter Pears's diaries of trips abroad, some carefully written up for private circulation, others very rough but supplemented with material from elsewhere; especially useful for Britten's and Pears's visits to Armenia and Russia.

White, E. W. *Benjamin Britten: His Life and Operas*, edited by J. Evans (London, Faber and Faber, 2nd edition, 1983)
A useful and thoughtful study of Britten's dramatic works.

Whittall, A. *The Music of Britten and Tippett: Studies in Themes and Techniques* (Cambridge University Press, 2nd edition, 1990)
A valuable study, fascinatingly comparing the two composers' reactions to musical challenges and stimuli. Inevitably 'technical' in its terminology, but original, important and thought-provoking.

Selective Discography

As conductor and as pianist Britten recorded a very high proportion of his output; his performances have unique authority, and in some cases are still unrivalled. The following list includes most of his currently available recordings together with others chosen either because they offer performances of a standard comparable to Britten's own but with a superior quality of recorded sound or present what seems to me a valid alternative view of the work in question. Where otherwise excellent recordings of short works are only available as part of collections devoted mainly to other composers I have usually omitted them. I have tended to prefer recordings which are usefully coupled with other works by Britten, and the numerous cross-references in the following list are intended to avoid unnecessary duplication. Works of secondary importance are usually omitted, except when they form part of a collection of major compositions. The list is intended as a reasonably comprehensive discography, not as a catalogue of those Britten performances that I admire. His folk-song arrangements, transcriptions of Purcell and other composers and music for film, radio and the spoken theatre are also omitted. Within each section works are listed in chronological order.

Stage Works

Paul Bunyan
Pop Wagner, James Lawless, Dan Dressen; Plymouth Music Choir and Orchestra conducted by Philip Brunelle
VIRGIN VCD7 59249–2

Peter Grimes
Peter Pears, Claire Watson, James Pease; Royal Opera House Chorus and Orchestra conducted by Benjamin Britten
DECCA 475 7712

Peter Grimes
Jon Vickers, Heather Harper, Jonathan Summers; Royal Opera House Chorus and Orchestra conducted by Colin Davis
PHILIPS 462 847-2PM2

The Rape of Lucretia
Janet Baker, Peter Pears, Heather Harper, Benjamin Luxon; English Chamber Orchestra conducted by Benjamin Britten; with Britten's *Phaedra*
DECCA 425 666–2

Albert Herring
Peter Pears, Sylvia Fisher; English Chamber Orchestra conducted by Benjamin Britten
DECCA 421 849–2

The Little Sweep
David Hemmings, Jennifer Vyvyan, Trevor Anthony; Alleyn's School Choir, English Opera Group conducted by Benjamin Britten
LONDON 436 393–2LM

Billy Budd
Peter Glossop, Peter Pears, Michael Langdon; London Symphony Orchestra conducted by Benjamin Britten; with Britten's *Holy Sonnets of John Donne* and *Songs and Proverbs of William Blake*
DECCA LONDON 417 428–2LH3

Gloriana
Josephine Barstow, Philip Langridge; Welsh National Opera Chorus and Orchestra conducted by Charles Mackerras
ARGO 440 213–2ZHO2

The Turn of the Screw
Peter Pears, Jennifer Vyvyan; English Opera Group conducted by Benjamin Britten
LONDON 425 672–2LH2

The Prince of the Pagodas
London Sinfonietta conducted by Oliver Knussen; with Britten's *Gloriana – Symphonic Suite*
EMI 3 52274–2

Noye's Fludde
Owen Brannigan, Sheila Rex; East Suffolk Children's
Orchestra and English Opera Group conducted by
Norman Del Mar
DECCA LONDON 436 397–2LM

A Midsummer Night's Dream
Alfred Deller, Elizabeth Harwood; Downside and
Emmanuel Boys' School Choirs, London Symphony
Orchestra conducted by Benjamin Britten
DECCA 425 663–2LH2

Curlew River
Peter Pears, John Shirley-Quirk; English Opera Group
conducted by Benjamin Britten
DECCA 421 858–2LM

The Burning Fiery Furnace
Peter Pears, Bryan Drake; English Opera Group
conducted by Benjamin Britten
DECCA 414 663 2LM

The Prodigal Son
Peter Pears, Robert Tear; English Opera Group
conducted by Benjamin Britten
DECCA 425 713–2LM

Owen Wingrave
Benjamin Luxon, John Shirley-Quirk; English
Chamber Orchestra conducted by Benjamin Britten;
with Britten's *Sechs Hölderlin-Fragmente* and *The
Poet's Echo*
LONDON 433 200–2LHO2

Death in Venice
Peter Pears, John Shirley-Quirk; English Chamber
Orchestra conducted by Steuart Bedford
DECCA 425 669–2LH2

Orchestral

Sinfonietta
Stuttgart Radio Symphony Orchestra conducted by
Neville Marriner; with Britten's *Sinfonia da Requiem*
and music by Honegger
CAPRICCIO 10 428

Simple Symphony
English Chamber Orchestra conducted by Benjamin
Britten; with Britten's *Young Person's Guide to the
Orchestra* and *Variations on a Theme of Frank Bridge*
DECCA 417 509–2DH

Variations on a Theme of Frank Bridge
(see *Simple Symphony*, above)

Piano Concerto
Sviatoslav Richter; English Chamber Orchestra
conducted by Benjamin Britten; with Britten's Violin
Concerto
DECCA 473 715–2

Piano Concerto
Joanna MacGregor; English Chamber Orchestra
conducted by Steuart Bedford; [a] with Britten's Violin
Concerto
COLLINS CLASSICS COLL 1301–2
[b] with original and revised slow movement,
unpublished music from Britten's *Paul Bunyan* and
work by Robert Saxton
COLLINS CLASSICS COLL 1102–2

Violin Concerto
Mark Lubotsky; English Chamber Orchestra conducted
by Benjamin Britten; with Britten's Piano Concerto,
see above
DECCA 473 715–2

Violin Concerto
Lorraine McAslan; English Chamber Orchestra
conducted by Steuart Bedford; with Britten's Piano
Concerto, see above
COLLINS CLASSICS COLL 1301–2

Young Apollo
Peter Donohoe; City of Birmingham Symphony
Orchestra conducted by Simon Rattle; with Britten's
*American Overture, A Ballad of Heroes, Diversions, The
Building of the House, Praise We Great Men, Suite on
English Folk Tunes, Canadian Carnival, Quatre
Chansons Françaises, Scottish Ballad, Occasional Overture*
and *Sinfonia da Requiem*
EMI CDS7 54270–2

Sinfonia da Requiem
New Philharmonia Orchestra conducted by Benjamin
Britten; with Britten's Cello Symphony and *Cantata
Misericordium*
DECCA 425 100–2LM

Sinfonia da Requiem
City of Birmingham Symphony Orchestra conducted
by Simon Rattle; with Shostakovich's Symphony No. 10
EMI ENCORE 5 86871–2

Diversions, for piano (left-hand) and orchestra
Julius Katchen; London Symphony Orchestra
conducted by Benjamin Britten; with Britten's
The Prince of the Pagodas
DECCA 421 855-2LH2

Diversions
Peter Donohoe; City of Birmingham Symphony
Orchestra conducted by Simon Rattle (see *Young
Apollo*, above)

The Young Person's Guide to the Orchestra
London Symphony Orchestra conducted by Benjamin
Britten (see *Simple Symphony*, above)

Cello Symphony
Mstislav Rostropovich; English Chamber Orchestra
conducted by Benjamin Britten (see *Sinfonia da
Requiem*, above)

Cello Symphony
Truls Mørk; City of Birmingham Symphony Orchestra
conducted by Simon Rattle; with Elgar's Cello Concerto
VIRGIN 5 45356-2

Suite on English Folk Tunes: 'A Time There Was ...'
City of Birmingham Symphony Orchestra conducted
by Simon Rattle (see *Young Apollo*, above)

Lachrymae
Roger Chase; Nash Ensemble conducted by Lionel
Friend; with Britten's *Phaedra, Sinfonietta, The Sword in
the Stone, Movement for Wind Sextet, Night Mail*
HYPERION CDA 66845

Choral

A Boy Was Born
Corydon Singers and Westminster Cathedral Choir
conducted by Matthew Best; with Britten's *Festival Te
Deum, Rejoice in the Lamb* and *A Wedding Anthem*
HYPERION CDA 66126

A Boy Was Born
The Sixteen conducted by Harry Christophers; with
Britten's *Hymn to St Cecilia, Five Flower Songs* and
choral dances from *Gloriana*
COLLINS CLASSICS COLL 1286–2

Hymn to St Cecilia
Emmanuel School Choir conducted by Benjamin
Britten (see *A Spring Symphony*, below)

Hymn to St Cecilia
The Sixteen conducted by Harry Christophers (see *A
Boy Was Born*, above)

Hymn to St Cecilia
Corydon Singers conducted by Matthew Best; with
Britten's *Saint Nicolas*
HYPERION CDA 66333

A Ceremony of Carols
Westminster Cathedral Choir conducted by David Hill;
with Britten's *Missa Brevis, Deus in adjutorium meum,
Hymn of St Columba, Hymn to the Virgin, Jubilate Deo
in E flat*
HYPERION CDA 66220

A Ceremony of Carols
King's College Choir, Cambridge, conducted by David
Willcocks; with Britten's *Saint Nicolas*
EMI 5 65112–2

Rejoice in the Lamb
Purcell Singers conducted by Benjamin Britten; with
Britten's *Saint Nicolas*
LONDON 425 714–2LM

Rejoice in the Lamb
The Sixteen conducted by Harry Christophers; with Britten's *Antiphon, Wedding Anthem, Te Deum* in C, *The Sycamore Tree, The Ballad of Little Musgrave and Lady Barnard, Advance Democracy* and *Sacred and Profane*)
COLLINS CLASSICS COLL 1343–2

Saint Nicolas
Peter Pears, David Hemmings; various choirs and Aldeburgh Festival Orchestra conducted by Benjamin Britten (see *Rejoice in the Lamb*, above)

Saint Nicolas
Robert Tear, Bruce Russell; various choirs and English Chamber Orchestra conducted by Matthew Best (see *Hymn to St Cecilia*, above)

A Spring Symphony
Jennifer Vyvyan, Norma Procter, Peter Pears; Royal Opera House Choir and Orchestra conducted by Benjamin Britten; with Britten's *Hymn to St Cecilia* and *Cantata Academica*
DECCA 440 063–2DM

Cantata Academica
Jennifer Vyvyan, Helen Watts, Peter Pears, Owen Brannigan; London Symphony Chorus and Orchestra conducted by Benjamin Britten (see *A Spring Symphony*, above)

Missa Brevis
King's College Choir, Cambridge conducted by David Willcocks (see *A Ceremony of Carols*, above)

Missa Brevis
The Sixteen conducted by Harry Christophers; with Britten's *Festival Te Deum,* Jubilate Deo in C, *Hymn to St Peter, Hymn to the Virgin, Hymn of St Columba, Sweet was the Song, New Year Carol, Shepherd's Carol* and *Ceremony of Carols*
COLLINS CLASSICS COLL 1370–2

War Requiem
Galina Vishnevskaya, Peter Pears, Dietrich Fischer-Dieskau; Bach Choir, Highgate School Choir, Melos Ensemble and London Symphony Orchestra conducted by Benjamin Britten
DECCA 414 383–2DH2

War Requiem
Heather Harper, Philip Langridge, John Shirley-Quirk; St Paul's Cathedral Boys' Choir, London Symphony Chorus and Orchestra conducted by Richard Hickox; with Britten's *Sinfonia da Requiem* and *Ballad of Heroes*
CHANDOS CHAN 8983/4

War Requiem
Elisabeth Söderström, Robert Tear, Thomas Allen; Christ Church Cathedral Choir, Oxford, City of Birmingham Symphony Orchestra and Chorus conducted by Simon Rattle
EMI CDS7 47034–8

Cantata Misericordium
Peter Pears, Dietrich Fischer-Dieskau; London Symphony Chorus and Orchestra conducted by Benjamin Britten (see *Sinfonia da Requiem*, above)

Sacred and Profane
The Sixteen conducted by Harry Christophers (see *Rejoice in the Lamb*, above)

Works for Solo Voice

Quatre Chansons françaises
Jill Gomez; City of Birmingham Symphony Orchestra conducted by Simon Rattle (see *Young Apollo*, above)

Quatre Chansons françaises
Felicity Lott; English Chamber Orchestra conducted by Steuart Bedford; with Britten's *Our Hunting Fathers* and *Serenade*
NAXOS 8.557206

Our Hunting Fathers
Elisabeth Söderström; Welsh National Opera Orchestra
conducted by Richard Armstrong; with Britten's
Serenade and folk-song arrangements
EMI CDM7 69522–2

Our Hunting Fathers
Phyllis Bryn-Julson, English Chamber Orchestra
conducted by Steuart Bedford (see *Quatre Chansons
françaises*, above)

Les Illuminations
Peter Pears; English Chamber Orchestra conducted by
Benjamin Britten; with Britten's *Serenade* and *Nocturne*
DECCA 436 395–2LM

Les Illuminations
Felicity Lott; Royal Scottish National Orchestra
conducted by Bryden Thomson; with Britten's *Quatre
Chansons françaises, Serenade*
CHANDOS 10192X

Seven Sonnets of Michelangelo
Peter Pears, Benjamin Britten; with Britten's *Serenade*
and *Winter Words*
DECCA 425 996–2DM

Seven Sonnets of Michelangelo
Philip Langridge, Steuart Bedford; with Britten's *The
Holy Sonnets of John Donne, Winter Words, The Children
and Sir Nameless* and *If it's ever Spring again*
NAXOS 8.557201

Serenade for tenor, horn and strings
Peter Pears, Dennis Brain; Boyd Neel Orchestra
conducted by Benjamin Britten (recorded 1944); with
Walton's *Façade*
DECCA 468 801-2

Serenade
Peter Pears, Barry Tuckwell; London Symphony
Orchestra conducted by Benjamin Britten (recorded
1963; see *Les Illuminations*, above)

Serenade
Philip Langridge, Frank Lloyd; English Chamber
Orchestra conducted by Steuart Bedford (see *Quatre
Chansons françaises*, above)

The Holy Sonnets of John Donne
Peter Pears, Benjamin Britten (see *Billy Budd*, above)

Canticles 1–5
Peter Pears, John Hahessy, John Shirley-Quirk, James
Bowman; Barry Tuckwell, Osian Ellis, Benjamin
Britten; with Britten's *A Birthday Hansel*
DECCA 425 716–2LM

Winter Words
Peter Pears, Benjamin Britten (see *Seven Sonnets of
Michelangelo*, above)

Nocturne
Peter Pears; London Symphony Orchestra conducted
by Benjamin Britten (see *Les Illuminations*, above)

Nocturne
Philip Langridge; Northern Sinfonia conducted by
Steuart Bedford; with Britten's *Phaedra* and *Serenade*
NAXOS 8.577199

Sechs Hölderlin-Fragmente
Peter Pears, Benjamin Britten (see *Owen Wingrave*,
above)

Songs and Proverbs of William Blake
Dietrich Fischer-Dieskau, Benjamin Britten (see *Owen
Wingrave*, above)

The Poet's Echo
Galina Vishnevskaya, Mstislav Rostropovich (see *Owen
Wingrave*, above)

Phaedra
Janet Baker; English Chamber Orchestra conducted by
Steuart Bedford (see *The Rape of Lucretia*, above)

Phaedra
Felicity Palmer; Endymion Ensemble conducted by
John Whitfield; with Britten's *Les Illuminations* and
folk-song arrangements
EMI CDM5 65114–2

Phaedra
Anne Murray; English Chamber Orchestra conducted
by Steuart Bedford (see *Nocturne* above)

Chamber/Instrumental

Phantasy for oboe and string trio, Op. 2
Douglas Boyd; Endellion String Quartet; with Britten's
String Quartets 1–3, String Quartet in D, Rhapsody,
Quartettino, Phantasy in F minor, Three Divertimenti
and *Alla Marcia*
EMI CMS 5 65115–2

Phantasy for oboe and string trio, Op. 2
Derek Wickens; Gabrieli String Quartet; with Britten's
Temporal Variations, *Insect Pieces*, Phantasy in F minor,
Three Divertimenti and *Alla Marcia*)
UNICORN–KANCHANA UKCD 2060

Suite for violin and piano, Op. 6
Alexander Barantschik, John Alley; with Britten's *Elegy*,
Cello Sonata and *Six Metamorphoses after Ovid*
EMI CDC5 55398–2

String Quartet No. 1
Belcea Quartet; with Britten's String Quartets 2 and 3
EMI 5 57968–2

String Quartet No. 1
Britten String Quartet; with Britten's *Simple Symphony*
and String Quartet in D
COLLINS CLASSICS COLL 1115–2

String Quartet No. 2
Amadeus String Quartet; with Britten's *Sinfonietta* and
String Quartet No. 3
LONDON 425 715–2LM

String Quartet No. 2
Belcea Quartet (see String Quartet No. 1, above)

Six Metamorphoses after Ovid
Sarah Francis; with Britten's Phantasy, Op. 2, *Holiday
Diary*, *Temporal Variations*, Five Waltzes, *Insect Pieces*
and *Night Piece*
HYPERION CDA 66776

Six Metamorphoses after Ovid
Roy Carter (see Suite, Op. 6, above)

Sonata for cello and piano
Mstislav Rostropovich, Benjamin Britten; with Britten's
Cello Suites 1 and 2)
DECCA 421 859–2LM)

Sonata for cello and piano
Alexander Baillie, Ian Brown; with Britten's Cello
Suites 1–3)
ETCETERA KTC 2006

Nocturnal
Julian Bream; with Britten's *Songs from the Chinese*,
folk-song arrangements, second lute song from
Gloriana and music by Walton, Seiber and Fricker
RCA 09026 61601–2

Cello Suites 1–3
(1 and 2 only) Mstislav Rostropovich (see Sonata for
cello and piano, above)

Cello Suites 1–3
Alexander Baillie (see Sonata for cello and piano, above)
Timothy Hugh
HYPERION CDA 66274

String Quartet No. 3
Amadeus Quartet (see String Quartet No. 2, above)

String Quartet No. 3
Belcea Quartet (see String Quartet No. 1, above)

Index

Page numbers in italics refer to
picture captions.

Aldeburgh 15, 62–3, 90, *95, 117, 121,
    124,* 156, 188–9, 196, 211
    Crag House 134, 137, 162–3
    Jubilee Hall 134, 161, 166,
    167, *167*
    Red House 163, *165,* 190, *191,*
    196, 211, *211*
Aldeburgh Festival 86, 134, *134,*
    136–7, 143, 146, 158, 172, 187,
    188–9, 192, *192,* 193, 196, 200,
    205, 206, 208–9
Alford, Violet 36
Alston, Audrey 19, 22
Amadeus Quartet 210
Amityville, Long Island 77, 80, 89
Anderson, Hedli 64
Anderson, Robert 187
Ansermet, Ernest 125, *129*
Aronowitz, Cecil 208
Ashton, Frederick 52
Aspen Award 187, 213
Astle, Ethel 18
Auden, Wystan Hugh 27, *45,*
    47–50, *47, 48,* 49, 52, 53, 58, 64,
    71, 77, 84, 85, 90, 92–3, 174
    The Ascent of F6 64, *64*
    The Dance of Death 48
    The Dog Beneath the Skin 48
    'For The Time Being' 93
    Hymn to Saint Cecilia (settings
    by Britten) 97–8
    Letters from Iceland 49
    Litany for St Matthew's Day 93
    Look Stranger 64–5

'Night covers up the rigid
    land' 49
    Our Hunting Fathers (text for)
    55–8
    Paul Bunyan 85–6, *86,* 88
    The Rake's Progress (libretto)
    93–4
    settings by Britten 54, 55, 64–5,
    97–8, 141–2, 166
    'Underneath the abject willow'
    45, 49
Auric, Georges 148

Bach, Johann Sebastian 19
    Christmas Oratorio 192
    St Matthew Passion 40
Baker, Janet *197,* 207, *208*
Baldwin, James
    Giovanni's Room 24–5
Baldwin, Stanley 54
Barbirolli, John 78
Bartlett, Ethel 84, 88–9
Bartók, Béla 42, 67
Basel Chamber Orchestra 166
Bax, Arnold 148
Beaumont, Francis
    *The Knight of the Burning
    Pestle* 141
Beecham, Thomas 146
Beethoven, Ludwig van 18, 19,
    26, 36
    'Appassionata' *42*
Belsen 118
Benjamin, Arthur 30, 37
Bennett, Richard Rodney 182
Berg, Alban 34
    Violin Concerto 57
    Wozzeck 58, 109
Berkeley, Lennox *58,* 59–60, 64,
    101, 134, 148
    Mont Juic (with Britten) 60
Berlioz, Hector
    Nuits d'été 206–7
    Symphonie Fantastique 36
Bernstein, Leonard 101

Bing, Rudolf 125
Birtwistle, Harrison 182
Blake, William *100*
    settings by Britten 99–100,
    188–9
Bliss, Arthur 108
Blitzstein, Marc
    The Cradle Will Rock 88
Bonasone, Giulio
    portrait of Michelangelo *83*
Book of Songs, The 147
Boosey and Hawkes 42, 78
Boston Symphony Orchestra 137
Boughton, Joy 143
Boulanger, Nadia 60
Boult, Adrian 35
Bowles, Paul 85
Brahms, Johannes 19, 36
Brannigan, Owen *160*
Bream, Julian 161, 186
Brecht, Bertolt 193
    Threepenny Opera 140
Bridge, Frank *18,* 19, 22–3, 28, 30,
    · 31, 38, 39, 40, 44, 54, 66–8, 71,
    74, 182
    Enter Spring 22
    Idyll No. 2 66
    Phantasm 35
    The Sea 22
    String Quartet No. 3 23
British Broadcasting Corporation
    (BBC) 64–5, 69–70, 77, 91, 97,
    104, *107,* 130, 193
Britten, Barbara (sister) *16,* 31
Britten, Benjamin *frontispiece, 11,
    16, 17, 18, 20, 22, 25, 26, 29, 30,
    31, 46, 77, 78, 95, 112, 114, 119,
    129, 150, 151, 154, 159, 170, 175,
    177, 181, 192, 195, 199, 210, 211,
    212*
    Abraham and Isaac 143–4, *175*
    Advance Democracy 55
    Albert Herring 15, *124,* 131–3,
    131, 134

An American Overture (An Occasional Overture) 89–90
The Ascent of F6 64, *64*
The Ash Grove 120
Bagatelle, for piano trio 27
Ballad of Heroes 55
The Ballad of Little Musgrave and Lady Barnard 103
The Beggar's Opera 137, *139*, 140
'Beware!' 18
Billy Budd 117, *117*, *124*, 140–2, 144–6, *145*, 150, 166, 169
The Bonny Earl o' Moray 120
A Boy was Born 38, 39–40, 42, 44, 50, 51, 56
The Building of the House 192
The Burning Fiery Furnace 184, *184*, 190
Canadian Carnival (Kermesse canadienne) 80
Cantata Academica, Carmen Basiliense 166
Cantata Misericordium 181, 182
Carols 118
Cello Sonata *168*, 170, 172
Cello Suite No. 1 188, 190
Cello Suite No. 2 192, 193
Cello Suite No. 3 200–1
A Ceremony of Carols 98, 101
A Charm of Lullabies 133
The Children's Crusade 193
The Company of Heaven 65–6, 69
Curlew River 15, 99, 183–6, *184*, 187
The Dark Tower 118–19
The Death of Saint Narcissus 205–6
Death in Venice 12, *12*, 198, 199, 200, 202–5, *203*, 206, 208
Dido and Aeneas (realization of Purcell's music) 142–3
Diversions 78–9, 81, 82–3
The Duchess of Malfi (lost) 130
The Eagle Has Two Heads 130
Elegy 28

Evening Hymn (realization of Purcell's music) 143
The Fairy Queen (realization of Purcell's music) 143
Festival Te Deum 107
Five Flower Songs 142
The Foggy, Foggy Dew 120
Friday Afternoons 50–1
Gemini Variations 186, 188–9
Gloriana 148–52, *149*, 154, 161, 191, 193
The Golden Vanity 191, 192, 193
Hankin Booby 191, 206
Holiday Diary 42, 50, 51, 187
Holy Sonnets of John Donne 118, *118*, 120–1, *121*
Hymn to Saint Cecilia 97–8, 118, 143
Les Illuminations 74, 75, 77, 118
Instruments of the Orchestra (film score) 119, 124
Introduction and Rondo Alla Burlesca Op. 23 No. 1 84–5
Johnson over Jordan 69
The Journey of the Magi 200
Lachrymae 142, 208
Let's Make an Opera! 124, 137
Love from a Stranger (film score) 58–9, 66, *67*
'masque and anti–masque' for *This Way to the Tomb* 118
Mazurka Elegiaca Op. 23 No. 2 85
A Midsummer Night's Dream 166–9, *167*, 192
Missa Brevis 166
Mont Juic (with Berkeley) 60
Night Mail (film score) 53–4, *53*
Night Piece 187
Nocturnal after John Dowland 186
Nocturne 163
Noye's Fludde 144, *160*, 162–3, 183
Occasional Overture in C 130
On This Island 64–5, 166

Our Hunting Fathers 38, 52, 55–8, 208
Owen Wingrave 193, 196–8, *197*, 200
Pacifist March 55
part-songs on poems by de la Mare 37–8
Paul Bunyan 85–6, *86*, 88, 205, 208
Peace of Britain (film score) 54
Peter Grimes 14–15, 59, 90, 91, 98, 99, 104–5, 107–9, 113, *114*, 116, 118, 119, 124–5, 129
Phaedra 207, 208, *208*
Phantasy Quartet 38, 39, 40, 42
Phantasy Quintet 37–9
Piano Concerto 68–9, 70–1, 78, 80, 81
Piano Sonata ('Sonata Romantica') 84
The Plough Boy 120
Plymouth Town 36
The Poet's Echo 189–90
Praise We Great Men 209–10
Prelude and Fugue 101
The Prince of the Pagodas 158–9
The Prodigal Son 184, 193
Quatre Chansons françaises 23–4, 25
The Rape of Lucretia 118, *119*, 125, *127*, 129–31, *129*, 153
Rejoice in the Lamb 99, 101–3
The Rescue 99, 104
Sacred and Profane 205, 206
Saint Nicolas 134, 136
Samuel 18
Scottish Ballad 89, 90
Sechs Hölderlin–Fragmente 163, 172
Serenade 98, 99–101, 163
Seven Sonnets of Michelangelo 81, 83–4, 96, 97, 98, 104
Simple Symphony 19, 42, 50
Sinfonia da Requiem 79, 80–2, 89, 92, 96–7, 121, *181*
42, 44

Six Metamorphoses after Ovid 143
'Sonata Fantasi' 18
Songs from the Chinese 161–2, 163, 172
Songs and Proverbs of William Blake 188–9
Spring Symphony 141–2, *181*
String Quartet in D 28, 205, 206
String Quartet No. 1 89, 90
String Quartet No. 2 118, 121, *121*, 124
String Quartet No. 3 207–8, 210, *212*
Suite on English Folk Tunes 12, 14, 205, 206, 207
Suite for harp 196
Suite Op. 6 42, 56, 57, 78
Sweet was the Virgin Song 192–3
The Sword in the Stone 70
The Sycamore Tree 193
Les Sylphides (reduced orchestration) 84
Symphony for Cello and Orchestra 182–3, 186, 187
Te Deum 42
Temporal Variations 58, 66
Three Divertimenti 50–1
Tit for Tat 37–8
'The Trees They Grow So High' 77
The Turn of the Screw 39, *147*, 153–8, *154*, *155*, 161, 166, 196, 202
Variations on a Theme of Frank Bridge 40, 66–8, 75, 78
Violin Concerto 74, 78, 79–80, 91
Voices for Today 188
'Waltzes' 19
War and Death (Russian Funeral) 55
War Requiem 166, 169–70, 172, *173*, 174–7, *174*, *175*, *176*, *177*,

180, 182, 183, 191
A Wealden Trio 193
A Wedding Anthem 142
Welcome Ode 209–10
Who Are These Children? 201–2
Winter Words 14, 152–3, *153*, 163, 205
The World of the Spirit 69–70
Young Apollo 74–5, 84
The Young Person's Guide to the Orchestra 119, 124
Britten, Beth (sister) 15, *16*, 17, 18, 31, 51, 59, 60, 80, 96
Britten (Hockey), Edith (mother) 15–19, *16*, 26, 27, 40–1, 46, 52, 60–1
Britten, Robert (Bobby) (brother) *16*, 40, 50
Britten, Robert Victor (father) 15–19, 24, 27, 29, 40, 46
Britten Award 211
Britten-Pears Foundation 211
Britten-Pears Library 211
Brontë, Emily
    'A thousand, thousand gleaming fires' 65
Brosa, Antonio 78, 79, 84
Burkardt
    portrait of Mahler *34*
Burns, Robert *206*
    settings by Britten 206
Burra, Peter 60, 62

Cable Ship (documentary) 46
Canticles 12, 133, 143–4, 152, 157, *157*, 175, 200, 205–6
Cardus, Neville 35
Cavalcanti, Alberto 46
CBC 74
Chagall, Marc 101
Chester cycle of mystery plays 143–4
Chopin, Frédéric 85
Christie, John 131
Clark, Edward 46

Cleveland Orchestra 89
Clytie (dachshund) *191*
Cobbett Prize 37
Cocteau, Jean
    The Eagle Has Two Heads 130
Coldstream, William *46*, 47
Colles, H. C. 57
Coolidge, Elizabeth Sprague 89
Copland, Aaron 71–2, *71*, 74, 77, *77*, 80, 88, 189
Cotton, Charles
    'Pastoral' 99–100
Council for the Encouragement of Music and the Arts (CEMA) 96
Coventry Cathedral *173*, 174, *176*
Crabbe, George 90, *91*, 140
    The Borough 14–15, 90, 95, 105
Cranbrook, Fidelity *134*
Cranko, John 158
Crawford, Michael *160*
Cross, Joan 104, 107, *114*, 124–5, *131*
Crozier, Eric 107, *114*, 124–5, *124*, 131
    Albert Herring (libretto) *124*, 132
    Billy Budd (libretto) *124*, 140
    Let's Make an Opera! (libretto) *124*

Dalí, Salvador 85
Darnton, Christian 38
Davies, Meredith *175*
Davis, George 85
Debussy, Claude 23
Delibes, Léo 159
Delius, Frederick 42
Deller, Alfred 168
Del Mar, Norman 148
de la Mare, Walter 50–1
    settings by Britten 37–8, 193
Donne, John
    Holy Sonnets 118, *118*, 120–1, *121*
Douglas, Basil *154*
Dowland, John
    'Come, heavy sleep' 186

'Flow, my tears' 142
'Lachrymae' 142
Duncan, Ronald *119*, 136, 142,
    157–8, 174
    Peter Grimes (libretto) 105
    This Way to the Tomb 118
    The Rape of Lucretia (libretto)
    118, *119*, 125, 129–30
Dunkerley, Piers 50
Dykes, John Bacchus 162

Eden, Anthony 54–5
Edinburgh Festival 192
Edwards, Len *195*
Einstein, Albert 77
Elgar, Edward 36, 42, 44, 133, 187
    The Dream of Gerontius 200
Eliot, Thomas Stearns 52, *200*
    'The Journey of the Magi' 200
    The Death of Saint Narcissus
    205–6
Elizabeth II *192*
    Coronation 148, *149*
    Jubilee 209
Elizabeth, Queen, the Queen
    Mother 206, *206*
Ellis, Osian 196, 205, 206, 208
English Opera Group 131, 133–4,
    137, 142, *154*, 157, 192, 196
Evans, Nancy 125, 133
Fass, Marjorie 71
Ferrier, Kathleen 125, 143
Festival of Britain 140
Fischer-Dieskau, Dietrich *175*, *177*,
    180, 188, 189, 212
Fletcher, John
    *The Knight of the Burning
    Pestle* 141
Forster, E.M. 90, 140
    Billy Budd (libretto) 117, *124*,
    140–1
Franck, César 44

gagaku (court music) 186
gamelan music 88, 98, 158, 210

Gas Association 52
Gay, John
    The Beggar's Opera 137, *139*, 140
Gilbert and Sullivan 133
Glock, William 108
Glyndebourne *frontispiece, 119*, 125,
    129, 131, *131*
Glyndebourne English Opera
    Company 125
Goehr, Alexander 182
Goodall, Reginald 125, *129*
Goodman, Benny 84
Goossens, Leon 40
GPO Film Unit 46–7, 52–4, *53*
Grace, Harvey 91
Grainger, Percy 12
Greatorex, Walter 26–7
Green, Kenneth *112*
Greene, Graham 52
Gresham's School 26–7, *26*, 28
Grierson, John 46
Griller Quartet 40
Gropius, Manon 57
Group Theatre 48, 52
Guthrie, Tyrone 137

Hardy, Thomas
    settings by Britten 12, 14, 152–3,
    153, 205
Harewood, Earl of 142, 148, 188
Harewood, Lady *see* Stein, Marion
Hemmings, David 157
Henze, Hans Werner 189
Hepworth, Barbara 52
Herrick, Robert
    'Welcome, Maids of Honour'
    142
Hesse, Prince Ludwig of 158, *159*,
    163, 202
Hesse, Princess Margaret of 158,
    159, 202
Hindemith, Paul 44
Hitler, Adolf 51
Hockey, Edith *see* Britten, Edith
Holland Festival 130–1, 141

Holst, Gustav 42
    The Planets 36
Holst, Imogen 136, 148, *150*, 154, 158
Homer
    Odyssey 99, 104
Hope-Wallace, Philip 146
Hopkins, Gerard Manley 84
Hugo, Victor
    'Nuits de juin' 23
Hussey, Walter 101
Hutton, John *173*

International Society for
    Contemporary Music (ISCM)
    40, 57, 59, 60, 63, 72
Ireland, John 28, 30, *30*, 39, 46
    The Forgotten Rite 36
    Mai–Dun 36
    Piano Concerto 36
Isherwood, Christopher *45*, 48, *48*,
    71, 77, 90, 104
    The Ascent of F6 64, *64*
    The Dance of Death 48
    The Dog Beneath the Skin 48
James, Henry
    Owen Wingrave 193, 196–8, *197*
    The Turn of the Screw 153–8, *155*,
    196
Jeney, Zoltán and Gabriel 186, 189
Joachim Quartet 22
Johnson, Samuel 101
Jonson, Ben 101

Kallman, Chester 85, 94
Kästner, Erich
    Emil and the Detectives 25, 50
Keats, John
    'Hyperion' 75
Keller, Hans 148–9, 207
Kodály, Zoltán 189
Koussevitzky, Serge 92, 104,
    137, 141
Koussevitzky Music Foundation 92
Kraft, Victor 74, *77*

Lamprecht, Gerhard
  Emil and the Detectives (film) 25
Lancing College 134
Landgraf, Ludwig 158
League of Nations Union 54
Lee, Gypsy Rose 85
Leeds Festival 153
Leeds Piano Competition 187
Left Theatre 52
Lemare, Iris 37
Lenya, Lotte 85
London Labour Choral Union 55
Longfellow, Henry Wadsworth
  'Beware!' 18
Lowell, Robert 207
Lowestoft 15, 15, 20, 31, 38, 40
Lumsden, Norman 131
Lutyens, Elisabeth 37
Luxon, Benjamin 197
'Lyke–Wake Dirge' 99–100

McCullers, Carson 85
Macdonald, Ramsay 51–2
Macmillan, Kenneth 160
Macnaghten, Anne 37
Macnaghten concert series 37–8
MacNeice, Louis 49, 85
  The Dark Tower 58, 118–19
McPhee, Colin 88, 98
Mahler, Gustav 34, 34, 66, 67, 68,
  193, 203
  Das Lied von der Erde 34, 141
Malcolm, George 148, 163, 166
Manchester School 182
Mann, Golo 85
Mann, Thomas 203
  Death in Venice 12, 198, 199,
  200, 202–5, 203
  Doktor Faustus 203
Marlowe, Christopher
  Dr Faustus 157
Matthews, Colin 208, 209–10
Maupassant, Guy de
  'Madame Husson's May King'
  15, 132

Maxwell Davies, Peter 182
Mayer, Elizabeth 77, 78, 88, 90, 92,
  97, 118
Mayers, Beata 80
Melville, Herman
  Billy Budd 140–1, 144
Menuhin, Yehudi 118
Mewton-Wood, Noël 157
Michelangelo Buonarroti 83
  Sonnets 73, 81, 83–4
Middleton, Thomas
  'Midnight Bell' 163
Mitchell, Donald 148
Moore, Gerald 37
Moore, Henry 52, 101
Mozart, Wolfgang Amadeus
  Die Zauberflöte 41
Musgrave, Thea 182
Mussorgsky, Modest 146

Nash, Paul 52
Neel, Boyd 66, 66, 67, 98, 101, 148
  Boyd Neel Orchestra 66, 67,
  101
Nerval, Gérard de 23
New English Singers 71
Newman, Ernest 34, 90, 108
New York Ballet Theatre 84
Nicholson, Ben 52
Night Mail (film) 53–4, 53
Noh theatre 15, 158, 183–4
Nolan, Sidney 198
Norfolk and Norwich Triennial
  Festival 55

Obey, André
  Le Viol de Lucrèce 125, 129
Ovid
  Metamorphoses 143
Owen, Wilfred 174
  Britten's War Requiem 174–7,
  180
Oxford University Press 37, 42

Paderewski, Ignacy 85
Parr, Gladys 131

Parry, Hubert 44
Parsons, William 131
Parte, Betsy de la 131
Peace Pledge Union 55, 133
Pears, Peter frontispiece, 12, 37, 60
  63, 61, 66, 71, 74, 77, 77, 78, 80,
  84, 88, 93, 98, 101, 104, 105, 107,
  118, 120, 125, 139, 142, 148, 151,
  154, 157, 158, 166, 175, 177, 180,
  184, 191, 192, 196, 198, 210–11,
  211
  works written for 62, 65, 81, 84,
  98, 101, 104, 136, 143, 161, 163,
  200, 201, 204, 205–6, 208,
  210, 212
Pepusch, Johann Christoph 137,
  140
Perahia, Murray 205
Piper, John 101, 136, 153, 154
  designs for Britten's operas
  147, 153
Piper, Myfanwy 24, 136, 153, 154
  Death in Venice (libretto) 198,
  199, 200
  Owen Wingrave (libretto) 197
  The Turn of the Screw (libretto)
  153–5
Plato 199
Playford, John
  The English Dancing Master 12
Plomer, William 154, 183
Potter, Mary 136
Poulenc, Francis 189
Priestley, John Boynton 70
  Johnson over Jordan 69, 70
Prokofiev, Sergey 79, 159
  Violin Concerto No. 1 36
Purcell, Henry 65, 96, 121, 124,
  134, 140, 152
  Dido and Aeneas 142–3
  Evening Hymn 107, 142–3
  The Fairy Queen 143
Pushkin, Alexander 173
  settings by Britten 189–90

Quarles, Francis
  'My Beloved is Mine' 133
  settings by Britten 39, 133
Queen Elizabeth Hall 191

Rachmaninov, Sergey 69
Racine, Jean
  Phèdre 207
radio scores 64, 65–6, 69–70, 84,
  99, 104, 118–19
Ravel, Maurice 23, 67, 79
  Boléro 36
Ravenscroft, Thomas 55
Redlich, Hans 148
Renard, Jules
  Poil de Carotte 25, 50
Richards, Ceri 101
Richter, Sviatoslav 180
Rimbaud, Arthur
  settings by Britten 74, 75, 77
Ritchie, Margaret *131*
Robertson, Rae 84, 88–9
Rodzinski, Artur 89
Rossetti, Christina
  settings by Britten 39
Rostropovich, Mstislav *168*,
  169–70, 172, 182–3, 187, 189–91,
  192, 200–1, 210, *210*, 213
Rotha, Paul *46*, 47
  Peace of Britain 54
Rothman, Bobby *73*, 77
Rothman, David 77
Royal College of Music 27–8, 30–1,
  30, *31*, 34, 36–7, 38
Royal Philharmonic Society 91
Rubbra, Edward 101
Rubinstein, Ida 36

Sacher, Paul 166
Sackville-West, Edward 84, 96
  The Rescue 99, 104
Sadler's Wells Opera Company
  104, 107, 108, 124–5
Sadler's Wells Theatre 108, *110*
Samuel, Harold 22, *22*

Sandburg, Carl
  The American Songbag 72
Schiøtz, Aksel 125
  First Chamber Symphony 39
Schoenberg, Arnold 23, 31, 42,
  68, 157, 166, 167, 182, 212
  Erwartung 31
  Pierrot Lunaire 26, 28, 31
  Six Little Pieces *42*
Schubert, Franz
  Die schöne Müllerin 107
Schumann, Elisabeth 41
Schumann, Robert
  Cello Concerto 172
  Scenes from Goethe's 'Faust' 202
Second Viennese School 23, 42
Shakespeare, William 163
  A Midsummer Night's Dream
  166–9, *167*
  'The Rape of Lucretia' 125
  Timon of Athens 48, 52
  The Winter's Tale 50
Sheppard, Dick 133
Shirley-Quirk, John 206
Shostakovich, Dmitry 34, *34*, 146,
  169–70, 172, 208
  Cello Concerto No. 1 169
  The Lady Macbeth of Mtsensk
  34–5, 62, 109
  Symphony No. 11 55
  Symphony No. 14 196
  Violin Concerto No. 1 80
Sitwell, Edith
  Praise We Great Men 209–10
  'Still Falls the Rain' 157, *157*
Sitwell family 46
Slater, Montagu 55, 72, 136
  Easter 1916 52
  Peter Grimes (libretto) 104–5
Smart, Christopher *100*, 101
  Jubilate Agno 101–3
Smith, Oliver 85
Snape
  Maltings 188–9, 191, *192*, 193,
  195, 196
  Old Mill 62–3, *63*, 96, 134

Solzhenitsyn, Aleksandr 200
Soutar, William
  settings by Britten 201
Soviet Union of Composers 189
Spence, Basil 174
Spender, Stephen 27, 94
Stanford, Charles 22
Stein, Erwin 134, 142, 148
Stein, Marion 134, 136, 142, 148
Stevens, Alfred
  'Dead Boy' 50, 143
Strauss, Richard 40–1, 79
Stravinsky, Igor 31, 34, 42, 65, 68,
  125, 144, 159
  Petrushka 31
  The Rake's Progress 93–4
  The Rite of Spring 31
  Symphony of Psalms 23, 31, 35,
  102
Sumidagawa (Noh play) 183
Sutherland, Graham 101
Swingler, Randall 55
Szell, Georg 84

Tallis, Thomas 162
Tanglewood 92, 104, 141
Tchaikovsky, Piotr Ilyich 44, 159,
  201
Tennyson, Alfred, Lord *100*
  settings by Britten 99–101, 163
Thompson, Leonard *114*
Thomson, Rita 206
Thomson, Virgil 85–6, 187–8
Thorpe, Marion *see* Stein, Marion
Thubron, Colin 160
Tippett, Michael 98–9, *98*, 101,
  108, 187
  Boyhood's End 98
  Concerto for Orchestra 99
Tudor, Anthony 52
Tusser, Thomas
  settings by Britten 39

United Nations 188
Uppmann, Theodore *145*

Valois, Ninette de 52
Vaughan, Henry
    'Waters Above' 142
Vaughan Williams, Ralph 28, 34,
    37, 39, 46, 108, 148, 187
    Five Tudor Portraits 56
    Fourth Symphony 42
Venice Biennale 154, 154, 156
Verdi, Guiseppe 146
    Falstaff 133
Verlaine, Paul
    'Chanson d'automne' 24
    'Sagesse' 11, 24
Vienna Boys' Choir 191, 192
Vishnevskaya, Galina 169, 170, 172,
    189–91, 212
Vyvyan, Jenifer 151

Waddington, S. P. 28
Wagner, Richard 18, 23, 41, 44
    Tristan und Isolde 31, 133
Waley, Arthur 147
Walton, William 36, 46, 101, 108,
    146, 148
    Belshazzar's Feast 36
    Viola Concerto 36
    Violin Concerto 79–80
Webster, John
    The Duchess of Malfi 130
Weill, Kurt 85
    Threepenny Opera 140
Weingartner, Felix 40–1, 41
Welford, Kit 93
White, T. H.
    The Sword in the Stone 70
Wilbye, John 151
Wilbye Consort 205
Williams, Grace 31
Williamson, Malcolm 182
Wittgenstein, Paul 78–9, 81, 82–3
Wolf, Hugo 96
Wolfsgarten, Schloss 202
Wordsworth, William
    'The Prelude' 163

Wright, Basil 47
Wyss, Sophie 56, 64, 74, 75, 77

Yeats, William Butler 155

Zeani, Virginia 188
Zurbarán, Francisco 210

Photographic Acknowledgements

Henry W. & Albert A. Berg
    Collection, The New York
    Public Library, Astor, Lenox &
    Tilden Foundations: 87
Courtesy Boosey & Hawkes: 153
Courtesy Britten-Pears
    Foundation: 17, 53,
Courtesy Britten-Pears Library: 11,
    15, 16, 20, 25, 29, 43, 45, 47, 63,
    64, 72, 73, 76, 135, 159
©Anthony Crickmay/Theatre
    Museum: 13
©Bertl Gaye: 212
Drawing by Kenneth Green
    ©Gordon Green: 112
Courtesy Gresham's School: 26
Hulton Getty Collection: 2, 19, 22,
    46, 48, 66, 70, 91, 95, 98, 99,
    100l+r, 101, 103, 106, 110, 114l,
    114–5, 117, 118, 119, 121, 122–3,
    124, 126–7, 128, 131, 138–9, 149,
    150, 151, 154, 155, 157, 160, 167,
    168, 171, 173, 174, 175, 177,
    178–9, 181, 185, 192, 194–5, 200,
    206
Photographs by Lotte Jacobi: 61, 78
The Kobal Collection: 67
The Lebrecht Collection: 30, 31,
    34, 35, 41, 59, 71, 203; NIGEL
    LUCKHURST/Lebrecht
    Collection: 199, 209, 210, 211
Maria-Astria Institute: 184
©Angus McBean: 145
©Jack Phipps: 164–5
©John Piper: 147
©The Royal College of Music:
    32–3
©Clive Strutt: 191
©Reg Wilson: 197